Goals and Purposes of Higher Education
in the 21st Century

of related interest

Academic Community
Discourse or Discord?
Edited by Ronald Barnett
ISBN 1 85302 534 8
Higher Education Policy Series 20

Higher Education and Work
John Brennan, Maurice Kogan and Ulrich Teichler
ISBN 1 85302 537 2
Higher Education Policy Series 23

University and Society
Essays on the Social Role
of Research and Higher Education
Edited by Martin A. Trow and Thorsten Nybom
ISBN 1 85302 525 9
Higher Education Policy Series 12

Graduate Education in Britain
Tony Becher, Mary Henkel and Maurice Kogan
ISBN 1 85302 531 3
Higher Education Policy Series 19

Academic Mobility in a Changing World
Regional and Global Trends
Edited by Peggy Blumenthal, Craufurd Goodwin,
Alan Smith and Ulrich Teichler
ISBN 1 85302 545 3
Higher Education Policy Series 29

Higher Education Policy Series 32

Goals and Purposes of Higher Education in the 21st Century

Edited by Arnold Burgen

Jessica Kingsley Publishers
London and Bristol, Pennsylvania

First published in the United Kingdom in 1996 by
Jessica Kingsley Publishers Ltd
116 Pentonville Road
London N1 9JB, England
and
1900 Frost Road, Suite 101
Bristol, PA 19007, U S A

Library of Congress Cataloging in Publication Data
Goals and purposes of higher education in the 21st century / edited by
Arnold Burgen.
p.   cm. -- (Higher education policy series : 32)
Includes bibliographical references and index.
ISBN 1-85302-547-X (hb : alk. paper)
1. Education, Higher--Aims and objectives. 2. Higher education
and state. I. Burgen, Arnold 1922- . II. Series.
LB2322.2.G62   1995
378--sc20   95-16486
                                                        CIP

British Library Cataloguing in Publication Data
Goals and Purposes in Higher Education in
the 21st Century. - (Higher Education
Policy Series,ISSN 0954-3716;Vol.32)
I. Burgen, Sir Arnold II. Series
378

ISBN 1-85302-547-X

Printed and Bound in Great Britain by
Biddles Ltd, Guildford and King's Lynn

Contents

Figures

Tables

Chapter 1

Introduction

The present attitude towards the prolongation of the educational period is of surprisingly recent origin. Strömholm records that as recently as 50 years ago in Sweden only 3 per cent of the relevant age group completed secondary school (most of these then went on to University). It is now accepted across Europe that it is obligatory for schooling to extend at least to 16; over much the same period a high proportion of those pupils have moved on into higher education and it would not be an improbable scenario if we were looking back just ten years from now, that we would be thinking it quite normal that virtually all the population had attended some form of higher education. Alongside this growth in education there has been an enormous change in lifestyle, as emphasised by Mayer. Whereas formerly children were employed part or fulltime on the farm or in commerce, this is no longer the case and we have moved to a position of later and later entry into gainful employment. At the other end of life, we have a far larger part of the population surviving to retirement age and indeed most of those retired remain mentally and physically active for another decade and many of these will be candidates for further education.

We also live in a period of extremely rapid technological change in which techniques and knowledge base learned earlier becomes obsolete quite early in a career; furthermore, many jobs are disappearing and entirely novel new ones appearing. This implies a new role for higher education in retraining and facilitating job switching into second or third careers.

The massive expansion of higher education has occurred largely within the university system, by expansion of existing institutions and the creation of new ones. The strain on the system has been very great especially as universities have had to change their mission to become providers of general education and vocational courses. There is indeed the question whether greater emphasis should not have been put on creating quite different structures; the 'Distance learning' developed in the Open Universities is an example of such a successful alternative.

The economics of an expanded higher education are important, resting, as they do, on a decreased size of workforce which has to support an enlarged part of the population that is not gainfully employed (this includes the enlarged number of retired persons).

These and many other issues were discussed at a workshop organised by the Academia Europaea and the Wenner-Gren Foundation, which was held in Stockholm in September 1994 and they form the basis of this book. We are very grateful to the Foundation and its Director, Professor Torvard Laurent, for their hospitality, excellent local arrangements and financial support.

Chapter 2

From Humboldt to 1984 – Where are We Now?

Stig Stromhölm

No sooner had I dispatched the letter proposing the journalistic, and thus pleasantly vague, heading of the present paper than I saw the trap I had set for myself. The title undoubtedly indicates an uninterrupted chain of events. Now, if there is one statement I dare venture on the history of learned institutions, it is that at one point in the contemporary development of the European university, the difference between the 19th century seat of learning and the modern institution – which had obviously grown wider all the time, but *then* slowly and successively – ceased to be a difference of degree and become one of kind. The transition from craft to industry had become completed. This juncture (which will certainly not deprive comparisons, between 'before' and 'after', of their great interest from the historian's point of view but which makes any comparison undertaken with a practical purpose difficult if at all meaningful) did not occur at the same time all over the Continent. The basic facts, however, were the same.

The most important single factor of change – there are others, but none even remotely similar in weight – is the quantitative explosion of the system. It can be illustrated by some figures chosen at random from the Swedish development. In 1931, a year in which I happen to take a special interest, the whole Swedish secondary school system (in a country with slightly less than 6 million inhabitants) counted 23,000 pupils. In 1991, the tertiary system – universities, university colleges and other public institutions requiring in principle successfully completed secondary school studies – comprised 230,000 persons (the population meanwhile having grown to 8.5 million). In an intermediate year, also of particular interest to the present writer: 1949, some 3 per cent of an age class completed secondary school and some 2.5 per cent continued into the university system. In 1991, more than 90 per cent of an age class pursued some kind of secondary school studies (important changes of terminology, mostly undertaken with vague 'democratic' and 'egalitarian' intentions and, as is usually the case, misleading, and precisely those whom the terminological base money coiners purport to help, make exact comparisons almost meaningless, but what is important is that roughly 30 per cent of an age class entered the tertiary system).

Beside this revolutionary change, the equally impressive revolution in the growth of research, and consequently of knowledge, is a less decisive factor from a strictly societal point of view. That there is an obvious and highly complicated causal relationship between the two revolutions is a fact that can only be taken passing notice of, and not further developed in the present context, where the emphasis should be on problems specifically facing the university as an institution. It is well known that research, after all, can be carried out in other kinds of establishments and that much high quality research is, in fact, conducted in special institutions. This is, of course, one of the questions that have to be considered when discussing in general terms the present situation of academia, but it is not specifically considered in the present paper.

Instead of indulging in a sterile analysis of the question whether it is the mass explosion of the university as an educational institution, or the progress of learning, that is the decisive, or most important single factor in the development of our sector of the community, I shall submit some observations on specific aspects of the research revolution which have immediate consequences on the educational system.

Be it said without cheap cynicism, it frequently occurs to a thoughtful observer that research has become, in the contemporary world, too successful an undertaking. The *Sorcerer's Apprentice* appears to the mind's eye. The enormous growth of accumulated knowledge in all fields has resulted in an inevitable specialisation which in turn has not only reduced the possibility of a reasonably broad overview, but has also trivialised the work of many researchers, in particular among the young. There are a great many secondary and indirect consequences which influence the world of learning and which will, in all likelihood have an impact upon the activity of the university as an educational and researching, or at least research-preparing institution. Thus, the capacity to survey large areas of knowledge is becoming more valuable and more appreciated, possibly at the expense of deeper but narrower knowledge.

A negative aspect of the societal success of research and its spokesmen in the last 50 years is that it sometimes seems to lead to a neglect, indeed a certain contempt, of professional competence as a legitimate goal of higher education. In fact, in their energetic and mostly successful plea for the dignity, value and – this is where it becomes most dangerous – exclusive virtue of research as a component in any training which has any intellectual value, they have managed to convince the heads, teachers and pupils of perfectly respectable educational establishments that the crowning glory of the training given there, irrespective of subject and purpose, is to add a generous helping of something called 'research', not unlike an ennobling clot of cream on top of an already substantial and well decorated cake. In fact, the glorifiers of research have successfully contrived to make non-researching but ambitious educators believe that full human maturity, full 'self-realisation' cannot be achieved without that miraculous elixir.

Dr Faust was far from harmless when gleaming in the minds of undergraduates representing 2.5 per cent of an age class. When introduced as a paragon for 30 per cent he becomes positively dangerous. The triumphs of 'research' as an ultimate goal of all higher education raise practical problems which can presumably be overcome with the usual verbal tricks – the term is given a suitably enlarged area of meaning in the rhetoric of educational policies – but the moral problems are less easily solved. If higher education is taken seriously, the goal of producing independent human beings must be recognised and earnestly pursued also in such branches of post-secondary school training as are principally, or even exclusively, intended to give highly qualified professional skill rather than an introduction to research. The best – possibly the only practically available way out of what is already amounting to a serious dilemma would seem to be that more generous elements of general culture are integrated into such professional courses. Again, it is of the utmost importance that the task be taken seriously, since adding general culture as an adorning clot of cream on the cake is in no way superior to making the same ornamental use of research.

A third consequence of the well-deserved but sometimes overexploited triumphs of research is that this once pure, distant, and little known activity has become a centre, at least one among several centres of power, and an activity largely taking place upon the public stage. Gone are, with few exceptions, the disinterested searchers for knowledge, gone the absent minded hermits, gone the lonely writers of monumental treatises. Present instead, obtrusively present, on the forum of the learned republic are the research managers, the laboratory imperators, the research council *condottieri*. Triumphs inevitably breed triumphators; the necessity to take an active part in a money and power game calls forth the strong and vital rather than the shy and hesitating; specialisation, as already said, gives added value to the generalisers, who mostly prefer to command and organise rather than to dip their fingers too deep into the test-tube.

To a great extent this development is inevitable. Too much public money is spent on research to allow it to remain an esoteric hobby pursued *in camera*. Moreover, the possible results of research may be of such immediate concern to the public at large that the whole activity has entered,as it were, the political sphere. The appearance of the politician type on the academic arena is a concomitant blessing!

For the purposes of the present discussion, which is devoted to the university, there are obvious, albeit problematic consequences to be drawn from this particular aspect of the triumph of research. Is it at all rational that the heaviest, the most costly and the most economically significant research be carried out in the university? How can it be co-ordinated with the teaching activity, in particular the mass teaching at relatively low levels? And how can that mass teaching be co-ordinated with the more qualified teaching which is intended to prepare for research and which must today, more than ever, start early? Playing two different games with players who consider themselves rightly or wrongly as essentially equal is an operation that invariably leads to tensions within a closed system. Further, what are the consequences for university leadership and for governing bodies inside academia?

A final remark upon the consequences of the research revolution: the increasing interest of industry and the business community, in general, in the doings of the university is flattering. The attention of that highly competent, well-informed and energetic community is a mixed blessing. It is a potential source of pressure which, when added to that exerted by the political powers, may become a very serious threat to the independence, not only of research but also of higher education.

To conclude this part of my paper: when putting together the mass explosion in the area of teaching, on the one hand and the quantitative and qualitative revolution in the field of research, on the other, we face a scenario so complicated both by virtue of its size, so fast moving and at the same time so important that a brutal question cannot be avoided: what men or women or what bodies of them are intelligent, well-informed, mature, determined and far-sighted enough to exercise legitimate power, or even control, over this fertile chaos? National politicians? European politicians or technocrats? The 'market'?

The probable answer is none (which may well be another way of saying precisely 'the market'). I have already humbly submitted, in previous publications, with regard to that modest microcosm, the Swedish higher education and research system, that this would be a most appropriate subject for the deliberations of an upper house; a body of experienced, independent and highly considered members from various fields – the learned republic, politics, public administration, business, culture – who would have the task of preparing all measures relating to research and higher education, of following continuously the national and international developments, of proposing measures, but first of all raising this area above the whims and quarrels of the daily political struggle.

One of the most fashionable words in Swedish public discourse in the last few years has been 'exciting' (Swedish '*spannende*', cf. German '*spannend*'). Few things have struck me as more thoughtless, coquettish and profoundly immoral. Those responsible for the organisation of higher studies and research activities which are of fundamental importance to young people, and through them to the future of Europe, and which demand considerable sacrifices from the working and tax-paying population, should exert themselves to find carefully prepared and planned, safe and reliable solutions, if possible tested by experience, and not gratify their own vanity and idle restlessness by looking for the 'exciting'.

Now, against this essential background here is a short account of the Swedish scene as it has developed over the last 30 years, selecting those elements which may be of interest for comparative purposes. Upon the whole, this is a story very similar to that which has occurred in other European countries, although possibly with some local differences.

First, it is important to remember that Sweden, although enjoying, particularly in the first 20 years after the Second World War, a reputation for wealth, is basically a poor country in those respects which are of decisive importance for the development of a system of research and higher education. Cars, refrigerators, TV sets, and holiday travels to the Happy Isles are not everything. In the present perspective the importance of these blessings is small. Sweden has a population of 8 million scattered over 450,000 square kilometres (not much less than France which has seven times the population). There is only one city with a million population. This means that for each km of telegraph wire, for each kilometre, of good road, for each bed in a hospital and for each high quality school, there are fewer arms and fewer heads than in countries where people live closer to each other, and also in a more clement climate. I insist this basic fact, because the habit of collective solutions – not least in the education system – and the habit of disciplined work were, and have to some extent remained conditions of survival and not expressions of any Socialist or collectivist frame of mind. The country got a good, but small education system earlier than most comparable states. A system of State financed medical care was set up in the 17th century. Institutions of this kind had to be created and run by the State; there was no 'market' particularly in the north, with less than one inhabitant per square km. Illiteracy was eliminated before the middle of the 19th century and political freedom and an unbroken constitutional tradition from the Middle ages are also elements to be remembered when characterising the point of departure of the modern developments.

In the university system this point of departure was clearly the neo-classical, humanistic, Humboldtian university. The system comprised, for all practical purposes, four general seats of learning. There was first the University of Uppsala, founded in 1477 and from the middle of the 17th century a fairly large seat of learning with very high quality teaching. Uppsala was and has remained the university of the kings and the aristocracy, the 'National university' with an emphasis on science, reflected in five Nobel prizes. Then there was the University of Lund (1668), smaller and more provincial until the middle of this century when other institutions were integrated with it and it then became the largest in Sweden, with many fine scholars on its staff. Then in the nineteenth century, the universities of Stockholm and Goteborg were created by the Liberal bourgeoisie and served as counterweights to the two older institutions. The foremost function of all the universities was to give enlightened, well-educated and loyal officials to State and Church, and this includes the secondary school system, which was with few exceptions run by the State (in close co-operation with the Established Church). Technical education was given by two high level Institutes of Technology, and business management was taught at two private institutions, on a good level and with distinguished teachers. There was also a forerunner of the present Swedish University of Agriculture.

In the national perspective, there was no doubt that the secondary school system, which was supervised by the Royal Board of Schools, guaranteed that all examinations and tests were on the same level throughout the country (in fact, the written school leaving examinations were held on the same day and even at the same hour, with the same texts throughout the Kingdom in the most important subjects, viz., Swedish essays, Latin, French and Mathematics) considered itself in the main purveyor of recruits for the universities. University professors were appointed censors at the oral examinations, and the senior teachers at the most highly regarded secondary schools were among the small group of scholars who were candidates for university professorships.

Within this framework, which it seems justified to call 'classical', it was natural that any student who successfully passed the final examination was entitled to enter a university. There were restrictions in subjects where teaching required laboratory space; the faculties and institutes of technology fell into that class, but these limitations did not constitute a matter of principle, but were dictated by practical needs. For certain studies there were requirements, such as Latin for law students.

The subsequent development can be described as an alternation of contraction and expansion. The thoughtful observer, whose reactions I have presumed to interpret once before in this paper, might find similarities with the breathing of a feverish patient; he may be right.

There are no reasons for going into details when describing these movements in the academic community of a small and peripheral community; I shall therefore be very laconic and highly schematic.

The first movement, or onslaught on the system, was clearly dictated by the great and, as it would seem, basically unforeseen growth of the secondary school system. This was in itself from many points of view an impressive development, an expression of the strong wishes of new strata in society to give their offspring a good education. The call for more schools was met by the creation, at an increasing rate, of secondary schools founded and financed by local authorities, usually city councils. This in turn created the need for more university trained teachers and the whole system underwent from top to bottom a very rapid and very extensive expansion. At this juncture, Sweden seems to have moved rather faster than most comparable countries.

As far as the universities were concerned, the expansion increased as a result of political measures, e.g. exceptions from the normal admission rules were made for those training as primary school teachers (a group favoured by Social Democrat education policies). One result of this very fast evolution was undoubtedly a lowering of standards in secondary schools (this is probably generally agreed today) which had to be manned with teachers who were insufficiently trained. Another result was that the universities had to make use of young and inexperienced instructors; mass teaching on a scale previously unknown was required to meet the most urgent needs. Yet, at first, there were no signs of abandoning the principle of open entry or of abandoning the Humboldtian ideal of university studies as a young person's pilgrimage to the pure springs of knowledge, a beverage to be drunk unmixed by the gallon in the company, and under the tactfully Socratic leadership, of scholars able to find open new wells indefinitely and indeed to engage unceasingly in that exalted pursuit.

Thus, the name remained unchanged: 'university studies'; and it exercised its powerful suggestion on all: politicians, university people, students, parents, while the thing underwent changes so deepgoing that the name gradually became a fiction and in the end a spurious certificate of origin and quality. On the other hand, for reasons which it is not necessary to develop, no one had an interest in exposing the widening gap. There are conspiracies of silence so fortunate that they are bound to be successful. When the question was raised what all these undergraduates were going to do with their depreciated BA, Social Democrat education politicians had ready answers such as: 'in the future it will be normal that a BA works at a petrol filling station'.

Under the influence of the mass invasion the university system reacted by finding new, less free and more school-like forms of teaching and by creating new kinds of teaching jobs. It was obvious that a professor with a legal obligation to lecture for 132 hours per year, was too exclusive a person to suffice, and it was equally obvious that creating new professorships on the required scale was too expensive. The new posts, lectureships, were intended exclusively for teaching, and the number of hours per annum required from the lecturer was so considerable that holders of this kind of post were practically prevented from doing serious research of their own. Thus, in fact, although not formally, the Humboldtian ideal of teaching by active researchers was abandoned. At the same time, an extremely serious source of discord and envy had been introduced into a so far relatively harmonious university system. Alongside the professor and the Docent (with a time-limited appointment and modest teaching load) there had been created a body of teachers who in the course of time considered themselves underprivileged and exploited, since they felt that they were carrying more or less alone the heavy burden of elementary teaching and examining, while the professors concentrated upon supervising graduate students and conducting their own research. There was clearly a difference in status between research and teaching and once appointed a lecturer, a position which carried tenure and hence security for life, a young academic would hardly have time to perform the research necessary to qualify for a professorial chair. He found himself caught in a trap. The university found itself divided into 'the researching guards brigade' and 'the grey teaching regiments' of the line.

The next movement, equally the work of Social Democrat education politicians, was a contraction of the system. Two obvious facts had emerged: the system could not go on growing indefinitely (it simply cost too much), and further, students could not choose to study any strange combination of subjects without paying some attention to the demands of the labour market.

The first problem took a good deal of time to be dealt with. It went naturally against the egalitarian grain of the governing party to close the 'Garden of Eden' to candidates. Over the years, all sorts of exceptions from normal admission rules had been invented and introduced in order to open the gates to the deserving, the culmination was a rule to the effect that anyone who had reached 25 years of age and had been working for five years had a right in principle to be admitted. The principle was, however, subject to some qualifications for most fields of study. Finally, however, rules on *numerus clausus* were successively introduced in most areas. Today, very few, if any disciplines are without restrictions in respect of previously acquired knowledge in specific subjects.

The second problem, that of organising the studies, must have been looked on with more enthusiasm by the education politicians. The task had an alluring element of hectoring, which was duly made full use of. A system of great rigidity emerged; in most faculties, lines of study were established which left little freedom of choice; a line was intended to transport the victims into a given sector of the labour market whose needs were taken care of in the teaching and recommended reading. 'Education committees' were set up in the various faculties and departments to facilitate contact between the ivory tower and the world outside.

Thus, the year 1977 is the point in the development of the Swedish university system which justifies the use of the ominous year 1984 in the heading of my paper. The story does not end there. Where are we now?

The university system, particularly in a country with a long constitutional and liberal tradition, is old, tough and complicated, full of strange loyalties, but also of equally strange and elusive resistances. Undoubtedly, the system we have sketched came into effect, and it worked, but there were various safety valves and methods of handling which reduced the effects considerably. A few years of exceptions and alternatives have deprived it of much of its content. It should be admitted that there were some good ideas that were helpful for disorientated young people in the original plan.

The final phase can be described as one of expansion, not in numbers but rather in liberty. Through legislation in the period 1991–4, the universities have been allowed to formulate their own criteria for admission and have been given extensive freedom to establish 'programs' (the successors to the 'lines'). It is premature to express an opinion on the results of these changes. They are in many respects less dramatic than might be expected, for the contracts between the Ministry of Education and the individual universities which lay down the obligations undertaken by each seat of learning and define the grants given in consideration, imply, in reality, fairly far-reaching restrictions on the liberty of action of the universities in framing their plans and their action in regard to teaching. The liberty with regard to research is larger but not unlimited.

The question remains open when this was written whether the new Social Democratic Government, that came into office in October 1994, will choose contraction or further expansion. The audible moaning of the patient shows that he is preparing himself for a new treatment!

Chapter 3

Creation, Transfer and Application of Knowledge Through the Higher Education System

Henk J. van der Molen

Introduction

The title of this book implicitly assumes that there is a future for higher education in the 21st century, but also, quite correctly, emphasises that goals and purposes might require reconsideration. This notion is supported certainly by the vast number of publications and meetings about the present state of affairs and about the future of higher education. During the past half year alone, I received in my personal mail announcements of several international meetings concerned with more or less the same aspects of higher education (Clark 1983).[1] Also, the opinion pages of, for example, the *Times Higher*, and other major newspapers in all European countries: *Nature, Science, New Scientist*,[2] etc., inform us every week about the concerns and disasters of higher education if no changes should be introduced (Clark 1994). Higher education has become a general public interest.

---

1 Recent meetings at about the same time as the present symposium, on the future of higher education include:
   • meeting on 'Changing relationships between the State and Universities', organised by the OECD Programme on Institutional Management of Higher Education; Paris, 5–7 September 1994.
   • 'Universities on the Eve of the Third Millennium AD: Problems of Unity and Variety' (Lomonosov – 94), Moscow, 17 – 19 October.
   • 'Higher Education Policy: International Trends', organised by the Centre for Higher Education Policy Studies (CHEPS), University of Twente, The Netherlands, 7 October 1994.
2 Publications in the *Times Higher, Nature* and *New Scientist* in summer 1994 illustrate the general interest and concern about higher education (*Times Higher Education Supplement* 1994; Maddox 1994; *Nature* 1994a, b)

The reasons are clear. Higher education is now inextricably linked to social and economic development and every respectable nation wants to be part of it. The resulting vast increase of student numbers in most developed countries places an enormous pressure on the institutions of higher education, as well as on the financial resources for these institutions and the students participating in higher education. This has led to uncertainty and unrest in several areas of society, not in the least in the higher education system itself; but also in the political arena and in governments, among prospective students and their parents, industry and the business world, which are the main financial supporters, as well as beneficiaries of higher education. All these issues have been presented in depth in several authoritative reports, by e.g., the Organisation for Economic Co-operation and Development, the World Bank, and the Memorandum on Higher Education in the European Community.

Universities in Higher Education

I have so far purposely used the term 'higher education' rather than 'universities', because the present discussions concern higher education as a whole. In this context, universities in most countries are part of a higher education system, which incorporates several other forms and institutions of higher education not included in or linked to universities. By far, the largest non-university sector in higher education concerns training of high level professionals with an emphasis on vocational skills and knowledge, rather than on scientific and cultural aspects and attitudes. In saying this, I realise that I am treading on dangerous grounds and that I am reflecting my background in a country which still operates a binary system in higher education, where universities are supposed to deliver academic training and institutions for higher education for many different professions. I hesitate to use the word 'polytechnic' any longer since the UK decided to abolish the binary system and installed a supposedly uniform university system, including the previous polytechnics. We all know, however, about the deviations from the theoretical distinction in terms of the so-called 'vocational drift' of the universities and the 'academic drift' of higher professional schools. It is not the typology of institutions (universities vs. polytechnics) that requires our attention, but much more the goals and purposes which are maintained by these institutions.

Universities have played an important, if not decisive role in the shaping of culture and civilisation of present day societies. There are those who wonder whether the universities under the present conditions will be able to continue to do so in the next century. It is my belief, that it is not so much the *institution* of the present university but the *idea of the university* that will have to be kept alive. Too often we discuss institutional and financial arrangements, when we pretend to discuss goals and purposes. Higher education throughout the centuries has always been concerned with: teaching of arts and sciences; training for professions (including the academic professions); and scholarship and research.

The institutional models of universities have developed through different models, which depending on societal and political attitudes emphasised different aspects of training and scholarship (e.g., the von Humboldt model, the British Cardinal Newman model, the North-American Clark Kerr multiversity model, the Napoleonic model).

From my experience in different capacities in the university system I have derived a few simple conclusions. The first is, that discussions on the purpose and goals of higher education are always with us and the future of higher education, and universities for that matter, will develop from existing institutions and experiences, and will be gradual rather than revolutionary.

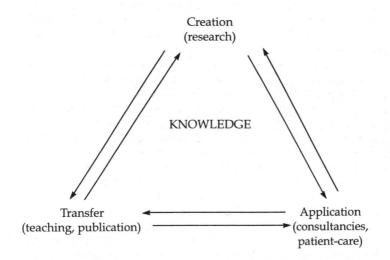

Figure 3.1. The creation, transfer and application of knowledge

My second thesis is, that all the important principles and possible solutions are internationally well-known and available. Any reform of higher education is not so much a question of developing new ideas but rather of implementation. The latter requires the conviction and actions of decision makers and the availability of sufficient financial resources, often dependent on or determined by political and government decisions.

The handling of knowledge, in my opinion, should be dominant in all activities of higher education institutions. In Figure 2.1, I have indicated the three main interrelated activities: creation, transfer and application of knowledge.

Depending on ambitions, strengths and weaknesses, individual institutions will create their specific profiles, e.g., dominant in research, dominant in teaching, dominant in market related applications, etcetera. Whether such institutions would or should be called 'universities', is, in my opinion, rather irrelevant. The concern for maintaining distinctive characteristics for the university in *sensu stricto* is expressed in many discussions and writings. In this respect, I support the general notion that an institution is recognised as a 'true' university when it concentrates more on developing attitudes and problem solving than on the accumulation of knowledge, and prepares for lifelong learning, rather than for specific jobs and functions. In their reactions on the memorandum on Higher Education in the European Community, the liaison Committee of the Rectors Conferences of the European Community (EC) and the Standing Conference of Rectors, Presidents and Vice-chancellors of the European Universities (CRE) have emphasised their concern that higher education in universities is almost exclusively treated in terms of servicing the economic community. They argue, that values which over the centuries have been associated with universities, such as independent judgement, creativity, cultural and ethical dimensions are probably equally, if not more, important and should be based on scientific knowledge.

Training Through Higher Education

In most countries, higher education depends to a large extent on the willingness of governments to pay directly or indirectly for the maintenance of higher education institutions. It is understandable, therefore, that the society as well as the individual (potential) student are interested in the requirements for and benefits of further training through the higher education system. This interest is determined by several parameters, such as: interests and ability of individual students; general academic and scientific attitudes; specific knowledge and skills; certification for professional accreditation; career linked continuing education; flexibility of the higher education system; and willingness/opportunities of students and employers (private as well as public) to pay for training.

In Figure 3.2, I have made an attempt to combine these requirements in an institutional framework, which, in my opinion, can serve as a blueprint for an integrated higher education system in the 21st century. The system would combine four different but interrelated higher education routes.

Separate in their goals, but interrelated in activities they are:

1. The first route aims to create a general academic training which would last 2–3 years and be completed with a certification that would be recognised in the employment market for a variety of lower/middle-management functions.

2. A second route requiring an additional 2–3 years would emphasise either training for specific professional degrees or training for a scientific degree. These degrees would qualify for a variety of functions.

3. A third route would aim for scientific scholarly work resulting (after an additional 3–4 years) in a doctorate.

4. Finally, a fourth route would be additional to all previous routes and concerns specialised further education and recurrent career training.

The inclusion of different routes of higher education in a comprehensive institutional framework would have great advantages for all parties involved; students as well as staff, employers and financing bodies. Students would be able to select within a single institution their personal study route(s) depending on ability, interest, financial resources and market expectations. Staff could apply their personal skills and maintain their interests in a much more flexible way than in a single level institution. Potential employers could interact more effectively with such comprehensive institutions in formulating specific requirements, which would determine the level of specific courses and routes of teaching and training. Financing bodies, whether public (governments) or private (industries, individuals) could negotiate with the institution about their needs and interests in financially supporting specific activities, rather than the institution at large. The existence of the institution in this respect would, in theory at least, not be dependent on a single source for financial support and not depend on a restricted scope of activities. This should result in more flexible market oriented institutions, marketing

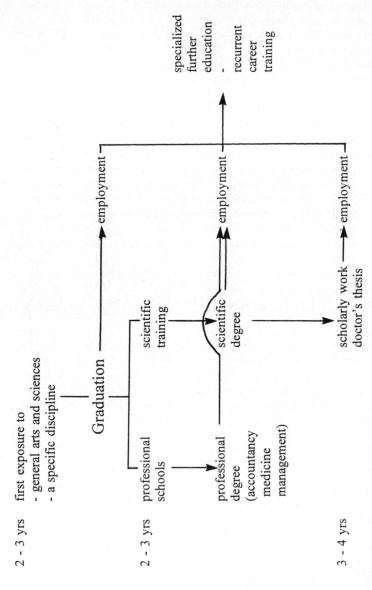

Figure 3.2. Higher education in the 21st century

knowledge and education in the best possible way, not under the threat of the collapse of a restricted market or the inherent risk of a single financing source. A judicious combination of the activities depicted in Figures 3.1 and 3.2 could, in my opinion, be the basis for comprehensive higher education institutions with quite different patterns of activities, depending on interests of all the parties involved.

There is always the problem, of course, that such comprehensive schemes ignore real life issues. If this would be a (theoretically) acceptable model, in which way should it be linked to secondary education and entrance requirements for students? Should such a comprehensive institution be called a 'university'? Would the prestige which is socially linked to the 'highest' scientific degree be influenced by the presence in the same system of degrees for more practical education? Would different routes require different degrees? These may be rather irrelevant issues in theoretical terms, but are ever so important in societies which value recognisable certification.

I have intentionally avoided using the word 'levels' in the discussion of the different and differentiated routes in Figure 3.2. The indication of 'levels' would unavoidably suggest that one particular route of higher education is 'lower' or 'higher' than another route. However, the appreciation of different routes on basis of the requirements of either potential students or potential employers of the graduates might be quite different. Hence, certification and awarding of degrees in such a comprehensive system should be handled with care, to avoid a prestige-driven system which would force students to aim for the highest diploma level, rather than the level most applicable to personal career development.

Towards a European Higher Education System?

In discussing the reality and advantages of a comprehensive higher education system, it is of interest also to consider the possibility of a more unified European system for higher education. Problems all over Europe appear to be similar with regard to development of élite to mass education, public vs. private (financial) responsibility, discrepancy between requirements of society and those of individual students and institutions. But it has to be accepted, also, that constraints in the development of a more united European system are rather prohibitive considering existing differences in:

1. historic development of national education systems
   (including higher education)

2. social/cultural appreciation of different forms of higher education
3. financial responsibilities (private vs. public) for higher education
4. political interest for and influence on higher education.

A practical example of different historic developments in different countries, is reflected in the time required/permitted in individual countries to obtain the highest degree before starting to work on a doctorate, as given in Table 3.2.

Table 3.1 Degrees in higher education

Belguim	Kandidant	2–3 years
	Licencié	+2–3 years
Denmark	Kandidat	5 years
Germany	Mag,art/diplom	5–6 years
England	Bachelor arts/science	3 years
France	Diplôme générale	2 years
	Diplôme de licence	+1 year
	Diplôme de maîtrise	+1 year
Netherlands	Doctorandus/meester ingenieur	4 years
Italy	Laurea de dottore	4–6 years

In reality, the body of knowledge taught and used in higher education all over the world has much more in common than the differences in study routes, certification and institutional arrangements would suggest. Even if institutional arrangements in different countries will develop from the existing historically determined situation, it appears safe to predict that higher education in the 21st century all over the world will move in a direction which will share common characteristics, such as:

1. changing relationships between public and private responsibilities of
   a) institutions (public-private money, autonomy of institutions)
   b) students (fees vs. student grants/loans)
2. changing teaching technologies (computerised information systems, telecommunication)

3. shorter and more diversified curricula (scholastic vs. market requirements)
4. international standards for quality and certification
5. Recurrent continuing education linked to career development and market requirements.

Discussions about these developments will undoubtedly start from the generally accepted view that education fulfils a social need and a functional role for the social, cultural and economic development of society, which warrants public financing. But that there is no convincing evidence, that the availability of more or less education would influence the growth of the national product. Developed nations become increasingly reluctant to pay from public resources for the high investment in higher education, although the added value of higher education for the individual is evident: better job prospects, higher income, more specialised higher level work, etc. The increasingly large numbers of students in higher education without predictable economic or other practical value for society at large, have made these societies more sensitive and reluctant to pay for higher education from public resources. It can be expected, therefore, that in the re-evaluation of responsibilities for higher education, there will be a greater emphasis on the interest and responsibility of the individual student (also financially) in choosing an education which is beneficial for him or her but not necessarily beneficial for society at large.

Conclusion

At this time, higher education systems in different countries differ so much that there is no single solution that will result in a uniform generally accepted model in the foreseeable future. Most societies and governments value higher education as beneficial for society at large, as well as for the individual. It is the success of higher education and the great interest in higher education that has put organisational and financial strains on institutions of higher education, as well as on governments and the individual student. The available information should make it possible, however, to devise workable arrangements, provided that there is the political and social support for such arrangements.

I share the views which were expressed in a report by the Bertelsmann Foundation (Mohn 1991) and the recent World Bank report, which concluded that all the important principles, problems and solutions for the future of higher education are internationally well-known and available.

For those who are reluctant or hesitate in the development or realisation of such plans, may I remind them of a saying of Seneca: *'Nolle in causa est, non posse praetenditur.'* ('The problem is that they *will not*, but they pretend that they *cannot* find a solution'). James Perkins, then president of Cornell University, probably gave the briefest summary of my belief in the future of the university, when he wrote in his 1965 Stafford Little Lectures, 'The university is the engine of change and is changed by it' (Perkins 1966).

References

Clark, B.R. (1983) *The Higher Education System: Academic Organisation in Cross-national Perspective*. Berkeley, Los Angeles, London :University of California Press.

Clark, B.R. (1994) *Places of Inquiry: Research and Advanced Education in Modern Universities*. Berkeley and Los Angeles: University of California Press.

Commission of the European Communities (1991) Memorandum on Higher Education in the European Community, November 1991.

Confederation of British Industries Report (1994) *Thinking ahead. Ensuring the Expansion of Higher Education into the 21st Century*. London: Ditchling Press.

Hague, Sir D. (1991) *Beyond Universities. A New Republic of Intellect*. London: The Institute of Economic Affairs.

Kerr, C. (1963), 'The Uses of the University', Godkin Lectures, Harvard.

Maddox, J. (1994) 'Can the research university survive?' *Nature*, 30 June.

Mohn, R. (1991) 'Evolution in higher education.' *Higher Education Management 3*, 306–309.

Nature (1994a) 'East Europe needs sustainable universities.' 23 June.

Nature (1994b) 'World Bank report slams Western-Style university model.' 21 July.

Neave, G. (1986, 1987) 'European university systems.' *CRE Information 75*, 1986; no 77, 1987.

Neave, G. and Van Vught, F. (1991) *Prometheus Bound: The Changing Relationship Between Government and Higher Education in Western Europe*. Oxford: Pergamon Press.

Perkins, J.A. (1966) *The University in Transition*. Princeton: Princeton University Press.

Reactions of the liaison Committee of EC Rector's Conferences and of the standing conference of Rectors, Presidents and Vice-Chancellors of the European Universities (CRE) to the memorandum on Higher Education in the European Community, 1992.

Times Higher Education Supplement (1994) 'Explosion that led to crisis.' (A commentary on the World Bank's report 'Higher Education. The Lessons of Experience', Washington 1994).

Wolff, R.P. (1969) *The Ideal of the University.* Boston: Beacon Press.

Chapter 4

Continuities and Change in American Higher Education

Martin Trow

Universities, as Clark Kerr and others have observed, are remarkably conservative and enduring institutions. In some important respects our contemporary universities are very much like their medieval ancestors: learned seniors spend their time reading books and talking to young men (and now young women), lecturing to them in large halls and talking more informally with them in small seminar rooms close to collections of books. These teachers – masters and doctors today as in the thirteenth century – are organised in groups of specialists around bodies of knowledge or professional practice, in what in many places are still called 'faculties'; departments came later. Young people still drink and wench too much, and neglect their studies, to their parents' disapproval, and still write home begging for money. Like their forebears 800 years ago, students entering higher education still have to show in some way that they are prepared to begin their higher studies, and on the successful completion of those studies are still awarded degrees which the university is specifically authorised by its charter to award; indeed, the power to award degrees is what legally, now as then, defines the institution's status as a university. Universities are still largely governed by the guild of teachers – the masters or professors – with a rector (or chancellor, vice-chancellor or president) presiding over the institution and managing its relations with its environment and its sources of support. The power of that officer is variable today as at the beginning, challenged both by the masters below and by the university's external governors and providers above. All this, of course, is our common heritage.

The biggest change in higher education over the past 800 years has been the invention of the research university, which added evidence to faith and reason as a basis for certifying knowledge. But even the research university, a far more complex institution than the medieval university, has been in place in Germany for nearly a 150 years; by the turn of the century almost everything we recognise as the American research university was already present.

But against this record of continuity is a parallel record of change. To remind ourselves of the difficulties of prediction, we might reflect on how well we might have predicted the situation in 1994 30 years ago. In 1964, mass higher education was just beginning to emerge in Western industrial societies (apart from the United States). The shock of the student disturbances and the cultural revolution of the late 1960s were ahead; the racial and sexual revolutions were just beginning in the United States; computers were big central number-crunchers, with no one anticipating the impact their development would have on communications, or on teaching and research. But with all that has happened, the institutions of higher education in modern societies are much the same today as then, in mission and organisation; somewhat changed in curriculum and finance; most sharply different in their more modest anticipations of the future. On the side of the technologies of instruction PCs are everywhere, along with faxes, e-mail, massive data banks, computerised library catalogues, and increasingly large parts of the libraries themselves on-line – all marking the beginnings of the revolution in electronic communication. But how much have they changed the working habits of scientists and scholars? My guess is not much, yet.

The history of higher education in Western Europe since the Second World War has largely been an account of the transformation of systems of élite higher education into systems of mass higher education, from small numbers of universities enrolling 3 to 5 per cent of the age grades to diverse systems enrolling 25 to 35 per cent of the age grades. That transformation has created severe problems for these systems in finance, governance, access, accountability, standards, the curriculum, graduate study and research – indeed in every aspect of academic life; problems with which these countries are still struggling. Just in the past few years, many European countries have started to grant their universities more freedom and autonomy, although tendencies in the opposite direction are also visible.

By contrast, the United States had a system of mass higher education in place over a hundred years ago, though the numbers that characterise mass higher education were still to come. In this brief summary, I would like to sketch the major defining characteristics of American universities and colleges, stressing the powerful forces of continuity which have marked this past century of American higher education. I then want to speculate about the immediate future, and the changes that we might anticipate over the next few decades.

Americans who have walked through the quads and gardens of Oxford and Cambridge, and who know that Harvard was modelled on a Cambridge college, often think of British universities as immeasurably older than our own. And so Oxford and Cambridge are. But higher education as a system is much younger in the United Kingdom than in the United States. The organisational revolution in American higher education took place about a hundred years ago, roughly between 1870 and 1910; the emergence of a British system of higher education is still underway. As Lawrence Veysey (1965) has put it, 'Looking back, it could be seen that the decade of the 1990s witnessed the firm development of the American academic model in almost every crucial aspect.' (p.339) By 1900, when only 4 per cent of Americans of college age were attending college, we already had in place almost all of the central structural characteristics of American higher education. Public and private colleges and universities occupied the same functional niches, with public and private funds mingled in both kinds. All American colleges and universities already had a lay board of trustees, a strong president and his administrative staff, and a well-defined structure of faculty ranks. In the selective institutions, academics sought promotion through a scholarly or scientific reputation linked to publication and a readiness to move from institution to institution in pursuit of a career. On the side of the curriculum, almost every institution embodied the familiar American pattern of two years of general education leading to two years of more specialised study in a discipline. Everywhere, both of these segments were based on the elective system, the modular course, credit accumulation and transfer based on the transcript of grades. All these were in place by 1900, as were the academic departments covering all known spheres of knowledge, and some not so well-known. In the universities, these departments were and are the centres both of specialised undergraduate and highly organised post-graduate studies, with today's degree structure already firmly in place, all taught by the same academic staff. Then, as now, all colleges and universities, except for the most selective, did a good deal of 'remedial' work to make up for the weakness of American secondary education. Underpinning all was the spirit of competition, institutional diversity, responsiveness to markets (especially the market for students), and institutional autonomy marked by strong leadership and a diversity of sources of support. The United States already had the organisational and structural framework for a system of mass higher education long before it had mass enrolments. All that was needed was growth.

What has happened since to American higher education? Of course, there was growth – an enormous expansion in the numbers of students, from a few hundred thousand to nearly 15 million in an enormous diversity of institutions, some 3700 of them offering credits towards degrees, with a commensurate growth of staff, research support, and everything else. And, of course, this tremendous expansion of access has changed the character of the student population, which reflects much more closely than it did even 50 years ago the characteristics of the society as a whole with respect to sex, race and ethnicity, age and social origins. Much of the growth in recent years has been from formerly under-represented groups – women, ethnic minorities, and older, working and part-time students.

But apart from expansion and growth, the most important structural change in this century, and a major force for the democratisation of the system, has been the development of the community college system, some of whose students earned credits accepted for transfer to four year colleges and universities; that has tied the four-year institutions and their degrees to the world of continuing and vocational education. Academic freedom is more firmly and broadly protected than at the turn of the century, thanks in part to the American Association of University Professors (AAUP). In addition, there is now broad federal support for student aid in the form of grants and loans, and this has supplemented, rather than replaced, other and earlier forms of student aid. Federal agencies support university-based research at a level that could hardly have been imagined a hundred, or even fifty, years ago. The machinery of fund-raising, the organisation of alumni and the associated development of big-time sports has gone further than one could have imagined, though the roots of all that were already in place at the turn of the century. And there are faculty unions in some hundreds of colleges and universities, though none in the leading research universities.

But what is impressive about American higher education at the end of the century is not how much it differs from the system that existed at the turn of the century, but how similar it is in basic structure, diversity, mission, governance and finance. An interesting question is how it came to be that a century ago the United States had already created a preternaturally precocious system of higher education with an enormous capacity for expansion without fundamental structural change. The basic explanations lie, as often, in the peculiar historical origins of the system, created in a European colony, on European models, but without the body of learned men who constituted European universities of the time. That fact gave a special pre-eminence and strength to the college president, at the beginning usually the only learned man, the only professor, on the college staff. And the strength of the American college president persists to this day. In addition, the weakness of government, both at the federal level and in the States after the Revolution, ensured that they could neither provide adequate higher education nor constrain other private groups and organisations from doing so. The resulting promiscuous chartering effectively removed American colleges and universities from the close control by central government that charters in Europe provided. In the new United States almost anyone could start a college that awarded degrees, and almost anyone did, without governmental approval (or support), or their setting of academic standards. Motives for founding colleges varied: supporting religious denominations, resisting the threat of barbarism at the frontier, even speculation in land, were among the motives of the founders of colleges. The result was a system of colleges marked by great diversity of standard, with a good deal of initiative but without much support; certainly without any adequate guaranteed support from the State. And that in turn led to a lively competition among the myriad institutions of higher education for support, and especially for students and their tuition payments which were crucial for the private colleges, and important for all. And this necessarily called for an entrepreneurial stance which strengthened the power of the college presidents. To many Europeans, this picture of higher education in America is marked by unnecessary diversity, lack of co-ordination or central control over quality, inefficient duplication, waste, and the absence of continuity. The standard American answer to all these criticisms is the answer of the market: 'We cannot be inefficient and wasteful, or we would not be able to survive.' And such an appeal to the 'unseen hand' reduces the need to develop a more elaborate educational, political or philosophical rationale; if students continue to enrol and pay, then the provision seems evidently needed and desirable.

That very partial explanation for the multiplicity and diversity of American higher education illustrates five characteristics of that system which are not shared in most European countries, and which help explain the peculiar form that higher and continuing education takes in the US:

1. Americans believe, as on the whole Europeans do not, that competition in higher education, as in other areas of organised social life, is the most effective way of planning for an unpredictable future. We believe so on the ground that despite the appearance of waste, it creates a diversity of

institutions some of which will be better fitted for future (as yet, unpredictable) conditions, demands and opportunities than any that can be designed by a central state authority.

2. A corollary of the acceptance of competition is the high measure of autonomy attached to our individual institutions, and their consequent ability to go into the market for students and academic staff without seeking approval elsewhere, in a ministry or a regional board.

3. Another corollary of competition is a perennial shortage of cash, since competition almost by definition makes current income inadequate to achieve ever higher aspirations. All American colleges and universities act as if they were poor even when they are very rich: Harvard and Stanford, for example, are always seeking more funds, always mounting new campaigns for contributions. And one strategy of American colleges and universities in that unceasing quest for more money is to provide services of all kinds to current and potential constituents in many areas of public and private life.

4. Central to our growth and diversity, both of student numbers and of institutions, is the broad assumption, in the US, very widely shared among all kinds of Americans, that education is intrinsically a good thing, and that everyone should get as much of it as they can be persuaded to enrol for.

5. Linked to that article of faith is that generally speaking there is no cap, no upper limit to the number of students who can be enrolled in the public institutions of higher education. There are, of course, limits on entry to specific colleges and universities, but almost always there is a place in some institution in the system, at costs that all can afford if they are prepared to work and study at the same time; and well over half our students in higher education are also employed during term time. This also implies no link between enrolments and the labour market except through the market. Higher education in the United States qualifies people for jobs, but unlike the case in Europe, it does not disqualify them for other jobs. That partly accounts for the persistently lower rates of unemployment among graduates than in the labour force generally; and also the peculiar fact that in the United States the income differential between graduates and non-graduates has substantially increased during recent decades while enrolments, and the numbers of graduates, have risen.[1] European systems of higher

education have refused to go down this road of uncontrolled market-driven competition. Nevertheless, the next decades of higher educational development in many European countries will be marked by strong tensions between diversifying forces within and between institutions of higher education, tensions arising out of the growing diversity of students and the explosion of knowledge on one hand, and the constraining forces of public authority on the other. The radical decentralisation and institutional autonomy that mark American higher education may come to seem more attractive the more complex the problems that emerge in European higher education, even as they resist emulating those models.

To this point, I have been suggesting a way of looking at the American higher education: in comparative perspective it is highly peculiar, unlike any other in quite fundamental ways. That is perhaps broadly accepted among Europeans. I have also argued, or at least asserted (the argument would have to be embedded in an historical account of the development of this peculiar system) (Trow 1993, pp.39–66) that American higher education has not changed fundamentally over the past century, but has simply fulfilled a potential for mass higher education that was inherent in it a hundred years ago. But the title of this paper involves change as well as continuity. One way to explore the possibilities for systemic change is to imagine what American higher education might look like two or three decades in the future.

It is a cliché, but with some truth in it, that the best predictor of the future is the past. But the truth in it decays the further we move into the future; and the rate of change of modern life, and the extraordinary and unanticipated events of recent decades should make any effort to peer some three decades into the future suspect. I am prepared to argue the case for our strong continuities with evidence; my notions about how the system might be changing should be seen as much more speculative. Predictions have often been used in the service of prescriptive planning, and since predictions beyond a few years about social trends and institutions are invariably wrong, certainly to the level of detail and precision which are required by

---

1   'In 1973, young men with a college degree earned only 19 per cent more per year than their counterparts with a high school diploma. By 1992, young male college graduates earned 70 per cent more per year than young high school graduates. Despite a substantial decline in the size of the traditional college-age population in the 1980s, full-time equivalent college enrolments rose 11 per cent between 1980 and 1990.'

social policies, policies based on those predictions are usually bad or ineffective. But as an exercise in another way of understanding an institution, the effort to imagine the state of higher education some decades ahead may be useful if it helps sharpen our efforts to see the forces working on its shape and character.

My guess about how American higher education will be developing could be put this way: if the past century has seen the United States develop the institutions of mass higher education more fully than anyone could have imagined, the next decades will see us develop what might be called a 'learning society', in which the forms and processes of higher education will be found in many institutions outside the boundaries of colleges and universities; a society in which most ordinary people will find themselves engaged in what we now think of as continuing education, primarily, but not exclusively, to equip themselves for work which will be in continuing and rapid states of change. I believe that our national values with respect to education, and the responsiveness (or vulnerability) of American colleges and universities to market forces will lead them to pioneer the institutions of a learning society based on patterns of interactive communication that we can now scarcely imagine.

But the fact that the Western university has survived in recognizable form for 800 years, and the modern research university for over 100, is no guarantee that it will survive in recognizable form for the next 30. Some trends in higher education can be predicted with some measure of confidence, rooted in deep-seated forces and trends in Western society that are not likely to be reversed in any foreseeable future. Chief among these are what Max Weber over 70 years ago saw as the master secular trends of our time – democratisation and rationalisation – processes which in higher education take the special form of massification. What does that mean, and how might those trends play out over the next three decades? Here are some guesses.

In 2025 in 'higher education' there will be more of everything: more institutions, more kinds of institutions, more students, and more diversity among them.

The development of the economy in advanced societies will continue to increase the demand for a labour force with more than a secondary school education, and reduce the size and number of the occupations that do not. But the demand for higher education will increase beyond what is 'required' by the occupational structure. Higher education's chief characteristic is that it gives its recipients a capacity to adapt to change; it will continue to be one of the few advantages parents can give to their children in a rapidly changing world, and more and more people will become aware of that. The technical upgrading of jobs, and the link between the success of a business and the training and skill of its labour force will accelerate the interest of industry in supporting and continuing the education of their employees. A good deal of advanced education already goes on in and around private firms; this will grow rapidly, as will the creation and development of 'learning centres' inside and outside of industry, serving a growing demand for the continuing education of the labour force.

Private business, industry and individuals will pay for what they want and need by way of further and adult education. Government in the United States at every level will be contributing a smaller proportion of the total costs of higher education; there are too many other demands on public money to support the continually growing demands of 'education' of all kinds. As a result, colleges and universities will become even more successful at selling their services and the knowledge their research generates to individuals and business interests. But governments will continue to be significant, indeed vital, to the support of certain kinds of higher education, particularly the special kind which continues to be provided in universities.

We are moving, I have suggested, toward a situation which might be described as a 'learning society', with very large parts of the population more or less continually engaged in 'formal' education of one kind or another. Under those circumstances, education will be widely distributed, taking many different forms in different locations, offering a variety of certificates and degrees. The growing distribution of higher, and especially of continuing, education will increasingly blur the distinction between education and the rest of society. Distinctions that we make today among 'higher' or 'continuing' or 'adult' or 'remedial' or 'further' education will be increasingly difficult to make as these activities are carried on, without being so identified or distinguished, as part of the ordinary activities of life in economic, political, military, and leisure institutions, as well as in places called 'colleges' and 'universities.' Moreover, the 'success' of such education will be attested not through examinations and certificates, but through the performance of an individual on a job, or of a unit performing a function or service. And that will make largely irrelevant the whole external assessment and evaluation industry – currently in some countries part of the government's efforts to maintain control over the uncontrollable.

In this web of educational institutions and activities, what will be the fate of the university? I suspect that in 2025 the university will be something like a knot in a web; places where education goes on somewhat more intensely than at other places, at higher levels of difficulty and complexity, and perhaps at higher levels of specialisation. Universities will not have a monopoly on research any more than they do today; research will be even more highly distributed throughout other institutions of the society, most of it done in the contexts of application.[2] But universities may retain a special preeminence in research for which little or no practical applications can be seen, and also for humanistic scholarship. Above all, they will retain a special hold on the post-graduate education of the most highly skilled and specialised scientists and scholars who go on to do research and teach in various distributed situations, not necessarily in universities.

The wild card in this scenario is technology, especially the technology of communications. Education, in recent decades, has seen enough announcements of abortive 'technological revolutions' to be properly sceptical of new announcements of yet another. But the one on the horizon really may be different. The fantastic development of computers, and more recently of interactive electronic communication, makes any predication about the future of education problematic. It seems likely that in the near future much of what is done today among people working in physical proximity may be possible to approximate through electronic links. This should affect many kinds of work, but education too at every level. Currently, big international firms are developing sophisticated systems for audio- and video-conferencing; as with all these developments, capacities grow as prices plummet. The interactive communications systems being developed for the lucrative business market is adaptable to higher education. Surely much of what is currently done in schools, colleges and universities will in the future be done through electronic links among people who are physically separated.

But I believe that people – teachers and students – will continue to come together in places called 'colleges' and 'universities' for longer or shorter periods, to study and learn together even when the same learning might be carried on at a distance. Even today we could imagine this conference being conducted through state of the art interactive technology. But even if technology were much further advanced, we would want to be in each other's company. Our wish to be in each other's presence, and the spontaneity of interaction and relationship that allows, cannot be duplicated by technology – or at least any that we are likely to see in place in the next 30 years.

Lionel Trilling once observed that for Jane Austen marriage was the most powerful educative relationship, combining love and learning. More generally, some kinds of education, perhaps the most

---

2   See Gibbons *et al.* 1994

important kinds, involve the shaping of mind and character and sensibility, not only the way we think but also the way we feel and see. For that kind of education to go on, I suspect, there need to be affective ties between teacher and taught; the people involved must care about one another beyond their usefulness to one another as carriers or recipients of bodies of information or skill. That kind of relationship is not likely to develop through electronic links; we need to be in each other's physical presence, at least from time to time, for such relationships to develop. Moreover, some of the most important kinds of knowledge are 'tacit', not fully articulated or rationalised, gained through direct apprenticeship and association with those who possess it. If that is true, then institutions very much like the colleges and universities we are familiar with, will survive at the centres of educative webs, surrounded by all the other kinds and places of advanced learning and education that will characterise the learning society of the future.

One warning of a development which may work at odds with the broadly optimistic picture I have been drawing. In a sense, the structural conditions and attitudes that are implicit in a learning society are already in place in the US, just as the institutions of mass higher education were already in place here a hundred years ago, just waiting for the mass expansion into them. The picture I draw of a learning society developing spontaneously in response to the demand of individuals and the economy will be hard for European societies to accept. In all of them, higher education has been a provision of government, largely central government, and it will be hard for them to let go. We are seeing in Britain a government that in its rhetoric seems to encourage university autonomy and responsiveness to social and economic demands, while it continues to try to steer and control the system through its funding mechanisms, intervening deeply into the private life of the institutions.[3] The result seems to be a levelling of the forms of higher education, with a concomitant tendency toward the deprofessionalisation of academic work, its transformation into just another public service closely managed by central government and its agencies. We have seen in the US the unhappy effects of tendencies toward the deprofessionalisation of the teaching profession in the schools. One can imagine similar developments accompanying the continued massification of higher education, with similar effects on its ability to recruit highly able people to teaching and university research, in competition with opportunities

---

3   See Trow (1994)

for better-paid work in more supportive institutions elsewhere. It is an open question whether élite forms of higher education, and particularly the highly selective and demanding research universities, can sustain their levels of intensity and creativity under the pressures toward levelling that accompany the growth of mass higher education.

The greatest danger to American higher education in the immediate future, one that it has not yet had to face, is the possibility that it will be asked to provide advanced and continuing education for everyone without the intellectual and moral resources of élite forms of higher education to draw on. Elite universities and their functions are vulnerable, both politically and financially; under enough pressure their research activities can move to industry and research laboratories, their humanistic scholarship to think-tanks, museums and foundations. The great research universities themselves will surely survive, but possibly with increasingly poorer staff-student ratios, more external 'accountability' and management, more and more the servants and instruments of other institutions, less and less able to define their own roles and missions. They would thus come increasingly to look like other institutions of mass higher education, different only in their historical and cultural pretensions. Democratisation, Max Weber once noted, has as one of its major characteristics cultural and institutional levelling, powered by the passions and forces behind the concept of 'equality'. If this process of levelling proceeds apace in the realm of higher education, it would reduce the difference between élite and mass higher education at the same time as the forms of mass higher education become more diverse. Higher education would then come to reflect and resemble the simultaneous standardisation and marginal differentiation of commodities in the global market. All this might happen just slowly enough, masked by the traditional forms, titles and ceremonies of university life on the one hand, and the revolution in communications on the other, so that our children and grandchildren may not even notice. I almost regret that I will not be here in 2025 to see what will have happened to the university of the twentieth century.

References

Gibbons, M. *et al.* (1994) *The New Production of Knowledge.* London: Sage Publications.

Harrington, P. (1994) 'Market demands higher education.' *Insight*, July 4.

Trow, M. (1993) 'Federalism in American higher education.' In A. Levine (ed) *Higher Learning in America*. Baltimore and London: The Johns Hopkins University Press.

Trow, M. (1994) 'Managerialism and the academic profession: The case of England.' *Higher Education Policy 7*, 2, 11–18.

Veysey, L. (1965) *The Emergence of the American University*. Chicago: University of Chicago Press.

Chapter 5

Unified and Binary Systems of Higher Education in Europe

Peter Scott

My theme is the differences between European higher education systems in terms of their structure and organisation: unified, or integrated, on the one hand; and divided, on the other (in England we would have used the word 'binary'), stratified, segmented. There are several other ways in which European higher education systems can be compared and contrasted. One is to distinguish between various systems in terms of their underlying value-structures. For example, Professor Claudius Gellert of the European University Institute has identified three main strands within the European university tradition (Gellert 1993, pp.237–238). The first, historically identified with Germany, places knowledge, its creation and transmission at the centre of the university's mission; the university is above all a *scientific institution*. The second, most completely realised in France's *grandes écoles* (although technically they lie outside the university system), emphasises the acquisition of high-level vocational skills; here the university is seen primarily as a *professional institution*. The third, the Anglo-Saxon (or, more precisely, the Oxford and Cambridge?) model, concentrates on the development of personality, or 'character'; the university is first and foremost an educational or, more broadly, a *cultural institution*.

Instead, I intend to concentrate on issues of structure and organisation, rather than of values and culture – for two main reasons. The first, and more trivial, is that my current work is as a policy analyst. And it is through policy analysis that we can obtain a forward look. Intellectual history, for all its charms, is inescapably retrospective. The second, is that it is no longer possible to concentrate narrowly on the European university tradition (Rothblatt and Wittrock 1993). The present age of mass higher education is heir to many different traditions, far more than the three identified by Professor Gellert – technical and technological education, adult education and so on. And, on the brink of a so-called 'Learning Society', new traditions are being added all the time – for example, the so-called 'corporate classroom', advanced training and R & D (research and development) in private corporations and public agencies. So-called 'short-cycle' higher education long ago ceased to be a residual sector (OECD 1973).

My paper is divided into four sections. The first is an attempt to describe the context in which unified and dual systems have developed. The second suggests a typology of European higher education systems. The third explores particularities, the national circumstances which have favoured one or other type of system, and commonalities, the factors which influence all systems, whatever their structure. Finally I will attempt to assess which, particularities or commonalities, are more influential in shaping the future pattern of European higher education and, too ambitiously, attempts to develop a general account of the dynamics of European, and other advanced, systems of higher education.

The Development of Unified and Dual Systems

In the 1960s and 1970s, many European countries reshaped their higher education systems. The extended systems created during this period replaced the much more narrowly based university systems typical of the pre-war era. They were developed in response to, first, the rapidly rising social demand for university-level education and, second, to the increasing demand for a more highly skilled labour force. This reshaping took various forms, but it was a general phenomenon across Europe (and the rest of the developed world) (Clark 1984). The fundamental imperatives were the same. They arose from the modernisation of society and the economy. My task is to analyse the differences. But it is at least as important to recognise the profound similarities underlying, apparently contrasting, national solutions.

In France, the reorganisation of the universities in the aftermath of the events of 1968 represented an overdue modernisation of structures which had changed little since the nineteenth century. Five years earlier in Britain, following the Robbins report, access to Europe's most selective university system was widened; in the later 1960s, the polytechnics were established as an alternative form of higher education (Scott 1984). In Germany, a twin-track policy was pursued. The universities were expanded and made more comprehensive, but the role of the *Fachhochschulen* was enhanced. In Sweden, a decade later, a unified system of universities and colleges was established. Outside Europe similar reforms were undertaken; the earliest and most notable being California's 'master plan' for higher education which created a three-tier system (Condron 1988; OECD 1989; Rothblatt 1992).

The goal of all these reforms was to widen access to higher education and to increase the production of graduates. This was done in one or both of two ways. First, existing universities were expanded and new ones created. Of the universities which are members of the Conference of European Rectors (CRE) more than a third have been established since 1960. The 1960s and the 1970s will be remembered as perhaps the most dynamic stage in the development of the European university. Second, greater emphasis was also placed on less traditional forms of higher education. It was argued that, even after the expansion of the universities, there would still be a demand for alternative models of higher education.

A variety of strategies was adopted to meet this demand. In some countries the creation of new forms of higher education was subsumed within the wider policy of expanding and reforming the universities. For example, in France the IUTs (Instituts Universitaires de Technologie) were designed to offer more vocationally oriented courses. But, as their name suggests, they were organically linked to the traditional university faculties. In Sweden, a more radical variant of this policy was pursued. After 1977, previously separate, and subordinate, institutions such as nursing and teacher training colleges were incorporated into the universities (Scott 1991).

In other countries an explicitly 'binary' policy was developed. The best example was Britain, where the polytechnics were conceived of as an alternative to the universities. Intense rivalry developed between the two sectors, although they had originally been seen as complementary, rather than competitive. In other parts of Europe, policies were adopted which incorporated features of both these approaches: the unified and the 'binary'. The superior position of the universities was confirmed, indeed enhanced, by the expansion of student numbers, but efforts were also made to upgrade technical high schools and similar institutions. This, broadly, was the approach in Germany and the Netherlands (Brennan *et al.* 1992; OECD 1993; Ministry of Education and Science *et al.* 1989).

But it is wrong to make too sharp a distinction between these different modernisation strategies. Even within formally unified systems, 'binary' characteristics could be observed. In Sweden, for example, the fault-lines within the expanded universities between the traditional faculties and recently merged colleges persisted, as did the distinction between the traditional universities, whether old ones like Uppsala or new ones like Umeå, and the smaller university colleges. Equally, no binary system was entirely consistent or logical.

In Britain, the former colleges of advanced technology, established in the mid-1950s outside the university sector, became technological universities in 1965, just when another tranche of alternative institutions (the polytechics) was being established. Whether institutions became universities or polytechnics was largely a historical accident. Also key institutions, like the Open University, lay in effect outside the 'binary' structure.

In Germany and the Netherlands, informal binary systems initially emerged, not as a result of deliberate policies to establish alternative institutions to rival the universities, but as the result of a gradual development of identifiably post-secondary education institutions, first within the narrow framework of technical education and subsequently on the larger canvas of professional education. The key change was not the reordering of institutions within higher education, still largely regarded as synonymous with universities, but the rearrangement of upper secondary education. In Europe, there was nothing to compare with the California 'master plan' (and similar reforms in other states), a sustained and sophisticated attempt to create a coherent higher education system out of the unco-ordinated fragments of university, technical and professional and post-secondary education.

Only later was this radical challenge addressed in Europe. The Swedish reform of 1977 came at the end of one phase and the beginning of another. In the first phase, higher education reforms were generally the product of *ad hoc* modifications of the inherited pattern of institutions. Even the most radical example (an apparent exception to this rule): the establishment of the polytechnics in England, had a much stronger political than educational rationale. In the second phase, starting with the Swedish reform, the inexorable consequences of earlier *ad hoc* adjustments began to be more systematically confronted. The predominant effect has been to produce a shift from dual, or 'binary', to more integrated systems.

In Britain, the inter-sectoral rivalry created by the 'binary' system ended by destroying it. In other parts of Europe, the outcome has been less dramatic but the trajectory of reform similar. In the Netherlands, it was recognised that the HBO sector (higher professional schools) could no longer sensibly be regarded as an extension of upper-secondary education. So the relationship between the HBO and university sectors had to be properly articulated. Although a dual system has been maintained (for the present), the two sectors are now embraced within a common legal framework. Because of close links between the English and Dutch higher education systems, the 'promotion' of the polytechnics has strengthened the resolve of the HBO sector to secure similar recognition. In Germany, the relationship between universities and the *Fachhochschulen* appears, for the moment, to be more stable.

Models of System Organisation

The second section of this chapter will consider various organisational models. These can be reduced to four broad types:

- The first model is a **dual** system. Universities and other post-secondary education institutions are regarded as entirely separate and treated differently, the latter typically less favourably than the former (although the non-university *grandes écoles* in France are an important exception).

- The second model is a **binary** system. Alternative institutions are deliberately established to complement (and rival?) the universities. It is the degree of deliberation which distinguishes binary from dual systems. Binary systems are designed as dynamic systems; dual systems represent the continuation of existing institutional patterns.

- The third model is the **unified** system. All institutions belong to a common system and are not formally differentiated. The best example is Sweden. Since 1992, Britain has also had a unified system of higher education – or, rather, three separate systems in England, Wales and Scotland.

- The fourth model is of a **stratified** system. Higher education is conceived of as a total system and institutions are allocated specific roles within it. The classic case remains California's 'master plan'.

However, as with the modernisation strategies, too sharp a distinction should not be drawn between these four models. In practice, the distinction between the first and second models, dual and binary systems, is often blurred. There is a tendency for stable dual systems, within which different types of institutions have inherited distinct and generally complementary roles, to develop into more volatile binary systems which encourage competition and permit rivalry. This is certainly true of the Dutch and, to a lesser extent, the German systems.

But it has not happened in France, where non-university sector institutions enjoy equal, or superior, prestige. The highly selective *grandes écoles*, designed to train the future 'leadership class', have no reason to envy universities obliged to admit all *baccalauréat*-holders.

The ability of even the less grand professional schools, particularly in business and management, and of the IUTs to select their students also places them in a stronger position than the traditional university faculties. Similarly, the mono-technic institutes of central and eastern Europe, established during the Soviet era, enjoyed more prestige, and were more generously resourced, than the old universities.

Neither the Swedish (since 1977) nor British (since 1992) systems are truly unified. In Sweden, the 13 universities remain a distinct group of privileged institutions. They receive the bulk of the available research income (Council for Studies of Higher Education 1994). In Britain, similar differences can be observed. Although all universities and higher education colleges are funded for teaching according to a common formula, research funds are distributed on an increasingly selective basis (Scott and Watson 1994).

There are no examples in Europe of stratified systems on the Californian pattern, but elements of stratification can be observed in many countries. The differences between full universities and university colleges in Sweden have already been mentioned. In most of Europe, universities retain a monopoly of doctoral programmes; in some countries this extends to all higher degrees. But none of these features is necessarily evidence of deliberate California-style stratification. An important distinction must also be drawn between anachronistic monopolies typical of dual systems, which are generally eroded in the transition to binary and/or unified systems, and the division of institutional labour and differentiation of missions typical of stratified systems.

So these four organisational models are probably too simple to capture the complexity of existing European higher education systems. Their relationship, if any, is also unclear. Are they independent models, genuine alternatives, or do they describe a dynamic sequence? In other words, are dual or unified systems stable, or do they have a tendency to develop into, successively, binary and stratified systems? The Dutch experience tends to support the latter interpretation. Not only have the HBOs been heavily influenced by the success of the English polytechnics, the inner dynamics of higher education in the Netherlands seem to be encouraging the development of a more coherent, and therefore more self-confident, non-university sector – for example, the aggregation of smaller and more specialist HBOs into larger and more comprehensive 'polytechnics'. (The English category has been widely adopted.)

A possible schema describing the development of European higher education systems is given in Figure 4.1. In Figure 4.2, I have tried, using this schema, to indicate the shifts which have taken place among selected higher education systems. However, it is important

University-dominated systems:
in which any other institutions are seen as part of the secondary or, at the most, technical education sectors, and in which the universities and these embryonic post-secondary institutions are regarded as separate sectors

Dual systems:
in which these other institutions are now acknowledged to be properly post-secondary and the need for co-ordination with the university sector is recognised, although the latter are still seen as structurally superior

Binary systems:
in which two parallel higher education systems, one consisting of the traditional universities and the other based on 'alternative' institutions, develop (there is a tendency for the relationship between these two systems to drift away from complementarity and towards competition)

Unified systems:
in which a comprehensive higher education system is created embracing both the traditional universities and other institutions, although important differences of status and reputation remain (particularly in respect of research)

Stratified systems:
in which a common system is maintained but the missions of individual institutions, externally and internally, become differentiated (this differentation may come about as a result of political action or through the operation of the market)

Figure 5.1. The development of European higher education

to recognise that, like all linear representations, this schema is much too simple. It cannot capture all the subtleties of policy change. First, it does not give insufficient weight to the circularities, or regressions, which characterise recent developments in some European higher education systems, notably in Germany. Second, the tendency for binary systems to reproduce themselves at lower levels when unified systems of higher education are being established is not covered. A good example is Britain, where the distinction between universities and polytechnics has been replaced by a new demarcation between higher education institutions and further education colleges. However, in time – and in turn – this new demarcation is likely to be eroded as unified post-secondary education systems develop.

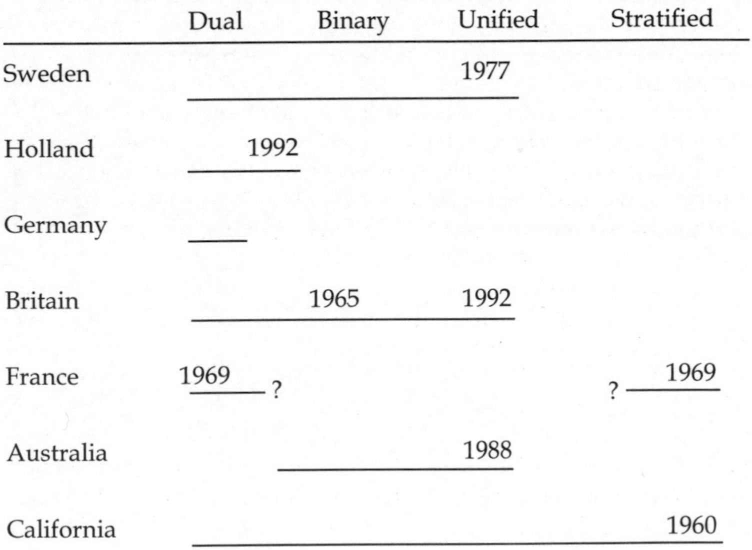

	Dual	Binary	Unified	Stratified
Sweden			1977	
Holland	1992			
Germany	—			
Britain		1965	1992	
France	1969 ?			? 1969
Australia			1988	
California				1960

Figure 5.2. The shifts which have taken place among higher education systems

Particularities and Commonalities

In the third section, the particularities and commonalities which have shaped European higher education systems will be considered. This may help to answer the question just posed – are these different organisational models mutually independent, or are they part of a sequence? Or, more simply, are present differences likely to persist, or is convergence likely to occur?

Particularities reflect the contingencies of national systems. Their structure grows out of national cultures – political, administrative, educational and cultural (ideological?). Generalisations, therefore, are suspect. The British binary system of 1965–92, for example, should not be compared too closely to the Dutch dual system because they grew up in very different circumstances and are/were subject to very different imperatives. If particularities are emphasised, only limited convergence is to be expected between higher education systems.

Commonalities arise from the over-arching trends which affect all higher education institutions and systems. These trends are political – the drive for wider access and, correspondingly, increased accountability; socio-economic – the role played by higher education in determining identities in a modern society which has transcended (or substantially modified) older demarcations of class, gender or ethnicity, as well as its role in producing a highly-skilled and adaptable labour-force; and cultural and scientific – intellectual trends sweep the world, while new configurations of science and technology are truly global phenomena (Gibbons *et al.* 1994). To the extent that these trends are represented and embedded in institutions and systems, convergence seems more likely.

The factors which I have called 'particularities', have clearly been important in shaping European higher education systems in the past. It is impossible to describe these factors in detail. I will just mention a few of the more important. One is the pattern of primary and secondary education. Especially relevant is the persistence, or otherwise, of divided secondary school systems (Commission of the European Communities 1990). Those countries with divided secondary school systems are more likely to have dual, or binary higher education systems. For example, in the Netherlands the HBOs, on the whole, recruit their students from the five-year vocational secondary school system, while the universities take most of their students from the six-year academic stream. On the other hand, those countries which have abandoned, or modified, the traditional demarcation between grammar schools, *lycées, gymnasia* and other, less noble, types of secondary education are more likely to have unified – or, at any rate, binary-higher education systems.

However, the articulation between comprehensive secondary education systems and unified higher education systems is far from straightforward. It applies to Sweden. But in France, where secondary education is more comprehensive than in Germany but less so than in Sweden or Britain, the picture is complicated by the presence of the selective *grandes écoles*. And in Britain during the 1960s, comprehensive reorganisation of secondary education and the establishment of the binary system in higher education were complementary, not contradictory, policies.

In any case, a more fundamental question can be asked. On a larger historical canvas, are the detailed differences between school systems: the particularities, more significant that their shared features: the commonalities? In outline, the evolutionary pattern was the same across Europe. All European countries developed universal systems of elementary education in the course of the nineteenth century. In the twentieth century these were extended gradually to the secondary level, either by incorporating existing academic secondary schools into a common system or by establishing new kinds of (comprehensive) school. Often the former tactic was a prelude to the latter. Perhaps the links between secondary and higher education are a better example of convergence than of difference?

A second is the contrast between 'northern' and 'southern' European higher education systems. Broadly, in northern Europe there are more examples of dual, or binary, systems, while in the south the university has remained dominant. Italy, Portugal, Greece and, less categorically, Spain, all have higher education systems in which alternative institutions are only weakly developed. There are, however, important exceptions. Sweden, and now Finland, have unified systems (although it can be argued that they represent post-dual, or post-binary, systems while in much of southern Europe there are pre-dual systems). Austria, unlike Germany, has no *Fachhochschulen* sector to complement the universities; a relic perhaps of its 'southern' orientation, although currently there are plans to develop institutions of this type.

The most obvious explanation of this north–south contrast is the different pace of industrialisation across the continent. On the whole, the industrial revolution came earlier to, and was more intense in, northern Europe. The growth of an industrial economy was the most powerful factor in both reshaping the university sector and stimulating the development of non-university higher education. In southern Europe, there was less pressure, until recently, to reform the universities. There was also less need to develop elaborate systems of technical education out of which alternative higher education institutions could grow.

However, these differences in industrial structure between northern and southern European countries, although still visible, have been very much reduced during the past 25 years. So, to the extent that choices between different types of higher education system are heavily influenced by these industrial structures, it might be expected that the broad division between the north, with its dual systems, and the south, with its university-dominated systems, would also have been eroded. There is some evidence to support this, notably in Spain where short-cycle academic programmes have been developed in the universities. However, this may point to an important generic distinction between northern and southern European higher education systems. In the south, a binary distinction is more likely to be created by establishing short-cycle programmes within universities, while in the north explicit binary systems based on institutional differentiation are more common.

A third factor is the influence of research organisation on the structure of higher education systems. In much of central and eastern Europe, and in the former Soviet Union, research is still dominated by the academies of sciences, and their associated institutes and units. The stake of universities, at any rate in cutting-edge scientific research and in technological development, is limited, although since the fall of Communism there have been moves in Poland and the Czech Republic to (re)integrate academy institutes into universities (hendrichová 1992). These moves have sometimes been resisted by the academies.

But this institutional separation between research and higher education is not confined to the former Soviet bloc countries. In France, the main agency for research is the Centre Nationale des Recherches Scientifiques (CNRS), and its linked laboratories; many of which, however, are sited on university campuses. Also, CNRS and university researchers actively collaborate (Neave 1993, pp.159–191). In Germany, high-level research is undertaken in the Max Planck institutes outside formal university structures. Even in Britain, there has been a proliferation of semi-detached research institutes which do not receive core funding from their universities (Becher, Henkel and Kogan 1994).

The organisation of research exercises an important influence over the structure of higher education systems. If most research is undertaken outside the university, or in loosely-linked research institutes, there is less incentive to establish a dual, or binary, system. However, if it is undertaken within higher education, the case for a unified system (or, at any rate, a system in which it is difficult to discriminate between institutions) is much weaker. But, as the British experience suggests, it may be more difficult to limit the ambitions of non-university institutions with regard to research within a rivalrous binary system than in a formally unified, but informally stratified, system.

A fourth particularity arises from the contrast between the different strands within the European university tradition identified by Professor Gellert. The influence of these models on the structure of higher education systems is significant. In those European countries where universities have become associated with the transmission of either a scientific or liberal culture, the incentive to develop a dual system has been strong. Motives have been mixed, to protect the university from 'sub-scientific' or philistine values or to bypass them by creating more socially and economically relevant alternatives, but the effect has been the same. In other countries, where universities have retained a more pronounced 'professional' orientation, the pressure to establish a powerful non-university sector has been much less.

Commonalities are both easier and more difficult to describe than particularities. They are easier, because the socio-economic environments in which higher education systems find themselves are becoming increasingly alike. The shift towards a knowledge-based and services-oriented economy, the rethinking of the welfare state in a post-scarcity age, the globalisation of culture, the acceleration of science and technology, the radical extension of the higher education 'franchise' – these are phenomena which affect every European country. As a result, the exceptionalisms of particular university traditions have been reduced.

The best example is British higher education, once sharply distinguished from other European systems in terms of access (more limited) and autonomy (more extensive). In the past decade, Britain has achieved participation levels broadly similar to those of other European countries and British universities have largely lost their privileged status. Also, the European Union, although only obliquely involved in higher education, has the potential to become a powerful centralising and homogenising force. As a common labour-market, and industrial, financial and social policies develop, the challenges which EU higher education systems face will become increasingly similar.[1]

Commonalities are more difficult to describe, because it is less clear that this convergence of socio-economic environments will necessarily lead to the convergence of higher education systems. Distinctive structural arrangements may be compatible with common missions. The result may be not so much convergence as fuzziness. Also, it has been argued that there is likely to be less emphasis on grand structural reform at times of slower growth, partly because there may be less need to diversify into new kinds of higher educa-

---

1   See de Witte (1993)

tion, and so to differentiate institutional missions, and partly because root-and-branch reform of the structure of higher education demands increased resources which are not available (Teichler 1993, p.31).

However, there is little evidence of a reduction in the complexity of the demands made of higher education systems, despite the slow-down in the growth of student numbers and restrictions on university budgets. And increasing complexity is the key to institutional and sectoral differentiation (Clark 1993, p.266). Also, the retreat from grand structural reforms is consistent with the schema of systemic evolution, which I described earlier. The shift from tightly structured dual – or binary – systems to more open – or fuzzy – systems, formally unified but actually stratified, is part of that schema. Finally, the erosion of dual, or binary, systems does not mean that the process of differentiation in European higher education systems has slowed; rather it has become too rapid and volatile to be expressed through sectorisation. Instead, differentiation has begun to operate at the institutional, or sub-institutional, level.

Conclusion

There is no Europe-wide model for the organisation of higher education systems. Particularities will inevitably persist. But are European systems on a convergent course? Certainly the inter-action between European universities and other higher education institutions has sharply increased during the past two decades – and at the level of policy and management, not only of scientific and scholarly ex-change. There is a heightened awareness of developments in other systems, which may provide the basis for convergent policies.

One possible interpretation suggests that dual systems developed and binary systems were established in many countries, to handle the heterogeneity which accompanied the rapid expansion of higher education in the 1960s; but that, as the inflexibility of these divided systems has become apparent and the prospect of mass higher education has appeared less forbidding, a drift to more adaptable forms of differentiation may be under way.

In the 1960s and 1970s, there were many reasons why European Governments preferred to articulate dual systems and/or create binary structures to cope with the strains of rapid growth. First, the traditional ethos of the universities was respected. With the move to much higher levels of participation there was a fear that universities would be contaminated by less 'scientific' values. Second, it was believed that undifferentiated systems inevitably produced 'academic drift' which undermined attempts to produce more vocational forms of higher education. There was a need, therefore, to create alternative institutional models.

Third, most institutions, universities and others, were small and homogeneous. Their managerial structures were underdeveloped. Large institutions with multiple missions were regarded as both undesirable and unworkable. The problem of complexity had to be addressed by establishing new, and new kinds of, institution. Fourth, the 1960s and 1970s were an age of enthusiasm for social and economic planning. This enthusiasm encouraged large-scale systems building rather than reliance on the initiative of individual institutions. Fifth, divided systems were the norm. In nearly every country, other higher (or advanced-level) institutions – colleges of technology, art and business, teachers' colleges – already existed alongside the universities. Dual, or binary, systems were simply rationalistions of the *status quo*.

Most of these reasons which persuaded European countries a generation ago to articulate dual systems or create binary structures are less persuasive today. First, dual and/or binary policies are difficult to reconcile with either democratic or 'market' values. This is especially true when, as is usually the case, there is a clear association between top-tier institutions, universities, and student recruitment from privileged social-economic groups. These policies are also seen as incompatible with 'market' values, because they inhibit institutional initiative and discourage entrepreneurial behaviour. Second, divided systems appear to have encouraged 'academic drift' rather than prevented it. Normally the university has remained the ideal model to which less 'noble' institutions continue to aspire, but it may have become a less dynamic institution because new challenges have been met by non-university institutions.

Third, significant changes have taken place in the relationship between universities and the State (McDaniël and Buising 1992). These changes have not been consistent across Europe. In some countries, notably Britain, the autonomy of the (traditional) universities has been sharply eroded; in others, like Sweden, universities have been granted increased administrative autonomy. Yet there is perhaps a common theme: the desire to recast universities as 'open' organisations rather than as 'closed' institutions. Fourth, universities have become large and complex organisations well able to handle multiple missions. The 'collegial' university, governed by the academic guild assisted by low-profile administrators has been succeeded by the 'managerial' university dominated by an increasingly expert cadre of senior managers. Finally, large-scale system-wide planning has gone out of fashion. The taste now is for 'market' solutions, even within state systems of higher education. This 'market' approach is difficult to reconcile with structured binary systems which assign missions to classes of institution. Instead, it encourages much finer grain and more flexible differentiation between and within institutions, regardless of their formal nomenclature.

These reasons do not, of course, carry the same weight in all European systems. Yet their influence is felt in all. In higher education systems, as in many other kinds of system, the growth of complexity has produced two very different responses. The first is the imposition of more elaborate control mechanisms – in areas like budgetary accountability, research selectivity and quality assessment. The second is an increase in volatility as institutions, and individuals, adapt to new environments; evidence of this is provided by the growing fuzziness of European higher education systems. If, as seems probable, this dialectic between control and volatility can be more easily reconciled, or expressed, within formally unified but highly differentiated systems than in dual, or binary, systems, European systems are likely to evolve in that direction.

There are intriguing correspondences between the growing fuzziness of European higher education systems and the increasing flexibility of the post-industrial labour force. Once, a clear distinction could be made in occupational structures between 'graduate' and 'technician' careers. So it made sense to train them separately, either on different courses or in different institutions. Today, it is more difficult to make this distinction, partly because credit accumulation and transfer systems have tended to erode the academic differences between different courses and qualifications and partly because the very notions of technical expertise and professional knowledge are being radically reconfigured.

How does this conclusion relate to the overall theme, the goals and purposes of higher education in the 21st century? Modern society is in the throes of profound transformations, technical and industrial but also cultural and moral. There is a superfluity of labels and slogans which relate to these transformations – the growth of post-industrial society, the construction of information super-highways, the decay of the welfare state, the progress of the gender revolution, the rise of post-modernism. In almost all of these diverse phenomena higher education is implicated, directly or indirectly. The university, as the key institution within even mass higher education systems, must be flexible and fleet-footed; it must be able to embrace intellectual ambiguity (even contradiction) and to take on multiple missions (Scott, forthcoming).

Yet, at the same time, it must preserve its status as a leading institution, perhaps *the* leading institution, of the modern system; an arena in which a synthesis is achieved between fundamental values, of rationality and perhaps morality, and the more fleeting imperatives of a new age. Perhaps it is coming to be recognised that this synthesis is more likely to be achieved within more flexible higher education systems, where a greater value is placed on institutional initiative than in planned systems where goals and mission are pre-determined. There are echoes of this growing recognition in the evolving structures of European higher education systems which I have tried to describe.

References

Becher, T., Henkel, M. and Kogan, M. (1994) *Graduate Education in Britain.* London: Jessica Kingsley Publishers.

Brennan, J., Goedegebuure, L., Little, B., Shah, T., Westerheijden, D. and Weusthof, P. (1992) *European Higher Education Systems: Germany, The Netherland, The United Kingdom.* London: Council for National Academic Awards and Twente: Centre for Higher Education Policy Studies.

Clark, B. (1984) 'Higher education systems: Organisational conditions of policy formation and implementation.' In R. Premfors (ed) *Higher Education Organisation: Conditions for Policy Implementation.* Stockholm: Almqvist and Wiksell International.

Clark, B. (1993) 'The problem of complexity in modern higher education.' In S. Rothblatt and B. Wittrock (eds) *The Europan and American University since 1800: Historical and Sociological Essays.* Cambridge: Cambridge University Press.

Commission of the European Communities (1990) *Structures of the Education and Initial Training Systems of the European Community.* Prepared jointly by EURYDICE, the European Information Network in the European Community, and CEDEFOP, the European Centre for the Development of Vocational Training (Brussels).

Commission of the European Communities (1991) *Memorandum on Higher Education in the European Community.* Brussels.

Commission of the European Communities (1993) *Guidelines for Community Action in the Field of Education and Training.* Brussels.

Condren, P. (1988) *Preparing for the Twenty-First Century: A Report on Higher Education in California.* Sacramento: California Postsecindary Education Commission.

Council for Studies of Higher Education (1994) *Swedish Universities & University Colleges 1992/93.* VHS report Series 1994:3/Short Version of Annual Report (Stockholm).

Gellert, C. (1993) 'Structural and functional differentiation: Remarks on changing paradigms of tertiary education in Europe.' In C. Gellert (ed) *Higher Education in Europe*. London: Jessica Kingsley Publishers.

Gibbons, M., Limoges, C., Nowotny, H., Schwartzman, S., Scott, P. and Trow, M. (1994) *The New Production of Knowledge: The Dynamics of Science and Research in Contemporary Societies*. London: Sage.

Hendrichovà, J. (1992) *Recent Developments in Higher Education in Central and Eastern Europe (Czech and Slovak Republics, Hungary, Poland, Romania and the Russian Federation)*. Prague: Centre for Higher Education Studies.

McDaniël, O.C. and Buising, W. (1992) *The Level of Government Influence in Higher Education in the US and Western Europe*. Zoetermeer and Twente: Delphi Research Project.

Ministry of Education and Science, HBO-Raad, VSNU, and NUFFIC (1989) *Higher Education in the Netherlands: Characteristics, Structure, Figures, Facts*. Zoeternmeer: Ministry of Education and Science.

Neave, G. (1993) 'Séparation de Corps: The training of advanced students and the organisation of research in France.' In C.C. Burton (ed) *The Research Foundations of Graduate Education*. Berkeley: University of California Press.

Organisation for Economic Co-operation and Development (1973) *Short-Cycle Higher Education: A Search for Identity*. Paris: OECD.

Organisation for Economic Co-operation and Development (1989) *Review of Higher Education in California*. Paris: OECD

Organisation for Economic Co-operation and Development and the Department for Employment, Education and Training (1993) *Post-Compulsory, Further and Higher Education in the Federal Republic of Germany*. Canberra: Centre for Continuing Education, Australian National University.

Rothblatt, S. (ed) (1992) *The OECD, the Master Plan and the California Dream: A Berkeley Conversation*. Berkeley: Centre for Studies in Higher Education

Rothblatt, S. and Wittrock, B. (1993) 'Universities and higher education.' In S. Rothblatt and B. Wittrock (eds) *The European and American University since 1800: Historical and Sociological Essays*. Cambridge: Cambridge University Press.

Scott, P. (1984) *The Crisis of the University*. London: Croom Helm.

Scott, P. (1991) *Higher Education in Sweden: A View from the Outside*. Stockholm: National Board for Universities and Colleges.

Scott, P. (forthcoming) 'The meanings of mass higher education.' *University of Leeds Review*.

Scott, P. and Watson, D. (1994) 'Setting the scene.' In J. Bocock and D. Watson (eds) *Managing the University Curriculum: Making Common Cause.* Buckingham: Open University Press.

Teichler, U. (1993) 'Structures of higher education systems in Europe.' in C. Gellert (ed) *Higher Education in Europe.* London: Jessica Kingsley Publishers.

Witte, de B. (1993) 'Higher education and the constitution of the European community.' In C. Gellert (ed) *Higher Education in Europe.* London: Jessica Kingsley Publishers.

Chapter 6

Who is Going to Study?

Staffan Helmfrid

I had the bad luck to bear the responsibility for a department, faculty and university at a time when the then political system saw reforms of the educational system in the perspective of a class struggle. I was Dean of the Social Sciences at Stockholm University at a time when 5000 out of 15,000 of its students were somewhat to the left of the communist party and an even greater proportion were anxious about their bleak prospects on the labour market.

It was also bad luck to be Vice-chancellor, in exactly the ten years when the 1977 reform incorporated universities into an unpopular, all-embracing factory-inspired production line system of post-secondary education, governed by an impenetrable hierarchy of decision making levels (seven!) of more or less corporate bodies. Life was unpredictable in those years, except for the annual budget cuts! In a way, it must have been more fun to be in office in earlier times when universities were respected, freer and well-endowed.

My hopes and fears for the future are thus solidly founded in experience. Some signals heard after the recent change in government in Sweden, alas, remind us that hot summers are often followed by cold winters!

Higher education, its goals and purposes can be looked at from two different angles: from the point of view of society, or from the point of view of the young individual facing a strategic choice in life. Most studies of higher education take the view of society and make statistics of students. But I have often had reason to reflect on the woes that meet the individual young boy or girl in secondary school, when having to answer to the 'why, what, where and when' of further education. And of course any such reflections must bear in mind the individual's environment, i.e., society, its possibilities and restrictions. What are the prospects for the beginning of the 21st century?

It is, of course, a romantic misconception that sudden changes occur at the turn of centuries. This is just a tribute to the decimal system. Past, present and future are somehow always present at the same time, spatially side by side.

No doubt we in advanced societies are now in the midst of the most revolutionary changes ever in working life, as we enter the information technology (IT) age. Young people today grow up in a social, technical and natural environment, more different from that of our own childhood than ours was from the Middle Ages. Nevertheless, we must also remember that significant parts of the world population, even today, still live in the Middle Ages and this can affect our future. Our Swedish future is probably already manifest somewhere on earth, if only we could be sure where! The world is a mosaic not only of different cultures, but also of cultures in different stages of evolution. This is what makes real communication so difficult and useful generalisations impossible. It is a common mistake of futurologists to neglect this geographical-time dimension. The more change accelerates in the centres of innovation, the larger are the gaps that exist in the world picture.

To those who study the world in curves it looks very simple and the near future almost foreseeable. For those who study the way human beings think, feel and react, their level of information when taking decisions, their relation to reason, knowledge, religion and superstition the world is complex beyond imagination and the way ahead is unpredictable. The greatest threat to our future right now may not be nuclear weapons but the growing gap between traditionalism and modernity inside all kinds of society or between the needs and expectations of the more and less developed countries. Our young generation meets a world in which infectious anti-intellectual movements and uncompromising fanaticism are rife – a market place for occultism and political, religious or just mad salvationists. In all conflicts between rationalism and fundamentalism, intellectuals are the first victims; we have seen societies eradicate their own educated people simply because they were educated. Thus, the basic aim of all education must be to broaden and deepen the base in which a rational, liberal, democratic society can flourish. In this perspective it is essential that every citizen should have an education based on scholarship and science. It is a more and more important mission of higher education to safeguard democracy and the development of society, to help people understand a changing world and to accept and facilitate both change and renewal of society.

As a preparation for future political decisions relating to post-secondary education in Sweden and with a clear ambition to raise the level of competence in Swedish society, the former Minister of Research and Education, Per Unckel, opened a wide-ranging public discussion and asked universities, academies and others to present their ideas about the future. This resulted in Agenda 2000. I have good reason to refer to the contribution by the Royal Academy of Sciences to this because it is, in my opinion, most comprehensive and constructive. Agenda 2000 was seen by the minister as:

> an enlargement and extension of recent reforms of the school system and of the system for higher education and research. Through these reforms, with quality and flexibility as key concepts, Sweden's capacity to handle and make use of the increasingly rapid knowledge production that is to be expected in the future will be strengthened.

> 'Of seminal importance to the scenario and the ensuing discussions,' wrote the Academy of Sciences, 'have been the global environmental perspective and more generally conditions of human life. Natural resources and the conservation of these resources, health problems and the battle against disease are central factors but cultural aspects, relations between people and nations and issues concerning values and human ethics are also included'...solutions on a national level are more or less impossible' and further 'the traditional Swedish educational structure with centrally planned nationwide comprehensive undergraduate programmes has recently been abolished and replaced by a structure that gives more freedom to universities and colleges to elaborate their own educational profiles and that allows students to combine subjects and courses across disciplinary and faculty borderlines. The actual choices of students have thus got an increased significance.'

It is helpful to consider the future from a long historical perspective, ignoring the short term perturbations, so let us take 150 years in three steps. In the pre-industrial society only 150 to 200 years ago, the vast majority of the population was engaged in agriculture. A small fraction of the total of people's time was devoted to other market production and very little to leisure. Almost all the time, apart from sleeping, was needed for subsistence. The universities emerged in this society and their task was limited to educating the higher ranks in State and Church administration. Vocational training was given within the farm or workshop from parents to children, from master to apprentice.

The industrial society was based on the more and more efficient use of steam power and power driven machinery with the transfer of manpower from agriculture to manufacturing and services. The increased efficiency of work gave more time for leisure. Vocational training for a growing number of areas was placed in new institu-

tions, and the universities grew in response to the demand for teachers, engineers, economists, physicians and lawyers. Student numbers
remained modest, just 2–4 per cent of an age group.

The evolving 'information-technology' society will mean further
fundamental changes with consequences that cannot yet be clearly
visualised, but it is obvious that robotisation of production and
computerisation of information services are rapidly reducing the
human input into production. The salaried working time is rapidly
being reduced, only part of that time is required for maintaining a
subsistence level; much time can be spared for unpaid work, travel
and leisure. It is evident that education and, in particular, higher
education should provide the tools so that everyone can benefit from
the richness of nature, culture, and society both at home and abroad.
The IT society needs more teachers and experts in the humanities and
social sciences, as well as highly qualified specialists in the professions. Education will take on new forms in new media and much
in-work vocational training at all levels will be offered within big
companies.

Towards the end of this century, we can expect the number of
students in post-secondary education to be the majority of an age
group. Again, the Academy of Sciences said, 'A general and significant trend in education seems to be the loosening of the once tight
coupling between kinds of higher education and career paths'. We
have to 'design educational programmes which prepare for a much
wider range of professions and which can serve as starting points for
on-the-job training and continuing education rather than as a finish-
ing school'; 'basic intellectual competencies and broad cognitive
profiles which include elements from several disciplines, even different faculties seem to be in line with future needs for competence both
in research work and in the general labour market'; '…people will
need a broader and better knowledge base to be able to orient
themselves culturally and politically in tomorrow's world, to be well
equipped for working life and to function as citizens in a democratic
society. Natural sciences and cultural sciences must then be kept
together higher up in the school system than they are today and more
students must have the opportunity to acquire deeper knowledge
and better qualifications'; '…should we simply expand the existing
system of higher education…or is it necessary to introduce a more
differentiated system of higher education and research with several
different tasks and ambitions? A system with other collective actors
than the state. Should we not much more seriously than before
discuss and treat the educational system as an integrated totality and
thus secure that the different levels are working well together…a
differentiated system of post secondary education that will meet the

demands from a larger and more heterogeneous group of students and to clearly define roles and responsibilities for the various actors in the educational arena'; '...a significant task is to define the role and missions of the traditional (discipline-based) university in relation to other institutions.'

The Why, What, Where and When of Studying; The Individual's Choice

Recent OECD statistics show that for most professions, post-secondary education in Sweden is relatively unprofitable and that this profitability for most professions has been falling over the past 20 years. The spread of salaries in Sweden is low in international comparisons; many countries have a higher proportion who have graduated from post secondary education. In the natural sciences and technology the Swedish deficit is more pronounced and especially so when it comes to PhDs. The Academy of Sciences comments: 'The present lack of competent teaching staff both in upper secondary schools and in educational institutions at the tertiary level will be even more detrimental in the future...there are unsatisfactory qualifications among schoolteachers particularly in the natural sciences.'

Why Should I Study?

Now let us turn to the girl or boy in secondary school aged 16–18 from families without experience of higher education. What are the incentives to undertake further years of study with its hardship, risk of failure and possible lifelong indebtedness? In a pre-industrial society the life of the student and the life of a farmhand was very much to the advantage of the student, provided someone supported the student during his studies. In an advanced industrial society, welfare state and leisure oriented modern society, the hardships of a student life are unchanged but are combined with rising personal indebtedness. His or her life for some years is more and more disadvantaged compared with the regulated working hours, leisure time and the possibility to accumulate resources of someone in employment; students and unemployed young people are the proletariats of today's society!

The simpler it is to find easy jobs giving enough money to provide a life better than that of the student, the more incentive is needed to recruit students for demanding studies. Attitudes to life and career are different in the first generations born into the welfare state from all earlier generations.

Recruitment in relation to social strata has been seen as a major problem in the past 35 years of university politics. All sorts of manipulations of the school system, matriculation rules and curricula (even at a time excluding compulsory study of foreign languages at university level) have ended in failure. The key problem may be prospects; both in relation to types of job and pay, on the one hand and financing of studies, on the other. Our system of financing study aimed at giving equal opportunities failed, I believe, because of loan burden.

There are very different attitudes towards loan and debt in different social strata. The well-to-do see favourable loan conditions and students with good job prospects see no problem in debt. Poor families feel the burden of debt, especially if low wages and a bleak labour market make the possibility of repaying the debt remote even in a lifetime. There is also the troubling fact that the merit value of postgraduate degrees seems to have little or no merit in many sectors of the labour market; indeed, this is reinforced by the negative attitude of society to intellectual work and superior knowledge. It is crucial that this attitude is changed.

In times of recession and high unemployment studies function as temporary employment; the queues for higher education and to the employment exchange are to some extent communicating vessels! Clearly we need better incentives for young people.

What Shall I Study?

The Academy stresses:

> It is necessary to take immediate measures against the existing lack of students in science and technology... Since the total number of students in relevant age groups will sink in years to come, the base for recruiting young people to undergraduate programmes in natural science and technology will be totally unsatisfactory in the very near future... Languages, mathematics and problem solving capabilities are basic needs in a future integrated European labour market.

These fields are obviously not the primary choice for most young people; their emotional preferences are towards different disciplines and types of profession.

Where Shall I Study?

The expansion of the post-secondary education system in Sweden has made higher education well-distributed geographically. Swedish students are also offered a broad choice in borderless Europe and already more than 20,000 Swedish students are studying abroad under the ERASMUS and other programmes. This is already more than the 10 per cent seen as a target. Also, a majority of high school students in Sweden is prepared to consider studies, jobs and careers abroad. How many will come the other way to Sweden? Language and climate must play a part.

When Shall I Study?

We are entering an era when lifelong education is a necessity for keeping up with developments within one's own profession. In earlier times, one could acquire the competence for lifelong professional work; now there is a growing gap between the knowledge of any individual and the frontiers of knowledge. The need for lifelong education is not just for professional reasons but also to enrich a long life in retirement.

So in the end the answer to the question I put as the title of this article, is that practically everybody is going to undertake some higher education provided that there are the right incentives and that suitable programmes of study are offered.

References

Royal Academy of Letters, History and Antiquities (1980) 'Man, landscape and the future.' Papers and Proceedings of a Conference in Stockholm 12–14 February 1979. *Academy Conference Proceedings, no.4.*

Chapter 7

Distance Systems in Europe

Walter Perry

I will start by asking, 'What is a system of higher education?' On the one hand, one can answer by saying that within the institutions of higher education there is actually a plethora of systems. They offer programmes of different structure and duration; they use different methods of communication and have staff and students of very different quality. I have no brief to discuss these various systems, but let me draw a couple of caricatures. In the ideal institution, the staff would all be internationally renowned scholars doing research at the frontiers of knowledge; they would meet highly intelligent students who had excellent school education on a one-to-one basis and would by encouragement, example and explanation, bring out the best scholarly qualities in their pupils. Real education only occurred, someone once said, when two fine minds rubbed together. This is a caricature of one system. My second caricature is of the poorest institutions, whose teachers' qualifications had been obtained maybe years earlier and never been updated; who gave dull lectures to large classes of students; who had acquired only minimal qualifications in school while managing to escape any real education; and who were barely numerate or literate. These students would feverishly take detailed notes of the lectures and in the end would regurgitate this information (right or wrong!) and pass the examination. If my first caricature is a pipe dream, the second is too true to be funny!

But I would actually answer my first question, 'What is a system of higher education?' in an alternative way. That is, because while there was until 1971 really only one system of higher education in Europe, there are now two after the Open University started operations.

The Open University, a distance education system, was different and new in principle and mode of operation. What were the essential characteristics that marked it out as a new system – a new species of university?

1. There were no entry qualifications except that all students had to be over 21 and have an address in the UK.

2. The students were not collected in one institution but could keep their jobs and stay at home, except for one week in the academic year at a summer school.

3. Apart from the summer school there was no requirement to ever meet a member of staff, although remedial tutorials were offered to those who wanted them.

4. The teaching received by the student was open to inspection by the public, by academics in other institutions, politicians, and by critics in the media. This was because the material was available in printed form in book shops and by public radio and television.

5. The courses were modular and each module was assessed independently.

6. All these characteristics were achieved without compromise in the quality of education as judged by external examiners from other universities and later by employers.

This new distance learning system did not originate with the academic establishment; the idea had been suggested by a few academics but the majority regarded it with profound suspicion. It was forced on the academic world by the then British Prime Minister, Harold Wilson. It was a remarkable act of political faith and his decision to gamble on its success demanded great courage and imagination. The fact that the Open University that emerged bore little resemblance to that in his original version in no way detracts from his vision. The changes were due to the impact of the small band of people who implemented the decision and were given both the time and the resources to turn it into a workable reality. Its history in the last 25 years shows how much of the academic world was, as a result, dragged sometimes kicking and screaming towards the 21st century.

I cannot resist recalling some of the remarks from newspapers and politicians before 1971. The proposal about the new university, then called the 'University of the Air', was published by the government in 1966. The editorial in the *Times Educational Supplement* began, 'Mr. Wilson's pipe dream of a University of the Air, now adumbrated in a White Paper (government report) as vague as it is insubstantial, is just the sort of cosy scheme that shows the socialists at their most endearing and impractical worst,' and ended with, 'can anyone by any stretch of the imagination justify a priority for this well-intentioned but untimely caprice.' In 1968, with the announcement of my appointment as vice-chancellor, the *Times* suggested that the success rate, if we were lucky, might reach 2 per cent and considered that there was little demand for the new institution. They ended, 'It is time for the planning committee and Miss Lee to convince us that the university is something more acceptable, feasible and desirable than just an expensive memorial to one who may have been its original mentor, that most brilliant of genuinely self-educated men, Aneurin Bevan.' This was particularly vicious since Jennie Lee was Bevan's widow.

In general, comments from all sides expressed extreme scepticism that the new venture had any chance of success, and while this was very discouraging it bred in the staff gathered around me a spirit of 'do or die' and in the event we failed the expectations of almost everyone because we did and we didn't die!

Courses were offered in six faculties: arts, social sciences, education, science, mathematics and technology. It was interesting to observe that when the results of students who had started without any formal school qualifications were compared with those who had the qualifications that could have gained them entrance to any of the conventional universities, there was no significance in the faculties of arts, social sciences or education. In science and technology, the qualified students showed a small but significant advantage, but in mathematics the difference was so great that we started to advise applicants to do a year's remedial study before starting.

Clearly one cannot teach at a distance subjects such as medicine, dentistry, or veterinary medicine where direct contact with patients is vital and there are areas of science and technology where success would be difficult to achieve. Laboratory experience in subjects such as chemistry, biology and/or electronic engineering can be provided by a combination of TV demonstrations (far more effective than ordinary laboratory demonstrations since every student has a front row view), home experiment kits hired out to students and a one-week intensive laboratory work during a summer school. Nautical, and aeronautical engineering, forestry and agriculture are virtually impossible to teach in this way, so there are limits to what is possible.

Each course was the equivalent of a full-time student load of study for either half or quarter of an academic year. Credits needed to be obtained in six of the half-year courses for a pass degree, or eight for an honours degree. Credit was awarded on a continuous assessment basis, by tutor-marked essays and multiple-choice papers marked by computer, together with a final written examination carried out under supervision.

Since there were no entrance qualifications students were admitted on a first come first served basis. The actual number admitted was limited by the size of the total government grant available, since fees provided only about 15 per cent of the total cost; this proportion has increased in recent years as insisted by the government. The modal age at entry was about 27 years. Most students were in full-time employment in occupations that were mainly middle class rather than working class. Since the university had been created by the Labour Party there was considerable criticism that it was not providing for the educationally disadvantaged; a survey revealed that at the age of 18 when they left school, 80 per cent had fathers in working class occupations. By the age of 27 they had become upwardly mobile, but found themselves in jobs with no prospects of promotion unless they acquired further qualifications. They were, therefore, committed students who worked very hard indeed. In this they resembled the ex-service students just after the war, who were similarly more motivated and committed than new school leavers. The result was that the success rate in attaining credits in individual courses was nearly 90 per cent and the final rate of graduation was just over 50 per cent of those who started as registered students. Many of the others formed a group who had succeeded in individual courses but were not concerned to obtain degree qualification because they had obtained the knowledge that they had sought.

After about five years, when the first degree programme had been accepted in the UK as being equivalent to the degree of the regular residential universities, a new programme of continuing education was started. In my view, this was a more important function for the OU than the first degree programme, but would have lacked credibility until the undergraduate programme had been established. Unlike the undergraduate programme, it is not subsidised by a government grant but is self financing from fees or from external sponsorship by employers; it has grown very rapidly since it started about 20 years ago. Whereas the first degree numbers reached a plateau of about 80,000, the continuing education group has reached about 120,000. The courses are updating, refreshing or retraining and cover such areas as advanced technology, business studies and community care as well as all the undergraduate courses taken at full cost.

The cost of the first degree at the OU is hard to estimate exactly, but is about 60 per cent of the cost in other universities. There are, of course, no maintenance grants supporting students during full time study and the capital costs are small since there are no teaching buildings. On the other hand, the OU is parasitic on other universities since it uses their accommodation for summer schools at relatively modest cost and employs many of their staff part time on a sessional basis as tutors and counsellors. It does not carry the pension or national insurance costs of those staff of which there are many thousands.

There are great economies of scale. To design and produce a new course with TV, radio, specially designed texts, assignments, summer school programmes and possibly a home experiment kit and computer learning, is very expensive indeed. It requires a course team consisting of academics, media producers, editors and educational technologists working usually over two years; but it costs just as much for one student as for ten thousand. There is no reason why such courses cannot be used in other universities with or without translation and this practice is growing especially in the field of continuing education.

While it took some five years for us to achieve academic respectability as a complementary system of higher education that actually worked, it has taken much longer for the characteristics that we pioneered, to be adopted by other universities. But once it started it has accelerated and at present 20 of our 100 universities offer some distance teaching, nearly 40 per cent of all UK students now study part time and the majority of students are now over 21 on entry; none of that was true in 1971.

All our courses are modular in structure. This was previously rare in England although common in Scotland, but is increasingly being adopted in universities and academics now talk freely of ODET – Open and Distance Education and Training. There has been a dramatic growth in the number of distance education institutions in Europe. Spain set up its National University for Distance Education in 1972 and there are now 15 such Open Universities in Europe and more than 50 worldwide. The nature of the institutions is not uniform in Europe; 11 are government run and four are private; three are run by consortia of regular universities and the courses are available to internal students; six have no entrance qualifications, but seven require entrance qualifications like the regular universities.

Back in 1978, there were already 14 institutions engaged in distance learning (five in Europe) so there seemed to be a good case for co-operation to share ideas about organisation, training and supervision of the huge numbers of part-time tutors, methods of examination and course production. There was also the possibility of cost saving by sharing courses. I, therefore, organised a conference, held at Creaton near the Open University and the executive heads of all 14 institutions attended. They were full of good intentions and the most important outcome was the setting up of an International Centre for Distance Learning at the OU which instituted a database that has proved to be of great value.

From the start, there has been close co-operation between the OU and the newer institutions; particularly in Germany and The Netherlands, and this led in 1987 to the formation of the European Association of Distance Teaching Universities. Furthermore, the International Council for Correspondence Education (ICCE) changed its name to the International Council for Distance Education (ICDE) and has become the forum for a great deal of activity. However, despite much useful discussion, almost no action has occurred on the most important objective – the sharing of courses. Multi-media modular courses of high quality are very expensive to produce even though modern technology, such as desktop publishing and hand held cameras, have reduced costs, so that economies of scale are most important. While these find favour with finance ministers and administrators, they find little favour with academics who all want to do their own thing. Where sharing has occurred, mainly between the OU and Eastern Europe, it has mainly been in the postgraduate area. It is doubtful whether the recent endorsement of distance learning in the new Article 126 of the European Union will change this.

What of the future? How will distance education affect the goals and purposes of education in the 21st century? I suspect that whatever we may plan in the academic world the real situation will be dominated and driven by the irresistible forces of communication technology, where the current rate of development is staggering and shows no sign of slowing. When the OU began teaching in 1972, many homes did not possess a TV set and there were large areas in the UK where the BBC2 signal could not be received. Since our philosophy was that our courses must be available to anyone who was a student wherever they lived, we supplied TV sets to every study centre and where the BBC2 signal did not reach, we supplied film loops of the TV programmes. Nowadays, almost every student's home has not only radio and TV, but also a video recorder and telephone and often fax and a personal computer, hence courses can take advantage of a more sophisticated distribution system. This is far from the case in most developing countries, but technology will become cheaper and AID programmes will lead to cabling institutions and homes there. With the communication superhighway, students will have access to courses being presented by gifted teachers all over the world, as well as to data banks, libraries, computer-based programmes and to individual tutors. The job of the academic will change and will not be easier as they guide students through the maze of material that will become available. We are all aware how difficult it is at present to keep up with the mass of material published in our own scientific areas. Things are going to get much worse! I find it ironic that having been partly responsible through the OU for bringing communications technology to the service of education, I am more than a little afraid that, like the *Sorcerer's Apprentice*, we will be unable to stop what we started. Indeed, it may be that an aim of the academic world, in preparing for the network revolution, should also be seeking a means of protection from it. It seems to me, that we will have to create islands of peace where we can have time to take thought and inwardly digest without continually ingesting more food; or to put it another way, the superhighway will get us more quickly to our destination but there may be more crashes on the way. Perhaps in the centres of excellence in the future, much of the staff will have to spend time filtering information so that others may have a manageable input to cope with and have some time to ponder. On the other hand, students will have a choice of teachers and should no longer be condemned to the poor teacher who happens to work in their local institution, but perhaps the choice will need to be limited by some local filtering mechanism.

I can see enormous advantages to education through life from the technological advances, but I can also see real danger to the quality of academic life as I have enjoyed it. I wish that I could see how to protect that quality and still retain the advantages.

Chapter 8

Education and Work in an Ageing Population

Karl Ulrich Mayer

Introduction

When Bismarck introduced the governmental retirement insurance for workers in Germany in 1889, the legal retirement age was set at 70. Bismarck's retirement insurance covered 54 per cent of those employed (almost entirely men) and the pension amounted to around 30 per cent of the worker's previous income. But not much more than a quarter of those insured reached the legal retirement age, and the survivors had a life expectancy of around eight years; women 8.5 years (Mayer and Müller 1986; Statistisches Bundesamt 1987, p.76).

The overwhelming majority of people who retired during Bismarck's time had probably worked as children, working full time starting at the age of 12 or 13 (at least in the country and in the summer). A law requiring seven years of compulsory school attendance was enacted as early as 1817, by Friedrich Wilhelm I in Prussia, but it was only generalised for the German Empire in 1890 (Leschinsky and Roeder 1976, p.137).

Only a small fraction of these workers had the benefit of occupational training in the sense of a trade apprenticeship, and such an apprenticeship had more the character of hard work than education. We have good reason to assume that the retired of 1890 attended school six to seven years, at best, and not the entire year and that only a tenth of them had received a secondary school education or occupational training (Lundgreen 1980; Müller and Zymek 1987). When they lived long enough, some of them had worked over 50 years (six days a week and ten hours a day) until they died. A small number of them experienced a short retirement phase.

The men born around the turn of the century went to school for at least eight years; 50 per cent completed an apprenticeship. Only very few had the benefit of a secondary school education. Their working life began at 17 (Blossfeld and Nuthmann 1989, p.862). On average, these men went into retirement at 60 years of age with a legal retirement age of 65 or 63 respectively (flexible old age pension after the pension reform of 1957); 43 per cent of them survived until retirement age and then had a life expectancy of 15 to 16 years. The lifelong working time had already been reduced to around 43 years for these age-groups, from which some years have to be subtracted for military service or captivity as a prisoner of war (Mayer and Brückner 1989, p.106).

Women who were born after the turn of the century started working one or two years earlier than men because fewer received occupational training (Blossfeld and Nuthmann 1989; Mayer 1981). Most of these women were only gainfully employed until they married (Handl 1988; Willms-Herget 1985). Women in these age groups could count on around 18.5 retirement years. Many of these women experienced exceptional hardships. They were frequently forced to work in the armaments factories and played a decisive role in the rebuilding after the war as *Trümmerfrauen*. Nevertheless, they often had no or only minimal rights to a pension of their own.

The retired of today, who were born around 1920, attended school for an average of 8.4 years, spent 3.6 years in occupational training, and were gainfully employed for 36.8 years. They interrupted or delayed their employment phase for 6.1 years during and after World War II (military service, captivity, etc.). They retired at an age of 61.1 and had a further life expectancy of 16 years. In the mean time, the median age of men when they retire from gainful employment has fallen to less than 60 years of age.

Women born around 1920 attended school on average for 8.3 years, spent 2.6 years in occupational training, and were gainfully employed for 22.2 years. To the extent that they had rights to a pension based on their own gainful employment and thus had worked in middle age or later, these women could retire at 60. They could then hope for a 21 year retirement phase. More than 40 per cent of the women in these age groups, however, did not retire until the age of 65 (VDR 1989), often due to the fact that they had not attained the minimum number of work years. We are thus looking back at a century in which learning and work, education and gainful employment were increasingly separated from each other and organised in a specific sequence in a person's lifetime: school, occupational training, gainful employment, retirement. This four-part sequence holds increasingly true, not only for men, but also for women. The length of the period of gainful employment of the men has diminished by almost one third. The average times for education and training has increased steadily but by no means dramatically.

How can we envision the future of education and work in an ageing society, in which the individual members live longer and the share of the elderly in the population as a whole increases? Three different solutions for this new life phase present themselves and are also being propagated: a lengthening of work life, filling this phase with education, or totally dissolving the rigid lifetime regime. Admittedly, none of these three variants is sociologically probable!

But how should this future then look and how can it be planned? This question does not only touch on the distribution of lifetime and the ages at which the transition between educational, work, and retirement phases takes place. It also refers to the quality of education and work and to the importance which both will have in a person's life. How must education be designed if it is not only meant to qualify a person for an entire working life, but should also be suitable for a long phase after retirement? Can such an education only take place in the youth phase? Is the rigid separation of working life and a long period of retirement humane? Which types of education, which types of work lead to a favourable ageing process, and which hinder it?

Two Perspectives: Differentiation of the Life Course and a Postindustrial Way of Life

Differentiation of the Life Course

Societal development can be understood as a secular process of differentiation and rationalisation. First, political authority is split from the family, then the economy and the place of work developed separately from the family and the household, and citizenship separated from clan and common origin. Finally, the educational system took over socialisation and training functions and the social welfare system took over the function of safeguarding against a number of life risks, above all income security in old age. Societal subsytems are thus separated more distinctly from each other (differentiation), and each individual segment is given an exact purpose (rationalisation): processes of societal differentiation follow the logic of the more efficient expedient rationality of reciprocally delimited institutional areas. At the same time, differentiation processes always also include the development of new integration mechanisms: government regulation and social policy are an important example of this (Mayer and Müller 1989).

For the individual person, this societal differentiation between institutions is reflected in the simultaneous participation in different social areas; this appears as role segmentation, but also increasingly as a sequence of different roles in one's lifetime (Mayer and Müller

1986). A lifetime is spent in different social contexts and institutions, in part in succession, in part simultaneously: preschool, kindergarten, elementary school, occupational training, gainful employment, retirement. The individual must deal with completing temporal claims and patterns of interpretation, in succession or simultaneously. It is not clear, though, whether this will lead to an increased pressure for individualisation or to a loss of individuality (Kaufmann 1990, Chapters 3 and 9).

The most recent development in this process of differentiation in life histories concerns the family: the partnership phase (in part, in the form of long-term non-marital relationships, in part as marriages without children) and the parental phase are separated clearly from each other and ordered temporally (Kaufmann 1990). The parental phase is shortened due to the reduced number of children. The 'empty nest' creates the possibility of a post-parental new partnership phase. Furthermore, a partial parallelism is developing out of the previous complementarity of the roles of men and women (Sørensen, 1990). The previous greater (and family related) comprehensiveness of the female life context (Simmel, 1986, p.136) is disappearing. The life of women is to an extent becoming much like that of men (Mayer 1991).

Education is principally seen as a preparation for work in one's profession, and retirement appears primarily as a relief from work. Occupational training provides the qualifications for a very specific profession. Under such a perspective, we could expect that an individual's work life would become increasingly shorter and – with a prolonged life span – the old age phase increasingly longer. The more rapidly occupational knowledge becomes obsolete, the greater the interest of the firms in dealing with the technological change at any one time with new workers who have received up to date training. Only a small share of employees take advantage of programmes for further education and occupational retraining. Moreover, the main share of occupational training takes place in the first working years.

There is considerable resistance on the part of employers against educational leaves of absence and sabbatical years. In the Federal Republic of Germany, only around one half of the measures for retraining the unemployed, which are financed by the *Arbeitsförderungsgesetz* (Work Promotion Act), reach their target group and are for many, especially older workers, only an intermediary step on the way to unemployment or retirement. This is understandable when qualifications are understood above all as human capital, as an investment in income returns which must be attained through gainful employment. The low interest in further training also comes from a weakness in the market mechanisms. The more income and job security are safeguarded collectively, the less they can be influenced and increased by individual efforts to attain further training.

In addition, tendencies toward institutional inertia in West Germany have led to the fact that the expansion of schools providing a general education and the dual system of occupational training have not reciprocally substituted each other, but tend to follow each other. Thus, for example, over one third of the *Abiturienten* (graduates of college preparatory schools) begin an occupational training (BMBW 1990, p.70). With largely unregulated durations of the course of studies at universities and increasing numbers of students, education time as a whole has been lengthened. The beginning of working life shifts more and more into the second half of the twenties, and for many into the first half of the thirties. After the emergence of childhood as an independent phase, the youth phase is being extended and is now lengthened by a phase of post-adolescence.

Despite the reduced working times, leisure time still primarily encompasses recreation and reproduction of the capacity for work, not least due to increased emotional burdens in the world of work. Leisure time is frequently filled out by commercially provided consumption and not by self-determined activities which further personal development.

A life course which is being regulated increasingly by external institutions also weakens a rational lifestyle as a self-reflective, internally guided planning and ordering of one's life (Mayer 1986), although, paradoxically, the safeguarding of social risks in the welfare state has increased the ability for individuals to make long-range plans.

A three-fold pressure for rationalisation works toward an early entry into retirement: first, the physical and, perhaps increasingly, emotional strains of a rationalised work life brings about health impairment. These are the most important causes for an early retirement. Second, employers have an interest in parting with older employees earlier in order to increase productivity. Unemployment affects above all older workers and is socially neutralised through early 'retirement'. Third, the level of prosperity of an effective economic order provides sufficiently high retirement incomes and thus allows workers to withdraw from gainful employment in part before reaching the maximum retirement age (Hainke 1990).

Reducing the Differentiation of the Life Course: The Postindustrial Way of Life

The sketch of an increasingly rationalised life course is, however, not only being increasingly questioned as a description of the present situation in our society. There are, above all, doubts as to whether it still holds true for the tendencies of a future society. Others see the contours of a post-industrial way of life to be already distinguishable in many places. I will sketch out this alternative point of view in the following.

Rigid patterns for organising one's lifetime are rapidly dissolving. The transitions between education and work, but also between gainful employment and retirement, are becoming fluid and reversible. Many return to improve their education after their first gainful employment. Not just women, but also men interrupt their employment or change professions. The career orientation within a single occupation and the commitment to a given firm loses influence. Phases of intense involvement with the children, going as far as temporarily reducing and giving up gainful employment, are not only becoming generally acceptable for men, but they are also being experimented with (Bielenski and Strümpel 1988). The greater involvement of women in gainful employment forces a greater flexibility in the organisation of life and working time for men, and it also makes it economically possible.

The reduced weekly and yearly working times support the shaping of a self-determined leisure sphere. Other orientations and capabilities can develop aside from work: 'The occupational society is not "passé", but loyalty to the work role is limited through demands, reservations, and preconditions. An "equilibrium ethic", which seeks to allow the different life areas to fully come into their own, is emerging among many people, especially those who are younger' (Bielinski and Strümpel 1988, p.4).

Institutions for 'lifelong learning' provide a freshening up of occupational knowledge, but also a systematic preparation for other life tasks – especially old age:

> What is wrong with taking one or more longer breaks in a 45 or even 50 year working life, to enjoy life, participate in further education, or to reorient oneself? The economic safeguarding of such time is solely a question of organisation. It is possible as well to structure the working time in one's life in such a manner that an adequate income can be earned in a thirty hour week (Miegel 1989, p.46).

An important motor of such a development for reducing a rigid organisation of the lifetime comes from the women's movement.

Each reasonable and conceivable model for better reconciling a family with children and an occupation, must lead to the demand that differences in the working time of men and women be reduced and that an increased involvement of men in family work be made possible. The institutional – temporal and spatial – separations between education/training and work, work and leisure will be weakened through the fact that more and more firms will carry out widespread further training efforts for their employees and bring back 'leisure activities', like health-promoting behaviour, sports, and social life into the work sphere.

The retirement age becomes more flexible in both directions and responsive to individual decisions. Some work until an age of 70 or longer, some treat themselves to a new educational phase in early retirement. Education becomes an important activity for, in part, younger, in any case more healthy and better educated, generations of older people. Especially couples who are oriented toward partnership also want to enter retirement together (Allmendinger 1990).

Such expectations and hopes for reduced differentiation in the life course are supported by differing conceptions: as a reasonable and inevitable adjustment to a longer life span (Imhoff 1988), as a financial remedy for safeguarding the systems of old-age pensions (Schmähl 1988), by the fear of structurally high unemployment (Dahrendorf 1982), by the programmes of psychological gerontological research (Lehr 1984), and by considerations of a structural mismatch between a society with a larger share of older people and institutions which are not suited for this.

The Importance of Education and Work

If we want to understand how such contrary descriptions of reality and expectations for the future could come about, we cannot only ask how much of the scenarios described above are already reality and how much wishful thinking. It is more fruitful to examine the 'theories' and 'ideologies' which, consciously or unconsciously, have inspired such theses and support their plausibility.

When we talk about education today – also about education for retirement or in retirement – we almost unintentionally use a concept of education which refers to the transmission of knowledge which has practical use. Education in this sense is instruction and training. The idea of training also frequently dominates the discussion about the proper time for education in the life course. It generally deals with occupational training, with retraining and acquiring new qualifications, with preparation for retirement, with the adjustment of the elderly to a modern world.

There is, however, a second meaning of education as the development of capabilities for taking part in a culture which has been handed down for generations, as a prerequisite for adducing sense and orientation capacities, and actively coming to terms with one's own environment and history:

> In addition to the attainment, maintenance, and fostering of cognitive capabilities, 'education' also includes the attainment of knowledge and experience as well as the development of interests. The formation of a motivational structure which awakes an interest in the contents of education and supports an active study of these contents is a central component of 'education' as well. In addition, the capacity to perceive one's own competencies and correctly judge the possibilities and limitations of the person is also a part of 'education'. (Kruse 1988, p.179)

In the German tradition, this concept of an all-round education goes back to Wilhelm von Humboldt: to develop within oneself is the highest purpose of a human being whose pursuits should never be considered to be simply a means to achieve a result (Humboldt 1960, pp.9–32; Lichtenstein 1971). Educated is he who attempts to '...grasp as much of the world as possible and connect it as closely as he can with himself' (Humboldt 1960, p.235): 'Education is the life-form-related medium in which the identity of the individual is developed in a rational culture and expresses this culture in itself.' (Mittelstrass 1989, pp.15–16).

These ideas become clear above all in Humboldt's conception of the university. The university as an institution oriented toward the education of a person through participation in pure knowledge and research is in fundamental contradiction with the needs of industrial society. More radically, what society needs from its educational system is precisely no longer only training, experiential and occupational knowledge, but a direct approach to reality which is only mediated through theoretical science and pure research (Ritter 1974, pp.105–106).

Depending on whether education is primarily considered to be 'training' or as a comprehensive 'all-round education' we will obtain different answers to the questions regarding the life phase in which education should take place and whether it should take place in institutionalised educational facilities. If education is understood in the sense of investment in human capital, this only makes sense for the individuals and society if returns can be expected. The shorter the expected 'period of yields' the less the inclination to invest in education. The concentration of educational efforts and expense on the youth phase then appears to be sensible. If, on the other hand, education is understood in the tradition of German idealism to be those activities and intellectual efforts through which the person acquires and secures his or her own identity by relating to the cultural universe, then old age is perhaps especially suited for this, as it is a life phase which is free from the necessity for training.

Finally, concepts of lifelong learning and education in old age are closely connected with the Neo-Hegelian idea of compensation through culture. On the one hand, older people can hardly keep pace with the rapidity of social and technological change and education in old age must compensate for such a disorientation. (Lübbe 1977, pp.326–327). On the other hand, the shortcomings of human beings are especially pronounced in old age. This also suggests education as a compensation.

Also, some of the objectives for education in old age which were developed in psychology appear in part to be characterised by instrumental ideas which aim at compensating for increasing losses (Lehr 1984): as training in how to deal with the mechanised environment; for communication with children and parents; as compensation for lost roles and function losses; as memory and intelligence training; as learning how to deal with new life situations (like retirement, moving into an old-age home, the death of a partner or sickness); finding a meaning in life and preparation for death, as the acquisition of new competencies of old-age wisdom.

Equally, our ideas about the desirable distribution and organisation of lifelong working time are shaped by fundamental concepts of human labour. If work is considered to be alienated wage labour and earning a living, which is connected in the extreme case with exploitation and physical and emotional wear and tear, then liberation from the burden of work in educational and retirement phases is a desirable, humane goal. The lifelong working time is considered as 'expropriated time', leisure time, time after work, as 'own time', as the share of time for 'being human' (Negt 1985, p.33). The human being can only pursue his own purposes outside of his or her gainful work. Work falls into the 'realm of necessity'. Only the liberation from the work-leisure division leads into the 'realm of freedom':

> The tendency toward a division of society appears to be unavoidable in all industrially advanced societal orders which are characterised by a high level of technological productive forces...but which hold onto the old time structures of work and a concept of work which emerged at the beginning of the bourgeois age and was the key institution of societal acceptance for centuries...

These are two different manifestations of one and the same societal structure: the maintenance of the old, basically capital-fixated
forms of work which give the appearance...as if it still depended
on the direct application of human labour to produce societal
wealth...and growing areas of society in which the people frequently enough, especially above a certain age and in certain
economically weak regions, were even degraded to lifelong ob-
jects of welfare... Work in the form of gainful employment is still
considered to be the basic medium for social acceptance, contacts
and the formation of an individual identity: work as such and also
not exclusively work which is fun and experienced to be satisfying. (Negt 1985, pp.39–46)

Consequently, it is one of the goals of trade union policy to create as
much work-free self-determined time as possible, to shorten the
weekly, monthly, yearly, and lifelong working time while simultaneously securing an adequate livelihood for its members.

In contrast to this, analyses based on Marx and Hegel developed
a utopia of work as a self-determined activity aimed not at the
production of exchange values, but of use values, and as the necessary precondition for human self-realisation:

Only when leisure has been completely uncoupled from work
time will it change its character – only then does it open the
chances which lie in it to actually be appropriated as time for
emancipation and societal orientation... Where work takes on a
creative character, then the abstract opposition of work, leisure,
and laziness is generally dissolved. Thus not only the traditional
working time is problematic, but also the traditional work. (Negt
1985, p.178)

In accordance with such a conception of work, the liberation from
work – also in old age – must then appear to be a dangerous loss if
work is considered to be a basic characteristic of human existence, as
a chance for a confrontation with and a structuring of the natural and
social environment. Just like the Hegelian/Marxist concept of unal-
ienated labour, Humboldt's concept of education arises from the
intellectual tradition of German idealism. Understood in this context,
education and work, as the inner self-realisation of a human being
through an active exploration of the environment, obtain a very
similar importance. Understood in this manner, education and work
become the necessary basic preconditions for an undistorted human
existence. An old age phase without education and work would be
beneath human dignity. If it is one of the anthropological purposes
of old age that a person should discover the essentials of his or her
human existence and person, then, according to this understanding,

acquiring an education without the intention of using it and working without intending to make money would appear not only a possible way to get there, but a necessary one.

We see that the conceptions of education as training, and work as gainful employment correspond to each other, just as the conceptions of an all-round education as self-development in confrontation with culture, and work as self-realisation in interaction with nature and the social environment. The utopia of old age as an educational phase could then only be judged in regard to the quality and extent of work in the phase of gainful employment. We are carrying the ballast of German idealism in our heads just as much as we have the ballast of the industrial society in our structures of lifetime.

Much speaks in favour of not getting bogged down with these traditional sharp conceptual dichotomies, especially in regard to the problem of the organisation of lifetime and the problem of the importance of work and education for old age. On the one hand, a training-related education also imparts competencies and skills which go beyond a specific occupation. Especially the German traditions of occupational training and the dual system for training apprentices aim at combining general and specialised competencies.

On the other hand, gainful employment in modern societies cannot simply be understood as alienated labour. Work can also impart more general competencies or coping with life which can be important outside of work and the employment phase. Longitudinal studies have shown that the autonomy and cognitive demands connected with gainful employment bring forth long-term effects in a greater intellectual flexibility and a greater general cognitive capacity (Kohn and Schooler 1978). In addition, modern forms of gainful employment presuppose a great degree of responsibility and self-control. These are capabilities which, on the other hand, could attain a great importance for actively and sensibly dealing with old age.

A scenario of education and work in an ageing population must thus inevitably become a bit of critical theory. On the one hand, it has to orient itself to the limitations of real institutional and material circumstances. On the other hand, it has to point out the still untapped possibilities of a highly developed society. These are, however, in contrast to the ideal type sketched out above, no longer simple occupational societies, but welfare societies in which life courses are not only, and perhaps not primarily regulated economically but also and increasingly politically (Mayer and Müller 1989).

Developmental Tendencies of Education and Work in their Importance for the Old Age Phase

In order to draw up a future for education and work in an ageing society which is probable and capable of being influenced, it is necessary to identify some ongoing developments which can be assessed and must be considered to be preconditions for this future. In this, we have a two-fold reference to the problem. On the one hand, it is the question of the importance of education and work for an increasingly large group of the elderly and for an increasingly longer old age phase. On the other hand, we have to consider how education and work change in a society in which the share of children and youths declines and the share of older people increases. In this context it is important that not only the demographic development be considered as the primary motor of the change. Such a trend-demographic determinism (Mayer 1989) would ignore the fact that when we look at the past there is very little proof to support the thesis that the speed of societal changes is determined entirely, or primarily, by demographic shifts. Economic development, the increase in the participation in education, or the rise in health care costs are examples of the fact that demographic changes are important, but generally not decisive. Though we have to add here that humanity has had very little experience with societies becoming demographically older. In the past, societies which became demographically older were almost always such in which the young people emigrated in large numbers, like Ireland, for example.

Life Span and Age Structure

In West Germany, 60-year-old men will be able to reckon with an average life expectancy of 18 years in the near future. Despite the controversies about the connection between morbidity and advanced age we can probably assume that those who survive until this age will, on the average, be healthy enough so that they would not rule out gainful employment from the outset, and that they would be healthy enough so that an active life planning, also in regard to educational activities, would be possible. Among women, the corresponding spans are around 22 years for the average life expectancy, 15 for the possible years of gainful employment, and 15 to 20 years of good health. In former East Germany the life expectancies at 60 are circa one and two years less respectively (Dinckel 1992). Although such numbers only express tendencies and are full of uncertainties there is no doubt, however, that a significant increase in 'gained years' (Imhof 1988) will be connected with old age.

The importance is not only life expectancy, but also the change in absolute numbers. The number of people over 60 years old in Germany will increase from around 13 million (1987) to around 21 million (including former East Germany, 25 million) in the year 2030; the number of those over 80 will increase from 2.2 million to 3.9 million (DIW, 1990). These numbers will hardly be influenced by immigration. This results in a critical order of magnitude for the needs, interests, and claims of elderly people. This holds true not least for the demand for cultural activities and other offerings.

Training and Change in the Educational System

A much greater proportion of the future elderly will have enjoyed a secondary education and a higher general school education, and, in addition, almost all of them will have completed a company internal or other type of occupational training (cf. Table 8.1). But not only the initial school and occupational educations have expanded in regard to the number involved and been lengthened, but also further education and training has increased rapidly just in the last few years. Edding (1991) estimates that the costs for further education and training increased from 1 to 3 per cent of the gross national product between 1970 and 1990 while the relative costs for schools and universities have gone down slightly (from 3.5 to 3.4%). Adult education has thus gained importance in comparison to youth education.

Table 8.1: General education and occupational training for selected birth years

| birth year | men | | | women | | |
	10 years of school	Abitur	company training	10 years of school	Abitur	company training
1910	13	8	64	17	5	32
1920	15	8	67	15	3	32
1930	11	6	69	13	3	28
1940	14	8	74	16	6	50
1950	19	18	71	18	15	52
1960	22	18	59	29	22	49
1970	24	24	57	35	24	60

(calculated using data from the Statistisches Bundesamt/ Federal Statistics Office [Mikrozensus-Zusatzerhebung 1971]; data from the life course study of the Max-Planck-Institut für Bildungsforschung 1981/82; BMBW 1989; the figures for the year 1970 were in part estimated or extrapolated.)

Becker (1991) has, however, shown that, on the one hand, offerings of further education are almost exclusively used by those who are already well-educated, and, on the other hand, that such activities are concentrated to a great extent in the age group younger than 35 years old. Finally, he could show that the participation in further education has sharply increased for the younger age groups which already had a better school education (cf. Table 8.1). There is, thus, a process of education accumulation, but also an effect of an accumulation of further education. In other words, people who have once taken part in further education activities also frequently do so again. Peters (1988) could show, as well, with data for the OECD countries that the share and number of adults taking part in post-occupational or supplementary courses of study at colleges and universities is higher the higher the proportion of students among the 19- to 25-year-olds. This is shown especially well in the US.

We can conclude from these findings that education is not only increasing in importance in the youth phase, but also in early adulthood. At least the potential of those interested in education in old age will thus increase enormously. At the same time, it becomes clear how differences in education tend to increase during the life course instead of evening out and being compensated for. A highly secure finding is also the fact that educational activities in the later life course can be best promoted through a good general education.

Furthermore, we can assume that educational activities in adulthood and old age do not only become more attractive due to better educational preconditions, but also due to the interests of the 'education providers'. The decline in the absolute number of pupils and students, but also of young adults in further education, produces an educational potential which is working less and less to capacity, and which could lead educational institutions to increase their offerings for older people.

Quality of Gainful Employment and the Expansion of Leisure Time

In the past, a large share of the generation of older people had direct experiences with practical activities: in farming, in handicrafts or producing trades, in their own garden, or in the home economy with a large share of self-production. These are experiences and activities which in part can be continued in old age and only have to be gradually reduced. A farmer who had passed the running of his farm on to the next generation could (and had to) help with the work for quite some time, as did the farmer's wife. A part-time farmer also knows what he will do when he retires from the factory. And even a coal miner from the Ruhr area – with a traditionally early retirement from gainful employment – has no difficulty in spending more time with his carrier pigeons in old age.

These opportunities for a direct connection of gainful employment and activity in old age have changed, and presumably worsened, with the change in the occupational structure. An increasingly larger share of those employed work in the service sector and in office professions. This makes it at least difficult for them to achieve a continuity between gainful employment and their activities in retirement. Voluntary work or hobbies could secure continuity here.

The tendency toward a decreasing share of self-employed people also counteracts a gradual end of work and a continuity of gainful employment in old age. Even today, we find high employment rates among the self-employed over 60 years of age, and in part also among those over 70. Many self-employed people work literally until they die. This is presumably not only because they have to work further for financial reasons, but also because they do not even know the difference between work and leisure time and because they do not want to give up what is for them the typical sphere of structuring opportunities and power.

Admittedly, we can argue against this that the longer periods of education and an independent leisure phase outside of work increasingly offer the opportunity to cultivate a multitude of activities which can be pursued further in old age. This applies perhaps less to the transfer effects from employment to retirement than to those from 'activities' which had already been pursued.

Jobs for Older People and the Demand for Older Workers

Two developmental tendencies determine the supply of jobs and the demand for older workers: rationalisation processes in work and the supply of workers, which is determined demographically and through migration. Technological rationalisation in production and, increasingly, also in the service sector means inevitably not only a higher productivity of labour, but also a reduced need for human work power. As there are – at least up until now – business management limits on the reduction of weekly and yearly working time, this results not only in a tendency toward a high level of 'structural unemployment', but also in a pressure for the firms to reduce the lifetime working time.

Standing in the way of this almost inescapable developmental tendency is the decline in the working population stemming from the reduction of the birth rate, as long as the declining share of youths and young adults is not compensated for by the influx of foreigners and Eastern Europeans of German descent. For the more probable case that the decline in the birth rate will quantitatively predominate we can reckon with a greater demand also for the work of older people. A smaller absolute number of people capable of employment would increase the relative supply of jobs for older workers, just as the willingness to invest in labour and keep older workers in the firms as long as possible: labour would be better paid and sought after more intensively; youths would be integrated into gainful employment more rapidly; the lifetime working time would be longer, the initial training time shorter, subsequent training would become more necessary. Up until now, there only seems to be a tendency in smaller firms to keep older workers as long as possible, whereas the opposite holds true for large corporations (Hainke 1990).

Demand for Jobs Among Older People

Will older people be looking for jobs in increased numbers? Due to the problems in financing old-age pensions and additional social burdens which were in part brought about by the ageing of the population, the available pension income will sink both when compared with their previous work income and compared with the income of those who are gainfully employed. German unification will increase the social burden additionally for some years and limit the rise of real net income. This will *ceteris paribus* increase the demand for gainful labour among older people as income, in addition to their pensions. As is already the case in the US, it could very well be the case that not only youths will work in the fast food chain, but also older people. Under these conditions, we could expect that the currently widespread, but invisible and statistically not registered, employment of older people, for example older cleaning women, would increase significantly.

An effect in the same direction will ensue from shortened and incomplete 'pension biographies'. Longer education times, periods of unemployment, voluntary breaks from gainful employment, and marginal employment situations, with or without little compulsory social insurance, will make the pension biographies of the men, and the pension claims and waiting times connected with them, rather more similar to those which women have currently. This will then lead to the similar compulsion of having to work longer.

The situation for single people is much different from that of married couples. Lower numbers of children mean that parents are also relieved of financial obligations for their children at an earlier age and thus have more income at their disposal. Added to this comes the fact that both men and women were gainfully employed among more married couples and thus have a higher income together. This will allow some of the men to retire earlier from gainful employment – even though the statutory regulations foresee a reduced pension for an early retirement (Allmendinger 1990; Matras 1990).

Social and Medical Services for Older People

The number of people employed in social services and the health care system more than doubled in former West Germany between 1960 and 1985 (Schmidt and Rose 1985). There were, thus, great efforts at limiting the financial expenditures in these areas in the last few years. The debates over the increasing costs of the welfare state were accompanied by warnings against bureaucratisation and too far-reaching professionalisation, as well as corresponding demands for increased volunteer services and non-professional help (Fink 1988).

Despite the general political climate which does not look favourable for a further build up of the welfare state, there can hardly be any doubt that the number of employees in the social and medical services for older people will increase by leaps and bounds if the quality of the care is to be maintained and improved. Thus the 'nursing care emergency' both in the in-patient and out-patient areas is a serious problem which will intensify further (Alber 1990).

Education and Cultural Activities in Old Age

Education and cultural offerings for older people have improved tremendously in just the last few years. The number of institutions and projects for this purpose which were created or developed in self-help has increased very rapidly (Council of Europe 1988).

There is still a great discrepancy between the thus growing opportunities to take up educational offerings and cultural activities, again or for the first time, in old age and the number and share of older people who take advantage of them. Although they have much free time at their disposal, older people are, for instance, by no means enthusiastic users of the public (and free of charge) libraries. Their share of library use is estimated at somewhat more than 10 per cent, despite the fact that the majority of the public libraries even have special offerings for older readers (Borchardt 1989).

Also, the current participation of older people in education, for example in Volkshochschule (adult education centre) and university courses for senior citizens, is far below their share in the adult population. Despite various efforts at establishing special cultural and educational offerings for 'senior citizens' (Kruse 1988; Lehr 1984), the demand is still rather low. But the frequency with which older people use the institutions open to all age groups is also below average. Thus, for example, out of the around 80,000 students of the British Open University only 2 per cent are over 65 years of age. Two per cent are also in the age group of 60- to 64-year-olds and 3 per cent are in the age group of 55- to 59-year-olds. Older students are not less successful, though: 5 per cent of the honours degrees and 2.6 per cent of the simple bachelor's degrees were awarded to people over 65 (Open University Statistics 1987, pp.20–47).

The few data dealing with the situation in West Germany reveal an inconsistent picture. An analysis of people auditing courses at the Bamberg University (Faber 1988) shows that the group of 31- to 45-year-olds has the largest share at 34 per cent and that their dominant motive is further occupational training. The second largest group, however, at 28 per cent, is people older than 60. The 'iron law' of education accumulation in the life course also reveals itself here: further education as an adult and in old age does not have a compensatory effect in the sense that people with little education would make up for this later, but rather those who are already educated acquire additional education. However, there also seems to be a 'generation effect' among those who are currently old. There is apparently a strong need for catching up, above all for those people in the birth years which could not obtain the education they desired due to adverse conditions from the world economic crisis up until the postwar era. In this group, there are above all also noticeable aspirations to be able to study subjects which had remained closed to them due to the practical constraints of preparing for a profession: 'Older auditors appear to see university study as an opportunity for a new concentration on themselves. Questions of self-interpretation, the meaning of life, and understanding the world explain their conspicuous preference for the humanities and thus for participation in the hermeneutic knowledge process.' (Faber 1988, p.117).

Forty-eight per cent of the students over 60 study history, the philologies come in second, art history and philosophy take third and fourth places respectively.

Judging from the openness of the access, the adult education centres, in particular, should be suitable institutions to open up educational opportunities for older people. The statistics of the *Deutscher Volkshochschulverband* (German association of adult education centres) reveal, on the other hand, that only 4 per cent of the participants in courses are over 65 years old. This share has not changed since 1978. This constant shares obscures an increase of 50 per cent in the absolute number from 145,000 to 213,000 people. As was the case for the auditors, the data for the adult education centres also show the greater interest of older people in general education offerings in the areas of history, geography/travel, and the humanities. Even when we look at the larger group of those over 50, we do not come up with more than about 15 per cent who attend courses at adult education centres, with a slightly increasing tendency over the years (Pehl 1989, pp.65–66).

The current German situation thus shows above all a distinct time-lag in the establishment of suitable institutions. The experiences in other countries, like the senior citizen centres in the US or the University of the Third Age in England, attest not only to the large potential of older people interested in education, but also to the fact that activities which they initiate and organise for themselves find greater demand than offerings where younger people 'look after' older ones.

Change in Values and Culture

Observations of a change in values as a precondition for the behaviour and attitudes of future generations of older people are difficult because the work done up to now in this area is characterised at least as much by speculation as by systematic longitudinal observations. The state of the literature is correspondingly controversial (Hondrich *et al.* 1988; Noelle-Neumann and Strümpel 1984). There is very much evidence, though, which suggests that basic orientations are shaped early in life and not decisively changed later. Accordingly, the values of the current adults and youths will be *grosso modo* the values of the future older people.

If this is true, then we can assume that a number of tendencies of value development could become important: from materialistic orientations focused on income, ownership, and standard of life to post-material orientations directed at individuality and self-realisation; from work and performance values to leisure and relationship values; from the emphasis on order, discipline, and sacrifice to pluralism, tolerance, and the right to develop one's own personality.

Very important for life in old age could be orientations which are directed toward a greater degree of social and political participation and are connected with concrete experience in this area. The future elderly will be better represented and much less privatistic. They will take responsibility themselves for matters which concern them and will be less inclined to let someone look after them.

There is little evidence, though, that the secular trend toward a higher valuation of youth and youthfulness will shift to a new esteem for adulthood and old age. Symbols of youthfulness belong rather to expected behaviour at least for the 'young elderly'.

Education and Work in Old Age and in an Ageing Population: A Future Scenario for an Active Societal Policy

We must first of all proceed from the assumption that the institutional framework of German society will remain relatively unchanged in the next decades. This thesis is supported not least through the manner in which West German institutions have asserted themselves in former East Germany. This means, for example, that the state would organise and finance the school and education phase in the first third of a person's life but will do relatively little in the area of supplementary or post-occupational education. In adulthood, the training and retraining of the workers will still be the dominant interest, be it within or outside the firms (via the *Bundesanstalt für Arbeit*/Federal Institute for Labour). Labour power will become scarcer for demographic reasons and education investments will thus be more lucrative. This will, however, nevertheless lead more to an intensification of initial education and generally shorter working times than to a loosening of the rigid sequence of education and work life. The inertial tendencies of the governmental education system and the forced pressure for rationalisation in the world of work will set narrow limits on lifelong learning, especially in the areas of general education and occupational reorientation. The unions, generally weakened by the competitive pressure in Western and Central Europe, will pursue predominantly traditional goals of shortening the weekly and yearly working time and will probably – except for the civil service unions – not make sabbatical years and the like the central object of contract negotiations.

The institutions of the social security system and their financial momentum will, next to the firms, continue in the future to be the most powerful actors which determine the retirement age and the amount of the pension income, and thus the personal scope for development in old age. The tax burden will shift from taking care of children to taking care of the elderly and thus from a direct, personal support for one's own children to an indirect, impersonal government redistribution via the pension scheme contributions. The increasing social burden will tend to slow down an increase in personal income in old age. The attempt in the last pension reform at achieving financial relief through increasing the effective retirement age will have only moderate success. The legal regulations and the financial control of the old-age insurance will be counteracted by the interests of the employers and employees in an early retirement from gainful employment.

The institutions of the social security system gladly accept the reduced expenditures due to increased gainful employment of women, but – except for the crediting of childrearing years – still use the traditional model of periods of full-time gainful employment which are as continuous and long as possible. Those who do not follow the traditional model are 'punished' with drastically reduced old-age income. As long as the economic situation does not allow the generation of large numbers of jobs which require the payment of social insurance, then primarily the women have to carry the costs (Allmendinger and Brückner 1991). The institutional rigidity sketched out here runs increasingly in contradiction to the interests, needs, values, and possibilities of women, men, and families.

The high level of education will surely increase the interest in educational activities during the phase of gainful employment and in old age. This trend will be supported by the fact that fewer births mean fewer children per family and this, on the other hand, leads to higher educational investments (and longer educational times) for each individual child. The longer life expectancy makes it worthwhile to also invest in training and retraining in adulthood. The goals of permanent education and recurrent education become more attractive: people want, in part, to work longer and they would like to interrupt work more frequently to undertake training and reorient themselves occupationally.

Such interruptions become more possible because the family income is not only earned by the man. Also, leaving gainful employment becomes a part of family life planning. The more that marriage is based on partnership, the more balanced the concern of the husband and wife for gainful employment and household tasks, the more similar their level of education, the more they will want to go into retirement together (Allmendinger 1990).

Men, or rather parents, do not have to support their children nearly as long as previously. This leads to a reduced necessity to participate in gainful employment. An increased tax burden reduces the attractiveness of gainful employment, above all in comparison to a retirement pension. This could also increase the inclination toward early retirement.

Because the content and meaning of work become more important as a value for themselves and a pure orientation on income will lose importance due to the additional income of women, then also the need for occupational reorientation in middle age will probably increase. The more satisfying the job, the longer people will want to work. Only when occupational reorientation is not possible for a person with an unsatisfying job will he or she want to flee into retirement from an unloved work situation.

It could also be the case that the greater amount of leisure time during a person's working life develops interests and activities for retirement early on. The greater the share of leisure time during one's working life the greater the inclination to make the leisure activities into an alternative, more attractive occupation through an early retirement. In the case of an early retirement, however, these 'private' wishes and needs must generally be paid for by a smaller pension.

A greater flexibilisation of old age in regard to entering retirement must not lead to older workers being forced from the firms against their wishes when the unemployment rate is high. The political challenge is, consequently, to become aware of and reduce these conflicts between the predominant interests of the world of work and the institutional inertia of the social security systems, on the one hand and the needs and wishes of the people, on the other hand. A strategy of many small steps and the support of, e.g., individual efforts at further education appears to be realistic. The first step could be to increase the quality and extent of general education in the first third of a person's life. This is surely the prerequisite for education to become a meaningful content both of adulthood and old age. Those who only have a narrow occupational training cannot find a new meaning in old age through education. Humboldt's educational ideal proves to be extremely practical in this regard for the development of an ageing population.

Moreover, the prerequisites must be created through governmental financing and governmental educational institutions so that educational phases can interrupt and change a period of gainful employment. These phases must be taken into account in the calculation of pension claims or the pension laws must be made flexible enough so that gaps in the payment of contributions can be closed later.

Workers and unions must use contract provisions to make retraining, educational leave, and sabbatical years possible. The adult education centres and universities must open up to a greater extent for older people, not only, but also, through special offerings. The model of senior experts, as is in part already being practised in regard to development aid and recently as in the transformation of former East Germany, must be enacted on a much wider scale.

In addition to the necessary, more intensive professionalisation in the social services, voluntary work and lay helpers should receive a better institutional anchoring and be rewarded through societal appreciation. The new social techniques of self-help groups should be used particularly for the many people who – frequently totally isolated – take care of sick and frail people until they themselves are old.

At present, older people are welcome customers for travel agencies, frequently for undemanding offerings. Demands will increase in the future, not least in regard to the educational content of travel.

Beyond this, older people could become an important consumer group on the private educational market. It is quite conceivable that, for example, *T'ai Chi* or Chinese shadow boxing, could become a popular activity in old age which would be arranged through private firms.

Not to be neglected, finally, is the fact that only a small proportion of older people live in old-age homes and nursing facilities, but that many older people will be doing this sometime in the future. Thus, the offering of good educational and cultural activities in old-age homes is an important task.

The reciprocal exclusion of life spheres and life segments produced by our economic system and welfare state cannot be totally reversed or set aside. It can be made more humane by creating more leeway for work as an activity which is satisfying in itself and education as pure self-realisation and participation in culture.

As a whole, it should thus have become comprehensible that societal development will by no means automatically produce those preconditions which support an active, productive, and meaningful old age phase. On the contrary, some developments will make old age into an even more precarious life phase. Very specific political and individual efforts are necessary, directed at the goal of a humane old age.

Summary

This chapter examines and assesses our understanding of changes in education, gainful labour, and old age in the context of the entire life course. It begins with a sketch of the two opposing perspectives which characterise the current debate: on the one hand, a more 'conservative' scenario of a further increasing differentiation of the life course, on the other hand, a more 'progressive' scenario of a radical change in the direction of a 'postindustrial' way of life. After this, the history of the basic concepts which inform these two differing views were illustrated. In a third step, I looked to see which tendencies of societal change in education and in the employment system can already be assessed with some degree of certainty. In this context I also pointed out the institutional approaches which already exist for promoting education in and for old age. Finally, a future scenario will be developed which is realistic in its preconditions, but does not do without normative criteria and seeking latitude for designing an active social policy.

References

Alber, J. (1990) 'Ausmaß und Ursachen des Pflegenotstands in der Bundesrepublik.' In *Staatswissenschaft und Staatspraxis 3*, S. 335–362.

Allmendinger, J. (1990) 'Der Übergang in den Ruhestand von Ehepaaren. Auswirkungen individueller und familiärer Lebensverläufe'. In K. U. Mayer (Hg.) *Lebensverläufe und sozialer Wandel*. (Sonderheft 31 der Kölner Zeitschrift für Soziologie und Sozialpsychologie). Opladen: Westdeutscher Verlag, S. 272–303.

Allmendinger, J., Brückner, H. and Brückner, E. (1991) 'Arbeitsleben und Lebensarbeitsentlohnung: Zur Entstehung von Ungleichheit im Alter'. In: K.U. Mayer, J. Allmendinger, J. Huinink (Hg.), Vom Regen in die Traufe: Frauen zwischen Beruf und Familie. Frankfurt am Main: Campus, S. 423–459.

Becker, R. (1991) Berufliche Weiterbildung und Berufsverlauf. Eine Längsschnittuntersuchung von drei Geburtskohorten in der Bundesrepublik Deutschland. *Mitteilungen aus der Arbeitsmarkt- und Berufsforschung 24*, 2, 351–364.

Bielenski, H. and Strümpel, B. (1988) *Eingeschränkte Erwerbsarbeit bei Frauen und Männern. Fakten – Wünsche – Realisierungschancen*. Berlin: Edition Sigma.

Blossfeld, H.-P. and Nuthmann, R. (1989) 'Strukturelle Veränderungen Jugendphase als Kohortenprozeß. *Zeitschrift für Pädagogik 35*, 6, 845–867.

Borchardt, P. (1989) 'Bibliotheksangebote für ältere Menschen – Sinnvoll oder überflüssig? Ergebnisse einer Umfrage der Deutschen Bibliotheksinstituts-Kommission für Öffentlichkeitsarbeit.' *Der Bibliotheksdienst 23*, 12, S. 1289–1299.

BMBW – Bundesminister für Bildung und Wissenschaft (Hg.) (1990) *Berufsbildungsbericht 1990*. Bonn.

Council of Europe (Hg.) (1988) *Adult Education and Social Change*. Strasbourg: Council for Cultural Co-Operation.

Dahrendorf, R. (1982). 'Wenn der Arbeitsgesellschaft die Arbeit ausgeht'. In J. Matthes (Hg.) *Krise der Arbeitsgesellschaft*? Verhandlungen des 21. Deutschen Soziologentages in Bamberg 1982. Frankfurt am Main: Campus, S. 25–37.

Dinkel, R. (1992): 'Demographische Alterung. Ein Überblick mit besonderer Berücksichtigung der Mortalitätsentwicklung.' In P.B. Baltes, J. Mittelstra (Hg.) *Zukunft des Alterns und gesellschaftlich Entwicklung*. Berlin, New York: de Gruyter, S. 62–93.

DIW – Deutsches Institut für Wirtschaftsforschung (1990) Szenarien der Bevölkerungsentwicklung in der Bundesrepublik Deutschland. *Wochenbericht 8/90*, S. 93–102.

Edding, F. (1991) Diskussionsbeitrag zum 3. Europäischen Weiterbildungskongre. Unveröff: Manuskript.

Faber, G. (1988) 'Was suchen die Gasthörer? Ergebnisse einer bundesweiten Erhebung und Erfahrungen in Bamberg.' In F. Edding (Hg.), *Bildung durch Wissenschaft in neben- und nachberuflichen Studien*. (Materialien aus der Bildungsforschung, Bd. 32). Berlin: Max-Planck-Institut für Bildungsforschung.

Fink, U. (1988) *Der neue Generationenvertrag. Ich für Dich. Die Zukunft der sozialen Dienste*. München: Piper.

Hainke, H. (1990) *Arbeitsmarktsegmentation und Rentenzugang. Eine empirische Analyse des Rentenzugangsalters von Männern in den Jahren 1957 bis 1987 mit den Daten des Sozio-ökonomischen Panels*. (Diplomarbeit). Berlin: Freie Universität.

Handl, J. (1988) *Berufschancen und Heiratsmuster von Frauen. Empirische Untersuchungen zu Prozessen sozialer Mobilität*. Frankfurt am Main: Campus.

Hondrich, K.O., Schumacher, J., Arzberger, K., Schlie, F. and Stegbauer, Ch. (1988) *Krise der Leistungsgesellschaft? Empirische Analysen zum Engagement in Arbeit, Familie und Politik*. Opladen: Westdeutscher Verlag.

Humboldt, W. von (1960) *Schriften zur Anthropologie und Geschichte*. Werke, Bd. I. Darmstadt: Wissenschaftliche Buchgesellschaft.

Imhof, A.E. (1988) *Reife des Lebens. Gedanken eines Historikers über das längere Dasein*. München: C.H. Beck.

Kaufmann, F.-X. (1990) *Zukunft der Familie. Stabilitätsrisiken und Wandel der familialen Lebensformen sowie ihre gesellschaftlichen und politischen Bedingungen*. München: C.H. Beck.

Kohn, M.L. and Schooler, C. (1978) 'The reciprocal effects of the substantive complexity of work and intellectual flexibility: A longitudinal assessment'. *American Journal of Sociology 84*, 24–52.

Kruse, A. (1988) 'Bildung im Alter'. *Zeitschrift für Gerontologie 21*, 4, 179–183.

Lehr, U. (1984) 'Zur Aktualität der Thematik "Bildung im Alter"'. *Erwachsenenbildung 30*, 3, 130–132.

Leschinsky, A. and Roeder, P.M. (1976) *Schule im historischen Prozeß*. Stuttgart: Klett.

Lichtenstein, E. (1971) Stichwort 'Bildung'. *Historisches Wörterbuch der Philosophie*, Bd. I, S. 921–938.

Lübbe, H. (1977) *Geschichtsbegriff und Geschichtsinteresse. Analytik und Pragmatik der Historie*. Basel, Stuttgart: Schwabe and Co.

Lundgren, P. (1980/1981) *Sozialgeschichte der deutschen Schule im Überblick*. Teil I: 1770–1918; Teil II: 1918–1980. Göttingen: Vandenhoeck and Ruprecht.

Matras, J. (1990) *Dependency, Obligations, and Entitlements. A New Sociology of Ageing, the Life Course, and the Elderly.* Englewood Cliffs, N.J.: Prentice Hall.

Mayer, K.U. (1981) 'Gesellschaftlicher Wandel und soziale Struktur des Lebensverlaufs', in J. Matthes (ed) *Lebenswelt und soziale Probleme.* Frankfurt am Main: Campus, S. 492–501.

Mayer, K.U. (1989) 'Das Altern der Gesellschaft: Theorie- und methodenkritische Anmerkungen'. *Zeitschrift für Gerontopsychologie und -psychiatrie 2,* 67–74.

Mayer, K.U. (1991) 'Vom Regen in die Traufe. Frauen zwischen Beruf und Familie', in K. U. Mayer, J. Allmendinger and J. Huinink (Hg.), *Vom Regen in die Traufe: Frauen zwischen Beruf und Familie.* Frankfurt am Main: Campus, S. VII – XXI.

Mayer, K.U. and Bückner, E. (1989) *Lebensverläufe und Wohlfahrtsentwicklung.* (Vols. I, II, III). (Materialien aus der Bildungsforschung Nr. 35). Berlin: Max-Planck-Institut für Bildungsforschung.

Mayer, K.U. and Müller, W. (1986) 'The State and the Structure of the Life Course'. In A.B. Srensen, F.E. Weinert, L.R. Sherrod (eds) *Human Development and the Life Course: Multidisciplinary Perspectives.* Hillsdale, N.J.: Erlbaum, pp. 217–245.

Mayer, K.U. and Müller, W. (1989) 'Lebensverläufe im Wohlfahrtsstaat', in A. Weymann (Hg.), *Handlungsspielräume.* Stuttgart: Enke, S. 41–60.

Miegel, M. (1989) 'Spät am Start, früh am Ziel. Die strenge Trennung der drei Lebensphasen muß gelockert werden'. *Die Zeit 13. 10. 1989,* S. 46.

Mittelstrauss, J. *Glanz und Elend der Geisteswissenschaften Oldenburg: Bibliotheks und Imformationssystem der Universität Oldenburg.* Reihe: Oldenburger Universitätsreden nr.27.

Müller, D., Zymek, B. (unter Mitarbeit von U. Herrmann) (1987) *Datenhandbuch zur deutschen Bildungsgeschichte.* Bd. II, Teil 1: Sozialgeschichte und Statistik des Schulsystems in den Staaten des Deutschen Reiches, 1800–1945. Göttingen: Vandenhoeck and Ruprecht.

Negt, O. (1985) *Lebendige Arbeit, enteignete Zeit. Politische und kulturelle Dimensionen des Kampfes um die Arbeitszeit.* Frankfurt am Main: Campus.

Open University Statistics (1987) *Students, Staff and Finance.* Milton Keynes: Open University.

Pehl, K. (1989) Statistisches Material zur Volkshochschularbeit 1962 bis 1987. (Arbeitspapier Nr. 113–6.89). Frankfurt am Main: Pädagogische Arbeitsstelle des Deutschen Volkshochschul-verbandes e.V.

Peters, O. (1988) 'Nicht-traditionelle Studien in der Bundesrepublik Deutschland und in den US', in F. Edding (Hg.), *Bildung durch*

Wissenschaft in neben- und nachberuflichen Studien. (Materialien aus der Bildungsforschung Nr. 32). Berlin: Max-Planck-Institut für Bildungsforschung.

Ritter, J. (1974) *Subjektivität.* Frankfurt am Main: Suhrkamp.

Schmähl, W. (1988) 'Alterssicherung und Familienlastenausgleich'. *Die Angestelltenversicherung 35*, 7/8, 318–323.

Schmidt, K.-D. and Rose, R. (1985) 'Germany: The Expansion of an Active State', in R. Rose (ed) *Public Employment in Western Nations.* Cambridge: Cambridge University Press, pp. 126–162.

Simmel, G. (1986) *Schriften zur Soziologie.* Frankfurt am Main: Suhrkamp Verlag.

Sörensen, A. (1990) 'Gender and the Life Course', in K.U. Mayer (ed) *Lebensverläufe und gesellschaftlicher Wandel.* (Sonderheft der Kölner Zeitschrift für Soziologie und Sozialpsychologie). Opladen: Westdeutscher Verlag, S. 304–321.

Statistisches Bundesamt (1987) *Statistisches Jahrbuch 1987.* Wiesbaden/Stuttgart: Kohlhammer.

VDR – Verband Deutscher Rentenversicherungsträger e.V. (1989) *Statistik Rentenzugang des Jahres 1988 in der deutschen gesetzlichen Rentenversicherung, einschlielich Rentenwegfall/Rentenumwandlung.* Frankfurt am Main: VDR.

Willms-Herget, A. (1985) *Frauenarbeit. Zur Integration der Frauen in den Arbeitsmarkt.* Frankfurt am Main: Campus.

Chapter 9

Higher Education and New Socio-Economic Challenges in Europe

Ulrich Teichler

Introduction

Any effort in discussing the future socio-economic conditions of higher education will face needs to be undertaken with caution. This is not only due to the fact that the social sciences do not have a strong record in predicting the future, but also that problems in the relationships between higher education and the subsequent tasks of graduates make it difficult and very risky.

Preparation for work is only one of the functions of higher education. The educational functions of higher education when viewed in relationship to employment are in principle general, professional, or academic. Higher education aims to provide a general enhancement of knowledge for students, and possibly a cultivation of values, attitudes and development of the personality. It is expected to provide a foundation of knowledge for the occupation that the student is likely to enter and in some areas a direct professional training. Institutions of higher education are also the training ground for scholars who are going to be the teachers of future generations of students. National higher education systems, disciplines and individual departments or institutions may vary in their emphasis on the balance between these functions but there exists a consensus among experts and politicians that a coexistence, rather than segmentation, of these functions is desirable at least in the high quality sectors of the higher education system.

In addition, higher education tends to be less directly and less clearly geared to occupational tasks than other forms of pre-career training. This is not only due to the combination of functions named above, but also to the curious fact that the more demanding the occupational task the less directly can it be trained for. Higher education also differs from late stages of other pre-career education in its critical and innovative functions. Graduates must be prepared not just to take on tasks and to apply existing rules, but they must also be capable and motivated to question established practices and to cope with unpredicted work tasks; that is, they must also anticipate and press for innovations.

Even if higher education was shaped strongly both quantitatively and qualitatively according to the needs of the employment system, imperfections in identifying future demands and corresponding education requirements would remain. Further, flexibility on the part of graduates can make up for imperfections in planning and forecasting. In considering higher education in the 21st century, I will begin with a cautious view looking back at the developments of the last three or four decades and by indicating some of the changes we can expect in the near future. At the end, I will discuss some changes which might be of long term relevance. The discussion will be confined to the educational function of higher education in relation to the subsequent work and other life experiences of graduates. I will leave to others the questions of the research and service tasks of higher education.

Major Trends in the Last Few Decades

Before getting into a discussion of the relationship between higher education and employment, we should be aware that a substantial part of the current debate does not focus on long-term trends but rather on short-term or medium-term cyclical changes. At times of problems in general employment or at times of rapid expansion of the graduate proportion among the whole new labour force, i.e., at times of the most visible mismatch between the output of education and employment, higher education is strongly under pressure to provide a response to presumed socio-economic demands. At times when the concerns of this kind are less, external pressures tend to be weaker. However, the cyclical concept based on economic market assumptions has been challenged in recent decades. Students have followed the cyclical market signals to a much lesser extent than expected on the various models that have been used, and socio-economic conditions have changed too fast.

There are three clear trends during the last few decades regarding the socio-economic challenges of higher education. First, we observe a secular trend to 'scientification' of employment and work. Production and services become more and more based on the results of research; a growing number of positions require high skills and the prospects become more and more dim for people who have not acquired a degree if they are aiming for responsible positions.

Second, we see that in the process of expansion, higher education assumes the function of serving the education and training of those employed in middle-level positions, in addition to the socialisation and selection of the social élite and the preparation for the professions that are highly demanding cognitively. This is the trend that has led to the pejorative term 'mass higher education'. The coincidence of the phenomena of scientification and massification of higher education has created a considerable mood of crisis not only among the academic but also in the highly educated professions. It is difficult for them to accept the fact that the more important higher education becomes for society, the less privileged are those within higher education and those who have been trained in higher education institutions. The growing expenditure on higher education has created pressure to justify the financial burden it gives to society. Apart from their efforts to increase efficiency, this pressure can lead administrators to demonstrate efficiency by favouring those activities which are of most usefulness to society and the economy.

In Europe, most governments have significantly reduced the unit costs per student of higher education and this has affected virtually all institutions. Many European scholars look with envy at the most prestigious section of higher education in the US, where some of the top universities have been protected from these pressures.

These trends undoubtedly have increased pressure on higher education to be more responsive to presumed trends in the employment system. Some authorities claim to observe an 'epistemological drift' in the educative function of higher education.

One has to take into consideration that there are also countertrends. Faith in the potential of external planning and steering of higher education has been eroded. This applies firstly to the ability to identify and forecast the requirements of the employment system. Secondly, it has turned out to be extraordinarily difficult to reach political consensus on either the underlying rationales or the measures that need to be taken. Those policies that have been implemented have not infrequently led to unexpected consequences. Thus the desire to shape education according to economic and social demands has been more or less counterbalanced by scepticism as regards its necessity, implementation and impact.

In various West European countries, we note that substantial changes in the steering, governance and administration of higher education has occurred since the 1980s. The classical distinction between external pressures and internal self-administration has become blurred, and has led to the latter being strengthened. The internal management is now expected to be the key negotiator between the forces exerted by the general, academic and professional functions. At the same time, some externals play a more active role, for instance as external members of boards and committees or through practitioners serving as part-time teachers. It remains to be seen how the balance will eventually be changed.

Expansion of Higher Education and its Implications

During the first decades of the second half of this century a rapid expansion of higher education has occurred. Among the corresponding age group in 1950, the quota of new entrants was 5 per cent or lower in most European countries. In various countries, the enrolment doubled several times during the course of ten years but this was not a smooth or continuous process. The Federal Republic of Germany showed striking discontinuities. After increasing from about 10 per cent in 1960 to 20 per cent in 1973, the enrolment remained virtually constant until 1985 and then almost doubled to 38 per cent by 1992 (this excludes the new East German *Länder*). Growing new entry quotas are not immediately reflected in the award of degrees. A new wave of massification is obviously on the agenda and not always explicitly recognised by 'higher education' policies.

It should be noted that the rapid expansion of higher education in Eastern Europe occurred in the 1950s and early 1960s and preceded that in Western Europe.

Growing new entry quotas have, of course, a delayed effect on the completion of degrees which are also influenced by the proportion of students completing, which is in the range 50–90 per cent. The proportion of the age cohort receiving a higher education degree was, according to OECD statistics, over 50 per cent in Norway, between 20 to 35 per cent in most Western European countries, lower in some, as well as in the majority of Central and Eastern European countries. Despite these differences in the actual expansion of the system, very similar stages of debate on the relationship between higher education and employment can be observed in all market-oriented industrial societies. Four stages can be resolved.

Initially, during the late 1950s and more so in the 1960s, most experts came to the conclusion that a substantial expansion of higher education was needed in order to stimulate economic growth. Soon thereafter, hope spread that this expansion would also help to reduce inequalities of opportunity, as well as strengthen a modern democratic society both economically and socially.

During the late 1960s and early 1970s this optimistic view was modified. The restructuring of the higher educational system was highlighted to meet the growing diversity of students, their talents, motives, and careers.

However, during the 1970s this optimism was replaced by serious criticism of the expansion which seemed to have led to overeducation, overqualification and other mismatches, such as graduate unemployment or underemployment. The critique went further that award of degrees was artificial (credentialism), had fuelled an unnecessary expansion and that the expansion had only a limited effect in reducing inequality of opportunity.

From the late 1970s and more obviously in the 1980s, the general atmosphere of crisis about the employment implications of the higher education expansion became more moderate. Mass higher education became accepted as an irreversible phenomenon. More attention was paid to three major issues:

1. The growing diversity of graduate careers and work according to the field of study, type of higher education institution, or rank of the individual and department.

2. The issue of preservation of quality of higher education and graduate competence during the process of quantitative expansion.

3. The changing role of higher education for middle-level jobs.

In the early 1990s, concern grew about the quantitative relationships between higher education and employment. On the one hand, unemployment increased in many West European countries, but graduation quotas were also rising. Most experts continue to assume that graduates will face a lower risk of unemployment than non-graduates and will expect more attractive careers; an absorption of the growing number of graduates in middle-level jobs is now more often regarded as beneficial than it was in the 1980s. However, most experts and politicians agree nowadays that structural and curricular initiatives, as well as supporting activities from higher education are needed in order to cope with changing socio-economic conditions.

It should be noted that the rather more favourable assessment of higher education and graduation quotas is not based on any single major assessment of socio-economic demand; rather, a multitude of assumptions, none of which are completely uncontroversial tend to be presented. There are some areas in which more specialists are needed; new technologies lead to a growing need for specialists in many fields. The growth of the service sector is accompanied by an increase in graduate positions. Growth in the need for co-operation among specialists are taken care of by establishing new positions.

Upgrading of middle-level positions is desirable following decentralisation of responsibilities, and the ageing of society can only be funded if labour is more highly qualified. A more complex knowledge base is more appreciated because it serves both qualification for employment and the ability to cope with more complex tasks in all spheres.

If we try to systematise the various arguments, we note four main possible directions, for expansion on the one hand, and possible consequences of expansion on the other:

1. New demands in the most intellectually demanding professional areas.

2. New ways of utilising knowledge in middle-level occupations.

3. A blurring of the division of labour and of the previously clear division between top and middle-level positions.

4. A growing complexity of work and other aspects of life calling for a general increase in the level of competencies.

We note an abundance of claims by experts in various fields detailing the new demands in well-established professions and disciplines. Researchers on higher education, including this author, find it difficult to evaluate these claims since their expertise does not rest in the individual areas but rather in issues relevant across fields.

We continue to hear sceptical voices in Europe about the role of higher education in preparing for middle-level jobs; for decades higher education was believed to be unnecessary for these occupations and one talked of 'overeducation' or 'overqualification'. Popular demand for higher education eventually forced graduates into these areas. The question remains whether the institutions of higher education will be able to develop concepts for the preparation of students for those positions, or whether middle-level jobs will more and more become a dumping ground for students who have mediocre success in reaching higher educational and professional levels.

The prevailing paradigm that a high level of competence is a scarce resource in higher education and that a clear hierarchy of status and responsibility should ensure the maximum use of the available talent, may collapse. Instead, society might be viewed as a highly educated one shaped by an abundance of talents. Responsibilities might be shared and decentralised and the degree of status difference between the former top-ranking and intermediate positions might diminish substantially.

The views about the level of competence needed to cope with a work task might lose weight in the debate about the required or desirable level of educational expansion, because the basic requirement of knowledge and understanding of the complex living environment for each individual might reach a level according to which tertiary education seems to be a desired good for almost everyone. The need to cope well with economic and social conditions, with the political system, with health and environment and with the risks and frequent changes in life rather than the demand of work might become the major rationale shaping education.

Diversified Structures and Graduate Employment

As already mentioned, the expansion of higher education was embedded in efforts to restructure it. This was based on the assumption that a growing diversity in student talents, motives and career prospects was better served by a diversity of institutions or a diversity of programmes. Around 1970, it became conventional wisdom that a diversified structure was necessary in order to protect élite higher education and to offer a suitable learning environment for motivating, and extending the capabilities and employment prospects of the new, previously disadvantaged or 'non-traditional' students.

Restructuring began outside Europe. In the late 1950s, community colleges in the US were the most rapidly expanding sector. In Japan, *Koto Senmon Gakko* were established in 1962 (technical colleges combining upper secondary with short cycle higher education), and junior colleges were granted permanent status in 1965. In Europe, new institutions surfaced in the 1960s and 1970s, for example, Polytechnics in Britain, *Instituts Universitaires de Technologie* in France, *Distrikt Hogskøler* in Norway and *Fachhochschulen* in Germany. Further restructuring was on the agenda in some other countries during the 1970s and early 1980s, but fewer measures appeared during this time, notably because the financial stringency made restructuring more difficult to implement.

Altogether, we note that diversification was regarded as either desirable or even indispensable. What remained controversial were the principles and structures for differentiation or diversification. Up to the present, no convergence of patterns of higher education has emerged, rather the pattern varies according to four dimensions:

1. Policies and actual developments varied regarding qualitative differences. In some countries there is a steep quality hierarchy in institutions, whereas in other countries the divergence was less.
2. Efforts were made in some countries to promote intra-institutional rather than inter-institutional divergences.

Models of the former kind as in the comprehensive higher education system in Sweden and the *Gesamthochschulen* in Germany remain the exception.

3. Institutional diversification could be arranged through a) quality and prestige differences between formally equal institutions (more pronounced in Japan and the US than in Europe), b) stages of course programmes and degrees (for example the *Cycles* in France, the lower and upper *Kandidatus* in the Scandinavian tradition or the Anglo-Saxon Bachelor and Master), and c) different types of higher education institutions, on the one hand universities, and on the other, *Polytechnics, Fachhochschulen,* and *Hogescholen.*

4. The different institutions and programmes might vary not only according to the duration of study but also according to the dominant curricular approach. In some countries the lower and shorter degree programme is the more general one and the longer one serves professional specialisation (this characterises the relationship between bachelors and masters in the Anglo-Saxon tradition), whereas in other countries non-university higher education is considered to be more vocational (e.g. Germany and the Netherlands).

In the late 1980s and early 1990s, restructuring of higher education became once more a key issue in many countries. On the one hand, this occurred in those countries in which the first degree involved a very long period of study; it is interesting to note the different options that were chosen. In Spain and Denmark, a bachelors degree is now awarded after three years. In Finland and Austria, new types of programme (*Ammattikorkealoulu* and *Fachhochschulen*) provide courses leading to a degree equivalent to the bachelor but with a more vocational emphasis. In Italy, separate university departments were established to provide very short programmes of up to two years. Similar debates occurred in Central and East European countries about diversification.

On the other hand, in the United Kingdom and in some other countries following the British model, the so-called 'binary' structure was discontinued; the Polytechnics were named universities and are likely to become similar to the previously established universities.

In addition, European Union policy may have an effect. In December 1988, the EU called for an equivalence of all European three-year programmes in terms of providing the basic entry requirements to the highly qualified occupations. As neither structural nor curricular convergence was visible, the duration remained the only undisputed criterion that could be agreed.

Most employers and politicians agree that the short and less academically oriented programmes (called 'alternatives to universities' in a recent OECD study) are most welcome for ensuring a better match between higher education and the human resource requirements of the employment system. Although the arguments are much alike internationally, the second or possibly third type of higher education institutions vary dramatically from one country to another. We might come to the conclusion that employers and politicians are more interested in stabilising the less academically oriented institutions than in the type of knowledge and competence provided by this sector.

In many countries, the graduates from the non-university sector of higher education seem to be rather well-received by the employment system. However, the data basis is sufficiently vague as to not allow an adequate comparison of employment and career of graduates coming through the two routes. Exaggeration of the success of the non-university graduates is obviously a widespread condition, as has been found by research in Germany on graduate employment.

We can note that there are two schools of thought about future perspectives. Some experts clearly expect an increasing stratification in higher education. Only a dozen universities might be really international, world leading institutions. Resources, as well as talent, would cluster around these institutions whereas others would narrow their objectives on specific national and regional tasks. Proponents of this view point to the high cost of resources in top science and engineering fields and the opportunities for cross-fertilisation within a leading institution.

Other experts point to a growing need for a wider dissemination of knowledge and consider this to be more influential for the future of an industrial society than competition in producing new knowledge. Concentrating resources and an increased stratification of higher education are regarded as counter-productive to the needs of a highly educated society. According to these views, it would be preferable to disperse talents and skills to spread knowledge rapidly.

By and large, scholars seem to cast a more favourable eye on stratified and hierarchical structures whereas politicians are more concerned about the improvement and stabilisation of the less prestigious institutions. I would argue that we notice in all European countries some diversification that accompanies expansion. We also notice a surprising stability of the dominant view over time in any given country. In countries where the system of higher education was quite hierarchical and stratified decades ago, further stratification is likely to be seen as a virtue, whereas in countries where more or less equal level of universities was held in high esteem, diversification is viewed with suspicion.

Curricula, Learning and Socialisation

Any effort at summarising the debates on curriculum reform, teaching, and learning considered as an appropriate response to changing socio-economic challenges turns out to be very difficult. Curricular rationales vary strikingly between disciplines and occupational areas, according both to the educational institutions and the historical goals of higher education; in each it is hardly possible to state anything, for instance which would apply both to medicine and the humanities. Expectations differ significantly in each country; French and German employers expect a high degree of specialisation and professional preparation, British employers prefer a trained mind and Japanese employers prefer to recruit graduates that can be considered as 'raw material' that they can train themselves.

Notwithstanding such diversity, the major focus of higher education curricula can be considered in terms of seven categories:

1. Curricula may be strongly directed towards preparation for research and the creation of knowledge or towards the reproduction and dissemination of knowledge that already exists.

2. Curricula may be closely geared to occupational preparation or not related to job roles at all.

3. Objectives of curricula differ remarkably according to the degree of specialisation intended.

4. Fields of study may be designed by discipline or be cross-,multi-, or inter-disciplinary.

5. Curricula may be completely field specific of provide a common core across disciplines ('general education' or something similar).

6. Educational goals might vary to the extent to which they are intended to shape personality development by other means than fostering cognitive, academic, or occupation related skills.

7. Higher education curricula vary in the extent to which they are expected to contribute to the cultural enrichment of society.

In the 1980s, we observed an abundance of dialogue between representatives of the employment system and higher education with
regard to socio-economic challenges; these were mostly disappoint-
ing to those who expected them to yield new recipes for the curricula.
This was not altogether surprising since surveys suggest that the
representatives of the employment system had little interest in the
minutiae of curriculum which concerned those involved with teaching.

Dialogues on the changing socio-economic challenges were successful in identifying some of the principal issues and my impression
is that five recommendations were frequently raised in latter years.
If taken into account they should be influential in the relationship
between higher education and employment in the early decades of
the coming century.

1. Higher education should become more flexible to reallocate
   resources and to regroup its potential in order to adapt to
   areas in high demand, such as those related to the growth
   areas of new technologies, for example, biotechnology,
   ecology etc.

2. Individual higher educational institutions and departments
   should be given more freedom in choosing profiles within
   disciplines. There should be less standardisation of curricula
   whether by governments, academic associations or
   professional bodies. Measures to stimulate student exchange
   and to establish common European curricula. Increased
   awareness should be encouraged of the fact that curricula
   are much less determined by disciplinary logic or the nature
   of job tasks than is commonly supposed.

3. Higher education should aim for a foundation on which to
   build rather than on a specified corpus of knowledge. There
   is a well-developed consensus that it should prepare
   students for lifetime but less agreement about how much
   direct professional preparation should be given and also
   doubts whether higher education institutions are suitable
   providing continuing education.

4. Higher education should aim to a lesser extent for a provision
   of a certain body of knowledge. There is an obvious
   consensus across industrial societies that higher education
   should play a more important role in preparing students for
   lifelong learning. There is a lesser degree of consensus,
   though, regarding the extent to which pre-career higher
   education should only lay foundations and refrain from any
   direct professional preparation. Consensus is even shakier

when one discusses the areas in which higher education institutions should provide continuing education for a college trained workforce.

5. Higher education should play a bigger role in shaping personality. Graduates are expected to be more loyal to their employing organisation, more entrepreneurial, better prepared for co-operation and to accept also the less demanding job roles, to be motivated towards problem solving and to be able to cope with unexpected demands.

Lifelong Education

Higher education is likely to play a more important role beyond pre-career education. Six interrelated developments support the view that institutions of higher education will play a growing role in this.

1. As the mood becomes favourable again for the expansion of education, the idea of lifelong education will gain ground.

2. We note that lifelong education does not mainly play a compensatory role benefiting those with a lower pre-career education level but actually reinforces differences in pre-career education. An expansion of adult education is likely to follow the expansion of higher education.

3. We note that continuing education is taking up some of the challenges to which pre-career education has been slow to respond to, for example, combinations of disciplines.

4. The more that lifelong learning becomes a system, the more likely it is that many individuals will change their learning patterns; the boundaries between pre-career and continuing education are becoming blurred. Many more students take part-time studies, interrupt and return and take advanced studies after a few years. More employers are making opportunities for part-time studies or study leave.

5. Politicians try to counter long initial study periods with concepts related to 'recurrent education'. The premise is that first degree programmes can be shortened and opportunities for later advanced study increased.

6. Institutions of higher education are themselves becoming more interested in playing an enlarged role in lifelong education. This has been driven partly by the pressure to relate studies to occupational opportunities as well as the continuing financial constraints.

One should bear in mind that many predictions about the dramatic scale of increase in lifelong education have not proved correct. There is an endemic overestimate due to the fact that any demands for new types of qualifications initially responded to by continuing education is soon also adopted into pre-career programmes; this means that these programmes have short periods before obsolescence. There are substantial differences in Europe in the involvement of higher education institutions in continuing education. Some believe that the growing speed of obsolescence is bound to lead to a greater involvement. If we present an extreme scenario and assume that half of a graduate's knowledge becomes obsolete within ten years, and if all graduate education is provided by institutions of higher education, they will eventually be applying more effort to this than to the pre-career period!

Long-Term Perspective

Most debates on future socio-economic challenges for higher education do not sound very futuristic; forecasts tend to be extrapolations with only small qualitative changes. However, I expect that there will be important changes in the relationship between higher education and employment.

First, internationalisation of higher education is growing. Many existing course programmes are quite national in character and notably, in the humanities and social sciences, rethinking is in progress. We also see a split occurring between jobs that are predominantly national and those that are international. In some areas, global approaches have already been achieved as in many areas of the natural sciences.

Equally important is the place of international mobility to change the horizons and cognitive maps of students. In our research on the Erasmus programmes we noted that the majority of students considered that their study abroad was superior to their study at home, even though only part of their performance abroad was recognised. Apart from a certain amount of overenthusiasm, this suggests that students appreciate the stimulus of studying abroad as a fresh look on their discipline or profession more highly than their teachers do. One could expect that this rethinking through novel experience and knowledge might be more systematically fostered in the future.

All curricular and structural concepts of higher education may well change very substantially once we view higher education as no longer being concerned with the selection and fostering of the scarce high talents, which are destined to take on the most demanding, rewarding, and responsible tasks in society, but is rather seen as concerned with providing a highly educated society. As higher education is viewed as directed to the masses, many basic concepts may change.

In Europe, it is generally assumed nowadays that those shaping the character of higher education systems, institutions and programmes are the key actors in determining the output of the system. Research on the impact of higher education on the achievements and careers of students cautions against this. Multi-variate analyses of college impact suggests that student achievements is determined more by the way students act during their period of study than by the formal structure of the higher institution;s provisions, programmes, teaching style etc.

Further, linkages between the competencies acquired during the course of study and job requirements are not automatically established. It seems rather that the search by graduates and employers have a dynamic of their own. We might view this as a shift from a 'delivery' model of higher education to an 'opportunity' model in the future. Students are key actors in selecting from what is available.

Institutions of higher education will probably put more effort into providing work experience, and in undertaking career placements. These changes signal a shift in responsibility to support of students with a decrease in the traditional role of instruction.

The future changes in occupation pattern will be of great interest. The current trend of decline in the opportunities for gainful employment have hardly affected the dominant interest in jobs and careers, but we tend to see a polarisation between those remaining in traditional occupations and those marginalised by the changes. We may be witnessing a substantial disappearance of the pattern in which an individual spends all of his or her life work continuously in one profession or in one institution. Perhaps, a person might spend half the week or half the day in one employing organisation and half in another. Moving in and out in certain professions might become a matter of course. The difference between the status of employee and the self-employed might be eroded. Changes in the organisation of work deserve more attention in scenarios about the future of higher education than they have had in the past.

Further Reading

Brennan, J., Lyon, E.S., McGeevor, P.A. and Murray, K. (1993) *Students, Courses and Jobs: The Relationships between Higher Education and the Labour Market*. London: Jessica Kingsley Publishers.

Education and the European Competence (1989) *ERT Study on Education and Training in Europe.* Brussels: Roundtable of Industrialists.

Commission of the European Communities, Task Force Human Resources, Education, Training and Youth (1991) Memorandum on Higher Education in the European Community. Brussels: HEFC.

Esnault, E. (1990) 'Les universités et l'évolution d'employ.' *CREaction 92,* 23–27.

Europäische Kommission (1994) Wachstum, Wettbewerbsfähigkeit, Beschäftigung: Herausforderungen der Gegenwart und Wage ins 21. Jahrhundert. Luxenburg: Amt für Amtliche Veröffentlichungen der Europäischen Gemeinschaften.

Higher Education and the Labour Market (1993) *Higher Education in Europe 18,* 2. (Special issue.)

Jonsson, B. (1993) Kompetensutveckling pa framtidens arbetsmarknad: en litteraturöversikt. Stockholm Universitets- och Hogskoleämbetet, (UHÄ projekt 1991: 3a).

OECD (1992) *Alternative to Universities.* Paris.

OECD (1992) *Education at a Glance: OECD Indicators.* Paris.

OECD (1993) *From Higher Education to Employment: Synthesis Report.* Paris.

OECD (1992) Recant Developments in Continuing Professional Education of Highly Qualified Personnel. Paris, mimeo. (DEELSA/ED/WE(92)10).

OECD (1993) Higher Education and Employment: The Case of the Humanities and Social Sciences. Paris.

Pascarella, E.T. and Terenzini (1991) *How College Affects Students: Findings and Insights from Twenty Years of Research.* San Francisco, Oxford: Jossey-Bass.

Pearson, R., Andreutti, F. and Holly, F. (1990) *The European Labour Market Review: The Key Indicators.* Brighton: Institute of Manpower Studies.

Sanyal, B.C. (1991) 'Higher education and the labour market.' In P.G. Altbach (ed) *International Higher Education: An Encyclopedia.* New York and London: Garland.

Schön, D.A. (1987) *Educating the Reflective Practitioner.* San Francisco and London: Jossey-Bass.

Schomburg, H. and Teichler, U. (1993) 'Does the programme matter?' *Higher Education in Europe 18,* 2, 37–58.

Staffenbiel, J.E. (1993) *Key Information and Jobs for the European Graduate 93/94.* Köln: Institut für Berufs- unde Ausbildungsplanung.

Teichler, U. (1990) 'The challenge of lifelong learning for the university.' *CREaction 92,* 53–68.

Teichler, U. (1991) 'Towards a highly educated society.' *Higher Education Policy 4,* 11–20.

Teichler, U. (1992) 'Occupational structures and higher education.' In B.R. Clark and G.R. Neave (eds) *The Encyclopedia of Higher Education*, 975–992. Oxford: Pergamon.

Teichler, U. and Maiworm, F. (1994) *Transition to Work: The Experience of Former ERASMUS Students*. London: Jessica Kingsley Publishers.

University Competence and Industry (special issue), *CREaction 92*.

Wijnards van Resandt, A. (ed) (1991) *A Guide to Higher Education Systems and Qualifications in the European Communities*. Luxembourg: Office for Official Publications of the Commission of European Communities.

Williams, B. (1993) *Higher Education and Employment*. Parkville: University of Melbourne, Centre for the Study of Higher Education.

Youdi, R.V. and Hinchliffe, K. (eds) (1985) *Forecasting Skilled Menpower Needs: The Experience of Eleven Countries*. Paris: International Institute for Educational Planning.

Chapter 10

New Perspectives of Learning and Teaching in Higher Education

Erik de Corte

Introduction

Due to the drastic social, economic, cultural and technical changes that are taking place in our modern world in general and in the European space in particular, the nature, the role, and the organisation of higher education have become the focus of critical analysis and discussion since the early 1980s. This has resulted in a series of rather severe criticisms of higher education in Europe. For instance, Buchberger, De Corte, Groombridge, Kennedy, and Vèhèsaari (1994) have recently listed the following criticisms:

- unclear and conflicting mission and goals, which may be seen in close relation with problems and discrepancies in study programmes and curricula
- inappropriate methods of teaching and learning
- inflexible curricula and programmes which lead to a high rate of drop-outs and a long duration of studies
- poor organisation of postgraduate studies and research training
- problems in the structures of administration and management
- a lack of co-ordination and co-operation both within and between institutions of higher education; a lack of internationalisation.

Probably as a consequence of a certain combination of these important shortcomings, students' outcomes in higher education, either in terms of measured achievement or in more qualitative respects, are also often not satisfying. For example, in my own country about 45 per cent of the freshmen fail at the end of their first year. This is certainly partly due to the absence of a selection procedure at the entrance of the university; as a consequence, the first year functions as a sieve. But free entrance to the university, conditional on having finished successfully secondary education, is not the only explanatory factor of the unacceptably high failure rate. Other causes seem to be inappropriate curriculum choices, weak teaching practices, and insufficient study guidance.

The relative dissatisfaction with the present state-of-the-art of higher education represents a major challenge at the threshold of the 21st century. Crucial aspects of this challenge are the necessity to make education more adaptive to the individual demands of, and the differences between students in initial higher education as well as in continuing education, on the one hand, and the requirement to respond appropriately to the new needs of society with respect to education and training at the tertiary level, on the other (see e.g., De Vocht and Henderikx 1993; OECD 1994). Achieving this will require a long-term, multifaceted approach.

This chapter focuses on only one facet, albeit it a major one, namely the teaching-learning environment at the classroom level, or more generally at the level of the learning group. It will be shown that research on learning and instruction has produced over the past decades an empirically underpinned knowledge base for designing more powerful learning environments that can lead to improvements in students' learning activities and outcomes, as well as in teacher's instructional practices. A comprehensive review of this field of inquiry, which has tremendously developed during the past two decades, is outside the scope of this chapter. Therefore, some significant aspects will be documented in an exemplary way, using as a frame of reference the three major components that can be distinguished in a theory of learning from instruction, namely a theory of expertise, a theory of acquisition, and a theory of intervention. A theory of expertise aims at analysing skilled performance in a domain. A theory of acquisition attempts to understand and explain the processes of learning and development that are conducive to the attainment of expert performance. Finally, a theory of intervention intends to design, elaborate and evaluate powerful teaching-learning environments for eliciting those acquisition processes.

A Dispositional View of Expertise

A theory of expertise should specify the knowledge, skills, beliefs and attitudes that students must acquire in order to become competent in a given domain. In addition, such a theory should identify possible initial misconceptions and defective skills that constrain the acquisition of competence. Starting from a research-based analysis of the aptitudes involved in expertise, this section will outline a so-called dispositional view of skilled performance in a domain.

Characteristics of Expertise

A major contribution to the elaboration of a theory of skilled and exceptional performance has come from the substantial amount of cognitive psychological research, in which expertise in a large variety of domains was analysed by comparing performance of experts and novices. Indeed, this work has resulted in the identification of a series of critical features of experts' performance that generalise across the distinct domains that were studied. In a summary of this research, Glaser and Chi (1988) describe the following key characteristics:

1. Experts excel mainly in their own domain.
2. Experts perceive large meaningful patterns in their domain.
3. Experts are fast; they are faster than novices at performing the skills of their domain, and they quickly solve problems with little error.
4. Experts have superior short-term and long-term memory.
5. Experts see and represent a problem in their domain at a deeper (more principled) level than novices; novices tend to represent a problem at a superficial level.
6. Experts spend a great deal of time analyzing a problem qualitatively.
7. Experts have strong self-monitoring skills.

Expertise and the Objectives of Higher Education

These findings do not only promote and deepen our understanding of the nature of expertise, but they are also very relevant from an educational point of view, because they contribute substantially to the clarification and definition of the objectives of higher education. Indeed, taking into account the results of the analyses of expertise, there is at present a rather broad consensus that becoming skilled in a given domain requires the integrated acquisition of four categories of aptitudes:

1. A well-organised and flexibly accessible domain-specific knowledge base, i.e., the facts, symbols, algorithms, concepts, and rules that constitute the contents of a subject-matter field.

2. Heuristics methods, i.e., search strategies for problem solving which do not guarantee, but significantly increase the probability of finding the correct solution because they induce a systematic approach to the task.

3. Metacognition, which involves knowledge concerning one's cognitive functioning, on the one hand, and skills relating to the self-regulation of one's cognitive processes, on the other.

4. Affective components such as beliefs, attitudes, and emotions relating to a subject-matter field.

Space restrictions do not allow the elaboration of each of these aptitudes in more detail (see De Corte 1994). Therefore, only the role of domain-specific knowledge and metacognition will briefly be discussed.

The Role of Domain-Specific Knowledge in Skilled Performance

As already referred to above, the important role of domain-specific knowledge in problem solving has well been demonstrated in the so-called 'expert-novice' studies (Chi, Glaser and Farr 1988). A representative example is an investigation by Chi, Feltovich, and Glaser (1981) in mechanics. They asked expert physicists (advanced graduate students) and novices (undergraduate students) to sort and classify mechanics problems. The novices based their classification on the apparatus involved (lever, inclined plane, balance beam), on the actual terms used in the problem statement, or on the surface characteristics of the diagram presented. Experts, on the contrary, classified problems according to the underlying principles needed to solve them (e.g., energy laws, Newton's second law). In other words, the experts constructed a totally different initial representation of the problems than the novices, reflecting differences in the content as well as in the organisation of the knowledge base of both groups. In a more recent study in the domain of physics De Jong and Ferguson-Hessler (1991) observed similar differences between good and poor novice problem solvers. It needs no argument that the quality, the completeness, and the coherence of the initial representation determine the efficiency of the rest of the solution process.

The important impact of domain-specific prior knowledge on study skills and academic achievement has been convincingly shown in a study by Minnaert and Janssen (1992) involving 161 psychology students in Belgium. Indeed, the results of a prior knowledge test explained a significant proportion of the variance in study success and progress after five academic years, being the nominal length of the curriculum.

The robust finding that skilled learning and problem solving in a given domain depends to a large extent on the availability of a well-organised and flexibly accessible knowledge base, is one of the major reasons underlying the scepticism concerning the possibility of enhancing problem-solving ability across domains through the mere teaching of general heuristics and metacognitive strategies. Indeed, when confronted with a problem in a relatively unfamiliar domain, the problem solver lacking sufficient domain-specific knowledge often does not know how to use the heuristics that he/she has in his repertoire, because he/she is unable to find the link between the problem situation and the appropriate heuristic that applies to it. Therefore, general heuristics are nowadays referred to as weak methods (Perkins and Salomon 1989).

The Role of Metacognitive Skills in Expert Performance

A major outcome that has emerged from the research during the 1980s relates to the crucial role of metacognition in learning, thinking, and problem solving (Brown, Bransford, Ferrara, and Campione 1983; Simons and Beufhof 1987).

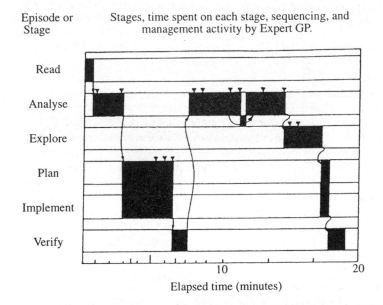

Figure 10.1 Expert mathematician solving a difficult problem

Schoenfeld (1992), for instance, observed that metacognitive activities constitute an essential component of expert problem solving in mathematics. This is illustrated in Figure 10.1 which shows a representative example of a time-line graph of an expert mathematician solving a difficult problem. As can be noted, this expert spent a substantial amount of time on analysing the problem in an attempt to understand what it is about, and on planning the solution process. Moreover, the expert continually reflected on the state of his problem solution; this is indicated by the inverted triangles in the graph, representing explicit comments by the expert during the solution process (e.g., 'I don't know where to start here'), followed by two minutes of analysing the problem.

This expert approach is in sharp contrast to the typical problem-solving behaviour that emerged from a large series of videotapes of college and high school students solving unfamiliar problems in pairs during 20-minute sessions. Schoenfeld (1992) found indeed that in about 60 per cent of the solution attempts self-regulatory activities, that are so characteristic of the expert approach, were totally lacking. The typical strategy in those cases is illustrated in Figure 10.2, and

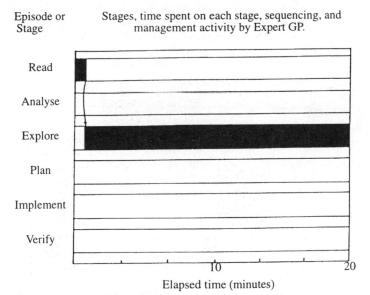

Episode or Stage   Stages, time spent on each stage, sequencing, and management activity by Expert GP.

Figure 10.2 College and high school students solving unfamiliar problems

can be described as follows: reading the problem, deciding to do something, and then keeping at it without considering any alternative even despite evidence that no progress is being made.

Similar results have been reported with respect to other content domains. For example, a review of the literature relating to computer programming by Dalbey and Linn (1985) clearly reveals that expert programmers, in comparison to novices, invest much more effort in metacognitive activities such as designing and planning problem solutions before coding the programme in computer language. Novices and poor performers tend to start writing computer code immediately.

But a second aspect of metacognition that influences students' learning and thinking activities in a negative way, should be mentioned here, because it is much less taken into consideration: namely certain naive, but incorrect, and motivationally important convictions that students hold – often more or less implicitly – about subject-matter domains. This is also illustrated by work of Schoenfeld (1985; 1988) showing that with respect to solving mathematics problems, less skilled students are afflicted with strange ideas like being able to solve a problem is merely a question of luck; when you have not found the solution of a problem after just a few minutes, it is useless to spend more time on it, and, therefore, you better quit. It is important to mention that Schoenfeld found that the students he studied acquired these ideas as a result of teaching that was generally considered successful. The title of one of his papers is: 'When good teaching leads to bad results: the disasters of 'well-taught' mathematics courses'.

Aptitudes are not Enough: Toward a Dispositional View of Expertise

The importance for learning and thinking of the four categories of aptitudes listed and exemplarily discussed above is undeniable. Nevertheless, it has also frequently been observed that even when those aptitudes are available to students, they often fail to apply them in situations where it is relevant to do so in solving an unfamiliar problem. To overcome this well-known phenomenon of inert knowledge, competence in a domain requires more than those four categories of aptitudes, namely the acquisition of a disposition for skilled learning and thinking. According to Perkins, Jay, and Tishman (1993) a disposition involves, besides the ability to deploy a certain behaviour, also the inclination to do so as well as the sensitivity for situations and opportunities where it is appropriate to do so. This implies that it is not sufficient for students to acquire certain concepts and skills, such as, for example, estimation skills in mathematics, but they should also get a feeling for task situations in which it is relevant and useful to apply these skills, and, moreover, become inclined to do so whenever appropriate. The acquisition of such a disposition – especially the inclination and sensitivity aspects – requires extensive experience with the four categories of aptitudes mentioned above in a large variety of situations. As such, the disposition cannot be directly taught, but has to develop over a rather extensive period of time.

Finally, referring to Boekaerts' (1993) model of the affective learning process, it should be taken into account that students can only be inclined and sensitive to use their available knowledge and skills if there are no emotional barriers, i.e., if a learning task or problem situation and its demands are not evoking negative feelings and expectations. If the latter is the case, students experience the situation as threatening or undermining their feelings of well-being, and tend to develop a coping intention rather than a learning intention: they are not primarily concerned about learning, but about restoring their well-being.

Constructive Learning as a Vehicle for Acquiring Competence

The major question of a theory of acquisition is the following: what kind of learning and developmental processes should be elicited in students, in order to facilitate the attainment of the intended disposition to skilled thinking and problem solving, resulting in competent performance in their domain? In this respect, a series of characteristics of effective learning processes have emerged from recent research on learning in educational settings. They can be summarised in the following definition of learning: it is a constructive, cumulative, self-regulated, goal-oriented, situated, collaborative, and individually different process of knowledge building and meaning construction. In this section the different aspects of this definition will be discussed.

Learning is Constructive

This major and overarching characteristic of (effective) learning is nowadays supported by robust empirical evidence. It means that students are not passive recipients of information, but that they actively construct their knowledge and skills (Cobb 1994; De Corte 1990; Glaser 1991). This feature of learning is, for instance, also convincingly shown in a negative way in the many misconceptions and defective skills in students that have been reported in a variety of content domains (see e.g., Perkins and Simmons 1988). A well-known example is that many students who engage in physics courses at the university level are afflicted with conceptions of motion that are not consistent, and even in contradiction with the principles of Newtonian kinetics. Their ideas seem to be much more in accordance with a pre-Newtonian impetus theory (Green, McCloskey and Caramazza 1985; Pozo and Carretero 1992; see Pfundt and Duit 1994 for an extensive bibliography on students' misconceptions and alternative frameworks in science).

While some scholars take an extreme or radical constructivist position by considering all knowledge as the result of a subjective and purely idiosyncratic cognitive construction, others – including this author – advocate a more moderate or realistic point of view that allows for the possibility of mediating and guiding learning through appropriate interventions and instructional resources (Cobb 1994). In spite of such differences in theoretical perspective, the constructivist view certainly implies that acquiring knowledge and skills is an active process, in the sense that it requires cognitive processing from the side of the learner (Shuell 1992). Referring to Salomon and Globerson (1987) it can be said that learning is a mindful and effortful activity. It is obvious that this conception contrasts sharply with the still prevailing, more or less implicit view of learning reflected in a lot of current teaching practice in higher education, namely as the transmission and rather passive absorption of knowledge gained and institutionalised by past generations.

Learning is Cumulative

This characteristic stresses the role of formal, as well as informal prior knowledge on subsequent learning (Dochy 1992; Shuell 1992). In fact, this feature is implied in the constructive nature of learning. Indeed, it is on the basis of what they already know and can do that students process actively the new information they encounter, and, as a consequence, derive new meanings and acquire new skills. Due to the fact that – as referred to above – students are sometimes afflicted by misconceptions, the influence of prior knowledge on future learning can be negative and inhibitory instead of positive and facilitating. In this regard, it is important to point to the fact that many misconceptions have been found to be very resistant to change (see e.g., Perkins and Simmons 1988).

Learning is Self-Regulated

This aspect refers to the metacognitive nature of effective learning, especially the managing and monitoring activities by the student (De Jong 1992; Shuell 1992; Simons 1989; Vermunt 1992). More specifically, this is manifested in such activities as orienting oneself to a learning task, taking the necessary steps to learn, regulating one's learning, providing for one's own feedback and performance judgements, and keeping oneself concentrated and motivated (Simons 1989). The more learning becomes self-regulated the more the students assume control over their own learning; as a consequence they are less dependent on external, instructional support for performing these regulatory activities.

An additional argument for enhancing students' self-regulation of their learning derives from the finding, that high levels of metacognition in students facilitate the transfer of acquired knowledge and cognitive skills to new learning tasks and problems. In other words, students having good metacognitive skills seem to be more able at using what they have learned in multiple ways to approach unfamiliar problems and situations (Brown 1989).

Learning is Goal-Oriented

Notwithstanding the occurrence of incidental learning, it is generally agreed that effective and meaningful learning is facilitated by an explicit awareness of and orientation toward a goal (Bereiter and Scardamalia 1989; Shuell 1992). Because of its constructive and self-regulated nature, it is plausible to assume that learning will be most productive when students choose and determine their own objectives; therefore, it is desirable to stimulate and support goal-setting activities in students. Nonetheless, learning can also be successful when objectives are put forward by a teacher, a textbook, a computer programme, etc., on the condition, however, that those objectives are accepted and adopted by the students themselves so that they generate in them a real learning intention.

Learning is Situated and Collaborative

The conception that learning and cognition are situated has emerged since the late 1980s in reaction to the 'strong' information-processing approach in cognitive psychology, which considers learning and thinking as highly individual and purely cognitive processes taking place inside the head, and consisting in the construction of mental representations (Brown, Collins and Duguid 1989; Greeno 1991, Lave and Wenger 1991; Resnick 1994). In contrast, the situated view proposes a contextualised and social conception of learning and thinking: it stresses that learning takes place essentially in interaction with the social and cultural context and artefacts, and especially through participation in cultural activities and practices. In other words, learning and cogniton are not 'solo' activities, but essentially distributed ones, i.e., the learning effort is distributed over the individual student, his partners in the learning environment, and the resources and tools that are available (Salomon 1993). This situated perspective obviously implies the need to anchor learning into authentic, real life social and physical contexts that are representative of the situations in which students will have to use their knowledge and skills afterwards. It also implies clearly the collaborative nature of effective learning reflected in such activities as exchanging ideas, comparing solution strategies, and discussing arguments. Of special significance is that interaction and co-operation induce and mobilise reflection, and, thus, foster the development of metacognitive knowledge and skills, and the self-regulation of learning.

Advocates of the situated cognition and learning paradigm have put forward the so-called cognitive apprenticeship view of learning and instruction as an approach that embraces the basic ideas and characteristics of situated acquisition of knowledge and skills (Brown *et al.* 1989).

Learning is Individually Different

The processes and outcomes of learning vary among students, due to individual differences in a diversity of aptitudes that affect learning, such as learning potential, prior knowledge, approaches to and conceptions of learning, interest, self-efficacy, self-worth, etc. (Ackerman, Sternberg and Glaser 1989; Marton, Dall'Alba and Beaty 1993; Snow and Swanson 1992).

For instance, in an investigation with Open University students in Britain, using the phenomenological approach, Marton *et al.* (1993) have identified six different conceptions of learning that fall into two main categories. In the first category the accent is on reproduction, namely increasing one's knowledge, memorising and reproducing, and applying facts and procedures; in the other three conceptions the focus is on meaning building, namely understanding, seeing something in a different way, and changing as a person. Marton and his colleagues have also found in higher education students two fundamentally different approaches to learning that are correlative with the two main categories of conceptions, namely a surface approach and a deep approach to learning. Students adopting the deep approach intend to understand the learning material; they try to relate new information to previous knowledge and search for relations within it. In contrast, surface learners accept information passively and focus simply on memorising it in view of mere reproduction (Marton, Hounsel and Entwistle 1984). Not surprisingly, the investigators observed a close relationship between students' approach and their learning outcomes: those with a deep approach outperformed the surface learners. In another study with freshmen taking a physics course, Prosser and Millar (1989) found that only those students who adopted a deep approach developed the more sophisticated, technical conceptions intended by the lecturer; those having a surface approach showed inadequate conceptions, creating increasing problems for them as the course progressed. This research outcomes indicate that individual differences do not only call for adapting teaching to student characteristics, but they are also orienting with respect to instructional interventions: passive, surface learners should be encouraged and supported to become active, deep learners.

Powerful Teaching-Learning Environments as Support

Taking as starting points the dispositional view of competent learning and thinking, on the one hand, and the realistic constructivist conception of effective learning, on the other, the challenge of a theory of intervention lies in designing and evaluating powerful teaching-learning environments, i.e., situations and contexts that can elicit and keep going in higher education students the appropriate acquisition processes and activities for attaining the intended disposition toward productive learning, thinking, and problem solving. This section will first, briefly, describe a series of design principles for powerful learning environments, that derive from the characteristics of effective learning processes, and that are at the same time in line with the dispositional view of expertise. Then, as an illustration of those design principles a representative example of an intervention study will be discussed.

Design Principles for Powerful Learning Environments

1. Learning environments should induce and support constructive, cumulative, and goal-oriented acquisition processes in students. But, conceiving learning as an active and constructive process does not exclude that knowledge and meaning building by students can be mediated by appropriate interventions and support by teachers, peers, and educational media. This principle implies that powerful learning environments are characterised by a good balance between discovery learning and personal exploration, on the one hand, and systematic instruction and guidance, on the other.

2. Learning environments should enhance students' self-regulation of their acquisition processes. This means that the external regulation of knowledge and skill acquisition in the form of systematic instruction should be gradually removed, so that students become more and more agents of their own learning. In other words, during students' learning history the share of self-regulation should progressively increase at the expense of external regulation.

3. Students' constructive learning processes should as much as possible be embedded in authentic contexts that are rich in resources, tools, and learning materials, and that offer ample opportunities for social interaction and collaboration. In order to foster the development in students of a disposition to productive learning and thinking – especially in view of the acquisition of the inclination and sensivity aspects of this disposition – learning environments should provide extensive opportunities for practice with the different categories of knowledge and skills in a large variety of situations.

4. To be able to take into account the individual differences among students in cognitive as well as in affective and motivational respects, learning environments should allow for the flexible adaptation of the instructional support, especially the balance between self-regulation and external regulation, and the alternation between cognitively-oriented interventions and emotional guidance, depending on whether the student is in the learning or in the coping mode.

5. Taking into account that domain-specific knowledge, heuristic methods, and metacognitive aspects play a complementary role in competent learning and problem solving, powerful learning environments should facilitate the acquisition of general learning and thinking skills embedded in the different subject matter domains of the curriculum rather than in a separate course.

These principles for the design of powerful learning environments are very much in accordance with the cognitive apprenticeship view of learning and instruction (Brown *et al.* 1989; see also de Corte 1990). They are also convergent with the design principles for so-called process-oriented instruction, proposed by Vermunt (1994).

A Powerful Learning Environment for Problem Solving in Mathematics

Schoenfeld's (1985; 1992) research relating to problem solving in geometry is one of the most representative examples of a powerful learning environment for the teaching of heuristic methods embedded in a metacognitive strategy, which is in line with the design principles described above. The starting point of Schoenfelds' work was the observation reported earlier that metacognitive activities which constitute an essential feature of expert problem solving, are mostly lacking in the approach of students. Therefore, he designed an environment focusing on the strategic aspects of problem solving. It is essential to mention here, that according to Schoenfeld it is not sufficient to teach students isolated heuristic methods. Indeed, such heuristics often are inert, because students are unable to decide which heuristic is appropriate for the problem at hand. That is why it is necessary to teach heuristics in the context of a metacognitive control strategy that helps the learner to select the right heuristic method to solve a given problem.

The exploration phase constitutes the heuristic heart of the strategy. Indeed, it is especially in transforming a problem into a routine task that heuristic methods are very helpful. But such thinking strategies are also useful in the problem analysis and verification stages. Table 10.1 gives an overview of the most important heuristic procedures that can be applied in those three phases.

The major components of Schoenfeld's learning environment can be summarised as follows. From the beginning, Schoenfeld orients his students toward the control strategy as a whole, although in a schematic form. Then, the different stages of the strategy – analysis, design, exploration, implementation and verification – are discussed consecutively, and the corresponding heuristics are explained and practised. In this respect, modelling is extensively used to demonstrate how an expert selects and applies heuristics methods. Afterwards, the students themselves are given ample opportunities to apply those methods under the guidance of the teacher who encourages them to use certain heuristics, gives hints, provides immediate feedback, and, if necessary, helps with the execution of some parts of the task which the student cannot yet carry out autonomously. In this way the problem-solving process is gradually turned over to the students, but sufficient support is provided when necessary. Besides modelling and class teaching, Schoenfeld also frequently uses small group problem solving. Acting himself as a consultant, he regularly asks three questions during group activities: 1. What are you doing? 2. Why are you doing this? 3. If what you are doing now is successful, how will it help to find the solution? Asking these questions serves

**Table 10.1. The most important heuristics
in Schoenfeld's (1985) problem-solving strategy**

Analysis

- Draw a diagram if at all possible
- Examine special cases of the problem
- Try to simplify the problem

Exploration

- Consider essentially equivalent problems by replacing conditions
  by equivalent ones, by recombining the elements of the problem
  in different ways, by introducing auxiliary elements, or by
  reformulating the problem
- Try to decompose the problem in subgoals, and work on them
  case by case
- Look for a related or analogous problem of which the solution
  method may be useful with a view of solving the new problem.

Verification

- Check whether all pertinent data were used, and whether the
  solution conforms to reasonable estimates and/or predictions
- Check whether the solution could have been obtained differently.

**Schoenfeld (1985) has elaborated such a metacognitive strategy
consisting of five stages:**

1. Analysis oriented towards understanding the problem by
   constructing an adequate representation.
2. Design of a global solution plan.
3. Exploration oriented towards transforming the problem into a
   routine task.
4. Implementation or carrying out the solution plan.
5. Verification of the solution.

two purposes: it encourages students to articulate their problem-solving strategies, and to reflect on those activities; in other words, it stimulates and fosters metacognitive knowledge and skills. Schoenfeld's ultimate goal is that students spontaneously ask the three questions themselves, and in doing so regulate and monitor their own thinking processes.

In a series of studies, Schoenfeld (1985; 1992) has shown that college students can acquire the metacognitive control strategy, as well as the heuristics involved in it. For instance, he observed that as a result of instruction students' problem-solving approach became more expert-like, and that less than 20 per cent of the solution processes were still of the kind that prevailed before instruction (60% as reported above). The number of correct solutions increased accordingly.

Although Schoenfeld's approach implies that heuristics and self-regulatory skills are explicitly taught, his learning environment is nevertheless essentially constructivist in nature. Indeed, the teacher does not give problem solutions nor imposes solution strategies, but supports students in their attempts at understanding problems, in articulating and discussing their beliefs about problem solving, in reflecting on their methods and strategies, and in interiorising valuable self-monitoring skills. In such an environment, students are not *learning* about mathematics, but they are *doing* mathematics. This involves learning how to use the tools of mathematics, and leads to the acquisition not only of mathematical concepts but also of a mathematical view of the world and a sense of mathematical practice and culture (Schoenfeld 1992). In summary, a real mathematical disposition is encouraged and fostered.

Successful learning environments that embody largely the same design principles have already been developed in other content domains. For example, Volet (1991; see also Volet and Lund 1994) elaborated an introductory course in computer programming involving the following main components: 1. acquisition by students of a five-step metacognitive strategy consisting mainly of a planning procedure with a monitoring and evaluation component, and taught embedded within the domain of computer programming; 2. the application of modelling and coaching instructional techniques in the context of an interactive teaching approach, in which students are stimulated to gradually take over from the tutor control over their learning; 3. a supportive social learning context encouraging collaborative learning, especially through discussion and comparison of problem-solving approaches and solutions. A study with 28 experimental and 28 matched control students in their first year at the university, showed that the course had significant positive immediate and long-term effects on the experimental subjects' understanding of programming concepts, their skills in solving new programming problems, their personal satisfaction with the learning experience, and their motivation for continued study in computer science. Another successful example is a learning environment described by Mettes (1987) for teaching first year university students a systematic procedure to solve thermodynamic problems. In this case, the systematic approach also consisted of a metacognitive strategy, involving the application of heuristic methods which were embedded in and adapted to the content domain.

Conclusions

Taking as a starting point the knowledge base that has emerged from research on learning and instruction over the past decades, a fundamentally new conception of learning and teaching in higher education has been elaborated in the preceding sections. In this alternative view, learning is not anymore considered as a highly individual activity, consisting mainly in absorbing a fixed body of largely decontextualised and fragmented knowledge and procedural skills transmitted by a teacher. To the contrary, learning is conceived of as an active, collaborative, and progressively more self-regulated process of knowledge building and meaning construction, based as much as possible on students' experiences in authentic, real-life situations and contexts.

Obviously this new conception of learning implies a major alteration in the position and the role of the students: not only do they have to engage in mindful and demanding learning activities, but they also have to become more and more agents over their own acquisition processes. However, one should realise that powerful learning environments, as described above, also require drastic changes in the role of the teacher. Instead of being the main, if not the only source of information, the teacher becomes a 'privileged' member of the knowledge-building community, who creates an intellectually stimulating climate, models learning and problem-solving activities, asks provoking questions, provides support to students through coaching and guidance, and fosters students' agency over and responsibility for their own learning. Putting this new perspective on learning and teaching into practice in higher education will take time and effort. Indeed, it is not just a matter of acquiring a set of new instructional techniques, but it calls for a fundamental and profound change in attitude and mentality on the part of the teaching staff. Achieving this will require a revaluation of teaching and tutoring in higher education, and especially substantial investments in the (re)training of teachers, and in sustained staff development.

References

Ackerman, P.L., Sternberg, R.J. and Glaser, R. (eds) (1989) *Learning and Individual Differences: Advances in Theory and Research*. New York: W.H. Freeman and Company.

Bereiter, C. and Scardamalia, M. (1989) 'Intentional learning as a goal of instruction.' In L.B. Resnick (ed) *Knowing, Learning, and Instruction. Essays in Honor of Robert Glaser*. (pp.361–392). Hillsdale, NJ: Lawrence Erlbaum Associates.

Boekaerts, M. (1993) 'Being concerned with well-being and with learning.' *Educational Psychologist 28*, 149–167.

Brown, A.L. (1989) 'Analogical learning and transfer: What develops?' In S. Vosniadou and A. Ortony (eds) *Similarity and Analogical Reasoning* (pp.369–412). Cambridge: Cambridge University Press.

Brown, A.L., Bransford, J.D., Ferrara, R.A. and Campione, J.C. (1983) 'Learning, remembering, and understanding.' In P.H. Mussen, J.H. Flavell and E.M. Markman (eds) *Child Psychology. Volume III: Cognitive Development*. (pp.77–166). New York: John Wiley.

Brown, J.S., Collins, A. and Duguid, P. (1989) 'Situated cognition and the culture of learning.' *Educational Researcher 18*, 1, 32–42.

Buchberger, F., De Corte, E., Groombridge, B, Kennedy, M. and Vëhësaari, J. (1994) *Educational Studies and Teacher Education at Finnish Universities, 1994. A Commentary by an International Review Team*. Helsinki, Finland: Ministry of Education, Division of Educational and Research Policy.

Chi, M.T., Feltovich, H. and Glaser, R. (1981) 'Categorisation and representation of physics problems by experts and novices.' *Cognitive Science 5*, 121–152.

Chi, M.T., Glaser, R. and Farr, M.J. (eds) (1988) *The Nature of Expertise*. Hillsdale, NJ: Lawrence Erlbaum Associates.

Cobb, P. (1994) 'Constructivism and learning.' In T. Husen and T.N. Postlethwaite (eds) *International Encyclopedia of Education. (Second edition)*. (pp.1049–1052). Oxford: Pergamon Press.

Dalbey, J. and Linn, M.C. (1985) 'The demands and requirements of computer programming: A review of the literature.' *Journal of Educational Computing Research 1*, 253–274.

De Corte, E. (1990) 'Acquiring and teaching cognitive skills: A state-of-the-art of theory and research.' In P.J.D. Drenth, J.A. Sergeant and R.J. Takens (eds) *European Perspectives in Psychology 1*. (pp.237–263). London: John Wiley.

De Corte, E. (1995) 'Fostering cognitive development: Perspectives from research on learning and instruction.' *Educational Psychologist 29*.

De Jong, F.P.C.M. (1992) *Zelfstandig leren. Regulatie van het leerproces en leren reguleren: Een procesbenadering.* (Independent learning. Regulation of the learning process and learning to regulate: A process approach.) Tilburg, The Netherlands: Katholieke Universiteit Brabant.

De Jong, T. and Ferguson-Hessler, M.G.M. (1991) 'Knowledge of problem situations in physics: A comparison of good and poor novice problem solvers.' *Learning and Instruction 1*, 289–302.

De Vocht, C. and Henderikx, P. (eds) (1993) *Proceedings of the European Conference 'Flexible responses in higher education'. Strategies and scenarios for the use of open and distance education in mainstream higher education. 13–14 December 1993, Brussels, Belgium.* Brussels, Belgium: Studiecentrum Open Hoger Onderwijs (StOHO).

Dochy, F.J.R.C. (1992) *Assessment of Prior Knowledge as a Determinant for Future Learning.* Utrecht, The Netherlands: Lemma.

Glaser, R. (1991) 'The maturing of the relationship between the science of learning and cognition and educational practice.' *Learning and Instruction 1*, 129–144.

Glaser, R. and Chi, M.T.H. (1988) 'Overview.' In M.T.H. Chi, R. Glaser and M.J. Farr (eds) *The Nature of Expertise.* (pp.XV–XXVIII). Hillsdale, NJ: Lawrence Erlbaum Associates.

Green, B.F., McCloskey, M. and Caramazza, A. (1985) 'The relation of knowledge to problem solving, with examples from kinematics.' In S.F. Chipman, J.W. Segal and R. Glaser (eds) *Thinking and Learning Skills. Volume 2. Research and Open Questions.* (pp. 127–139). Hillsdale, NJ: Lawrence Erlbaum Associates, Inc.

Greeno, J.G. (1991) 'Number sense as situated knowing in a conceptual domain.' *Journal for Research in Mathematics Education 22*, 170–218.

Lave, J. and Wenger, E. (1991) *Situated Learning. Legitimate Peripheral Participation.* Cambridge: Cambridge University Press.

Marton, F., Dall'Alba, G. and Beaty, E. (1993) 'Conceptions of learning.' *International Journal of Educational Research 19*, 277–300.

Marton, F., Hounsel, D.J. and Entwistle, N.J. (1984) *The Experience of Learning.* Edinburgh, Scotland: Scottish Academic Press.

Mettes, C.T.C.W. (1987) 'Factual and procedural knowledge: learning to solve science problems.' In E. de Corte, H. Lodewijks, R. Parmentier and P. Span (eds) *Learning and Instruction. European Research in an International Context, Volume 1* (pp.285–295). Oxford/Leuven: Pergamon Press/Leuven University Press.

Minnaert, A.M. and Janssen, P.J. (1992) 'The causal role of domain-specific prior knowledge on study skills and curriculum outcomes after five academic years.' *Tijdschrift voor Hoger Onderwijs 10*, 134–142.

Organisation for Economic Co-operation and Development (OECD) (1994) *Towards Mass Tertiary Education. Individual Demands for Access and Participation. Orientation Note for the Preparation of Country Contributions.* Paris, France: OECD, Directorate for Education, Employment, Labour and Social Affairs.

Perkins, D.N., Jay, E. and Tishman, S. (1993) 'Beyond abilities: A dispositional theory of thinking.' *Merrill Palmer Quarterly 39*, 1–21.

Perkins, D.N. and Salomon, G. (1989) 'Are cognitive skills context-bound?' *Educational Researcher 18*, 1, 16–25.

Perkins, D.N. and Simmons, R. (1988) 'Patterns of misunderstanding: An integrative model for science, mathematics, and programming.' *Review of Educational Research 58*, 303–326.

Pfundt, H. and Duit, R. (1994) *Bibliograpy: Students' Alternative Frameworks and Science Education, 4th edition, Bibliografie: Alltagsvorstellungen und naturwissenschaftlicher Unterricht, 4. Auflage.* Kiel, Germany: Institut für Pèdagogik der Naturwissenschaften/Institute for Science Education.

Pozo, J.I. and Carretero, M. (1992) 'Causal theories, reasoning strategies, and conflict resolution by experts and novices in Newtonian physics.' In A. Demetriou, M. Shayer and A. Efklides (eds) *Neo-Piagetian theories of cognitive development. Implications and applications for education.* (pp.231–255). London: Routledge.

Prosser, M. and Millar, R. (1989) 'The 'how' and 'what' of learning physics.' *European Journal of Psychology of Education 4*, 513–528.

Resnick, L.B. (1994) 'Situated rationalism: Biological and social preparation for learning.' In L. Hirschfeld and S. Gelman (eds) *Mapping the Mind: Domain Specificity in Cognition and Culture.* (pp.474–493). Cambridge, England: Cambridge University Press.

Salomon, G. (ed) (1993) *Distributed Cognitions. Psychological and Educational Considerations.* Cambridge, England: Cambridge University Press.

Salomon, G. and Globerson, T. (1987) 'Skill may not be enough: The role of mindfulness in learning and transfer.' *International Journal of Educational Research 11*, 326–637.

Schoenfeld, A.H. (1985) *Mathematical Problem Solving.* New York: Academic Press.

Schoenfeld, A.H. (1988) 'When good teaching leads to bad results: the disasters of "well-taught" mathematics courses.' *Educational Psychologist 23*, 145–166.

Schoenfeld, A.H. (1992) 'Learning to think mathematically: Probem solving, metacognition, and sense making in mathematics.' In D.A. Grouws (ed) *Handbook of Research on Mathematics Teaching and Learning.* (pp.334–370). New York: Macmillan.

Shuell, T.J. (1992) 'Designing instructional computing systems for meaningful learning.' In M. Jones and P.H. Winne (eds) *Adaptive Learning Environments: Foundations and Frontiers.* (NATO ASI Series F: Computer and Systems Sciences, Vol. 85, pp. 19–54). Berlin: Springer-Verlag.

Simons, P.R.J. (1989) 'Learning to learn.' In P. Span, E. De Corte and B. van Hout-Wolters (eds) *Onderwijsleerprocessen: Strategieæn voor de verwerking van informatie.* (Teaching-learning processes: Strategies for information processing) (p. 15–25). Amsterdam/Lisse: Swets & Zeitlinger.

Simons, P.R.J. and Beukhof, G. (eds) (1987) *Regulation of Learning.* (Selecta.) Den Haag, The Netherlands: Instituut voor Onderzoek van het Onderwijs.

Snow, R.E. and Swanson, J. (1992) 'Instructional psychology: Aptitude, adaptation, and assessment.' *Annual Review of Psychology 43,* 583–626.

Vermunt, J.D.H.M. (1992) *Leerstijlen en sturen van leerprocessen in het hoger onderwijs: Naar procesgerichte instructie in zelfstandig denken.* (Learning styles and regulation of learning processes in higher education: Toward process-oriented instruction in independent thinking.) Amsterdam/Lisse, The Netherlands: Swets and Zeitlinger.

Vermunt, J.D.H.M. (1994) 'Design principles for process-oriented instruction.' In F.P.C.M. de Jong and B.H.A.M. van Hout-Wolters (eds) *Process-oriented Instruction and Learning from Text.* (pp.15–26). Amsterdam, The Netherlands: VU University Press.

Volet, S.E. (1991) 'Modelling and coaching of relevant metacognitive strategies for enhancing university students' learning.' *Learning and Instruction 1,* 319–336.

Volet, S.E. and Lund, C.P. (1994) 'Metacognitive instruction in introductory computer programming: A better explanatory construct for performance than traditional factors.' *Journal of Educational Computing Research 10,* 297–328.

Chapter 11

The French University System
Assessment and Outlook

Daniel Bloch

The recent history of higher education in France has been marked by two periods of intense growth. The first one took place in the 1960s, when the number of students registered in universities alone grew from 215,000 in 1960 to 732,000 in 1972; in other words multiplied by 3.5 in 12 years. The second major growth period started in 1987, when the university student population was 980, 000 reaching approximately 1,400,000 today with the prospect of arriving at 2 million by the end of the century.

These increases are the result of a particularly strong social and economic demand both in the middle of the 1950s and in the middle of the 1980s.

Thus in 1985, the year of the European Act, the abolition of foreign exchange controls, and price deregulation within the country itself, France realised that it was still poorly prepared to face international competition. The country set itself two 15-year objectives, that is by the end of the century, to lead the entire young generation to a recognised professional qualification and 80 per cent of youths to complete the final year of secondary school. The creation of the vocational *baccalauréat* in 1985 constitutes an essential tool for the achievement of these two objectives.[1]

As for the social demand, a single example can demonstrate its strength. The orientation towards short-term technological and professional training at the end of the second year of secondary education collapsed, not through any deliberate programming by those responsible for the education system, but due to parental refusal to consider this for their children.

---

1 Basic statistical information can be found in documents published by the Direction de l'Evaluation et de la Prospective of the Ministry of National Education.

Nevertheless, it has taken over 45 years to achieve a 4-year common-core syllabus in the first cycle of secondary education. The reluctance of the teaching profession is undoubtedly not the only cause of the excessive length of time taken to establish this 'common core', but it is certainly one of the main reasons. The stages of increase in the number of secondary school graduates can easily be interpreted as the result of the actual application of the common core, with a further acceleration due to the introduction of the vocational baccalauréat.

The number of students in higher education (essentially public) continues to increase by 100,000 students per year, and the 2 million mark has already been passed at the start of the 1993–1994 university year. This is why the French higher education system is often referred to as 'mass education', a term which is not innocent and which carries with it the age-old opinion of a level which is falling and memory being lost.

The future of our universities will depend on the manner in which the following points are addressed:

1. Their means of existence – which today are considerably lower than those which prevail in other OECD countries.
2. Their role in scientific research – somewhat weakened today by the development of specialised research organisations.
3. Changes in educational procedures – which today are far too directive and impersonal.
4. Their function in professional training – too many students today are engaged in programmes with insufficiently ambitious disciplinary content or insufficiently defined professional objectives.
5. The way in which they respond to the necessity of a regional development policy while maintaining the required university standards.

The Baccalauréat, the Entrance Ticket to Higher Education

The baccalauréat is the name of the diploma which marks the end of secondary school education in France. The baccalauréat qualifies the students for entrance to university without any legal restriction, and for this reason it is reasonable that the presidents of the juries that deliver this diploma are university professors There are three types of baccalauréat:

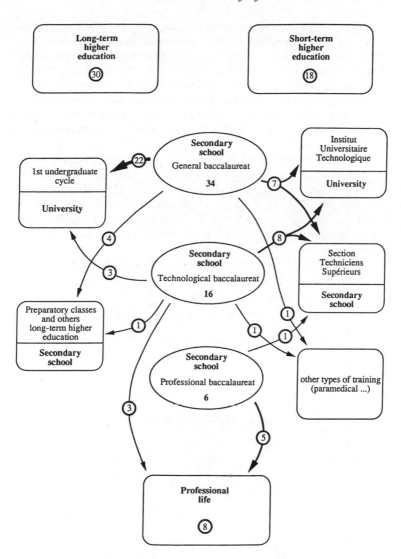

Fifty-six of them obtain a baccalauréat and 48 continue on into higher education programmes. Among these, 18 go into short-term programmes and 30 into long-term programmes. We can also distinguish baccalauréat holders according to whether they go into university (29) or into a non-university establishment, namely the preparatory classes in secondary schools or a professional college (19)

Figure 11.1 Fate in higher education of 100 French youths born in 1975

1. **The vocational baccalauréat** certifies a specific qualification allowing immediate entrance into professional life. Only 15 per cent of the holders of this diploma carry on into higher education, and those who do so register for the most part in a non-university short-term technological training programme. The vocational baccalauréat was created in 1985 and since then the number of diplomas delivered has increased rapidly to 52,837 in 1993 – representing 6 per cent of the age group – and this number is expected to reach 80,000 by the end of this century.

2. **The technological baccalauréat** was obtained in 1993 by 122,344 young people which corresponds to 15 per cent of the age group. Some of them stop their education at this point to take a job (19%), and a decreasing number of them (25%) enter higher education programmes, essentially at university. The technological baccalauréat is particularly adapted to continuation in short-term higher education, which in fact approximately 56 per cent of these diploma holders do. These short-term higher education training programmes can take place in:

   a) secondary schools in what are known as STS (sections de techniciens supérieurs) which can be translated as 'higher or qualified technician training sections'

   b) an Institut Universitaire de Technologie – (IUT, University Institute of Technology)

   c) specialised vocational colleges such as those which train for paramedical activities.

3. **The general baccalauréat** represents the largest proportion of students and is the preparation for long-term higher education. This diploma was obtained in 1993 by 283,664 young people, which corresponds to 34 per cent of the age group. Only rarely does a student end his/her education with this diploma. Some of them go on to short-term forms of higher education (24%), but the majority enter long-term higher education in the form of first-year undergraduate courses mainly in universities (66%), but also in preparatory classes for the '*grandes écoles*' system (10%). These preparatory classes take place in secondary schools.

Eighty Per Cent of Baccalauréat Holders?

Not all the students in the final year of secondary school obtain the baccalauréat. Given the present success rates, the objective set in 1985 of 80 per cent of the age group going into the final year of secondary school has actually only reached approximately 70 per cent. In 1982 the proportion of the working population with a diploma at least equivalent to the baccalauréat was 22.5 per cent; in 1990, it was 30 per cent and should be close to 40 per cent in the year 2000.

This is not just a mechanical effect due to the increased offer of diploma-holders. In a job market which is not very open to young diploma-holders, it is those who hold a higher education diploma who experience the least difficulty in finding a job.

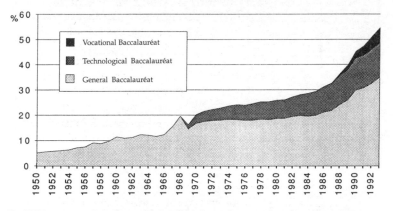

In 1975, one youth in four obtained the baccalauréat in 1987, one in three; as in 1994, the score is almost three out of five. Over two out of every three young people should obtain a baccalauréat in the year 2000. The number of young people arriving at baccalauréat level will have at least doubled in 13 years

Figure 11.2 Proportion of age group obtaining the baccaluauréat.

A Diversified Training Offer

The programmes of higher education to which baccalauréat holders have access are offered in establishments whose administrative structures, entrance conditions and organisations all differ considerably, which results in a relatively complex higher education landscape in France.

The universities accommodate two thirds of the students. But almost one student in five is registered in a vocational college outside of the university system and one in six in a secondary school-type structure. The number of students registered in the French higher education system has increased by approximately 100,000 per year in the course of the past few years. The majority of these students attend public establishments.

Table 11.1 Evolution in level of training of the working population. Whereas in 1982 worker without professional qualification predominated, as the year 2000 approaches they only represent one third of the working population

Level / Year	Higher education diplomas	Baccalaureat and intermediate professional training	No professional training	Total
1982	2 440 784 11,5%	7 157 832 33,5%	11 873 168 55%	21 471 784 100%
1990	3 622 078 16,5%	9 208 275 41,5%	9 239 977 42%	22 070 330 100%
2000	5 067 000 20,5%	11 673 000 47,5%	7 886 000 32%	24 626 000 100%

Higher education diplomas

Baccalaureat and intermediate professional training

No professional training

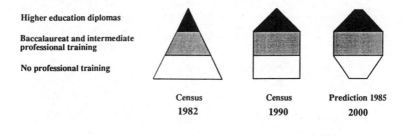

Census 1982   Census 1990   Prediction 1985 2000

One of the characteristics of the French higher education system is the relatively small share provided by private establishments; public establishments accommodate the majority of students (85%). Most of these establishments are under the authority of the Ministry for Higher Education and Research (all the universities, and some engineering colleges). But we have already pointed out that within secondary schools, which come under the Ministry of National Education, there are some programmes of higher education whose courses last two years. Several public institutions with a specific professional orientation are under the authority of 'technical' minis-

Table 11.2 Distribution of students among the various types of higher education establishments 1992–1993

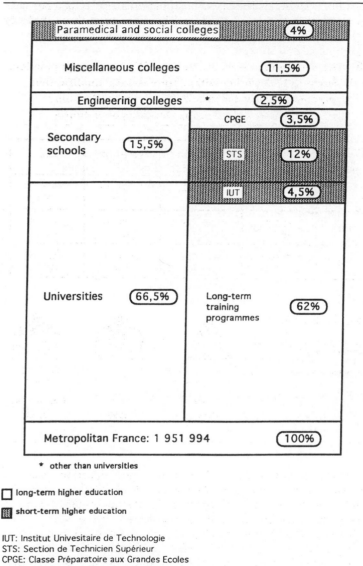

Paramedical and social colleges		4%
Miscellaneous colleges		11,5%
Engineering colleges *		2,5%
Secondary schools 15,5%	CPGE	3,5%
	STS	12%
	IUT	4,5%
Universities 66,5%	Long-term training programmes	62%
Metropolitan France: 1 951 994		100%

* other than universities

☐ long-term higher education

▦ short-term higher education

IUT: Institut Univesitaire de Technologie
STS: Section de Technicien Supérieur
CPGE: Classe Préparatoire aux Grandes Ecoles

Various colleges: commerce, management,
teacher-training, art, architecture, ... etc

tries: Ministry of Health (for paramedical training), Ministries of Industry, of Culture, of Agriculture, Defence, Telecommunications, etc., Tuition is free in public establishments as a rule. Private establishments mainly train for the tertiary sector (for example, sales or secretarial training) and are in many cases administered by Chambers of Commerce and Industry. Others are of a denominational nature. Tuition is paid in these institutions (typically about thirty thousand French francs per year). Since 1993 we have seen a decrease in the numbers of students in private higher education, and short-term technological training programmes for the most part in favour of public establishments.

Within the higher education system, we must also distinguish between short and long-term programmes. Approximately two baccalauréat holders out of five go into short-term higher education programmes and the remaining three into long-term programmes. Ten years ago, only one student in four went into short-term higher education. Short-term higher education programmes last two to three years after the baccalauréat. They train middle managers or senior technicians, providing them with a sufficiently extensive professional qualification to allow them to enter a professional activity, but the general education they receive in these programmes also allows them to continue in further studies. Nowadays, almost one student out of every four graduating from short-term higher education continues in another higher education programme. It should be noted that the differences in salaries and careers between degree-holders in short-term higher education and those from long-term higher education are too great and encourage this trend.

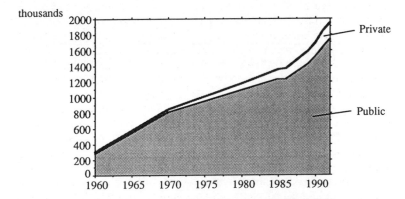

Figure 11.3 Evolution of number of students in public and private higher education establishments between 1950–1992

There are two major means of access to long-term higher education; the most common one gives admission to the first year of university to successful baccalauréat candidates. Theoretically, any baccalauréat holder can enter any first year university course, no matter what kind of course they took in secondary school. In practice, there are in fact strong correlations between the type of baccalauréat with its predominating subjects and the first year courses that are chosen. At this same level of studies, but housed in secondary schools, there also exist the preparatory classes for entrance examinations to the 'grandes écoles'. Entrance into long-term higher education is divided between 85 per cent for universities and 15 per cent for the preparatory classes. The first university degree is received after a two-year programme and the programmes of the preparatory classes are also designed to last two years. However, the majority of students in both cases takes three years to successfully complete this first cycle.

The Universities

The rise in the number of students at university, close to 6 per cent per year, results not only from the increase in the number of baccalauréat holders, but also from the growing attractiveness of universities and prolonged studies in general, due partly to the difficulties in finding employment. Over the past ten years, the distribution of students in the main sectors of study has changed. In particular, the numbers of students in health-related disciplines has declined, in direct relation to the lowering of the *numerus clausus* and hence the numbers of students allowed to enter the corresponding programmes. Numbers of students in economics and legal studies have increased moderately, in arts and social sciences the increase is considerable and in pure sciences even stronger. This is a result of a deliberate policy between 1985 and 1988 giving priority to the development of the scientific sections in secondary education. It should be said that between 1960 and 1975 the proportion of students engaged in scientific studies had fallen by half. Students enrolled in University Technology Institutes are divided approximately equally between the secondary or industrial activities sector and the tertiary activities sector.

To give an alternative idea of the numbers involved, we can say that at the end of the 1980s, 360,000 general and technological baccalalauréats were completed each year. In 1992, the students coming out of higher education heading for professional life numbered 100,000 with a short-term programme diploma and 160,000 with a long-term programme diploma. Although some 75 per cent of the baccalauréat holders who enter higher education do complete a degree, it is too often after several failures and successive reorientation. This is partly the price that is paid for the freedom of choice for baccalauréat holders who have not necessarily acquired suitable qualifications to enter various higher education programmes. The student population can be of very mixed levels and the first year of university, therefore, often consists of a year of reorientation.

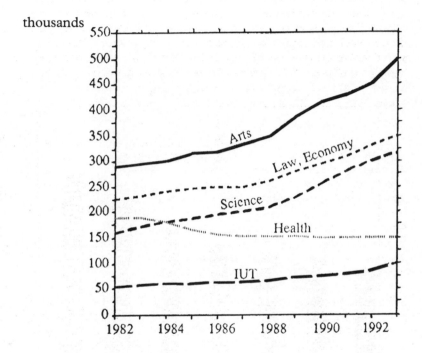

Figure 11.4 Evolution of numbers of university students according to field of study

The Major Challenges for Universities

French universities have managed to adapt to the demographic surge each year since 1987 without lowering their ambitions. They have successfully combined their local responsibilities with their national roles. Their autonomy has developed via the implementation of contractual relations with the state, a mechanism which theoretically enables them to carry out their specific, self-defined mission. Their public image has improved, even if it is not yet what they would like it to be. Their future will, nevertheless, depend on the manner in which they take up the following five fundamental challenges:

The first challenge is one of financial resources: the percentage of the GDP devoted to higher education is considerably lower in our country than in those of our principal competitors, reaching only 75 per cent of the average level in OECD countries. This results in inadequate ratios of training and administrative staff, particularly in arts and social sciences, and rarely adequate working conditions (library facilities, practical laboratories) in all fields. Although a significant effort towards improvement of these standards occurred between 1988 and 1993, this effort has not been maintained. Compari-

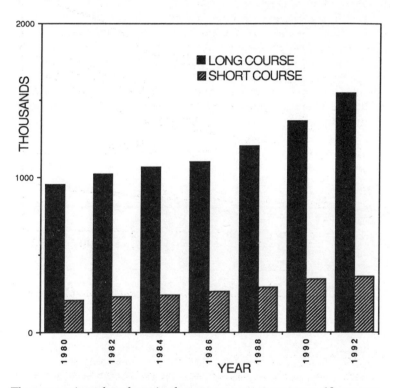

The proportion of students in short-term programmes was 18 per cent in 1980. In 1992, they represented 25.5 per cent

Figure 11.5 Evolution of number of students in short and long-term higher education programmes from 1980 to 1992.

sons on an international basis show that France does not have 'too many students'. But there is a need to provide each student with suitable working conditions, to aim for excellence. Who will assume the cost of bringing this situation up to standard; the state, local governments, or the students themselves?

The second challenge concerns the universities' share of the country's research activities. A characteristic of the French research scene is the importance of public, non-university research organisations whose aim is to develop research, including cognitive research within the organisation itself, whereas research within the universities is insufficiently organised and poorly armed to be able to defend itself collectively. But a divided system with professional researchers on one side and professional teachers on the other can only lead to lower quality both in research and in training.

The third challenge concerns a clearer definition of the role of the universities. Should the university do everything? For example, should the university further develop long-term professionally-oriented higher education more than it does today? Perhaps short-term vocational programmes should take place primarily outside the university and long-term programmes within the university could be built on the basis of the potential developed within the short-term programmes.

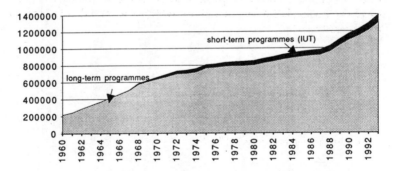

In the course of the last few years the number of students in higher education has increased at an average of 100,000 each year. The bulk of this additional responsibility has been assumed by the universities with 75,000 additional students each year. The total number of students registered in French universities reached 1,400,000 at the start of the 1994–5 university year

Figure 11.6 Evolution of the number of students in university between 1960 and 1993.

The fourth challenge directly concerns the organisation of university education. The overly complex higher education system needs to be simplified, programmes need to be individualised, more attention needs to be paid to the preparation for a professional activity, and a greater contribution needs to be made to the acquisition of a wider cultural base. University programmes in France are too often excessively specialised and designed without sufficient reference to the 'outside' world. Evaluation, whether internal – in particular by the students – or external – in particular based on the performances of the university's diploma-holders – is practically non-existent.

The fifth challenge concerns regional development, with the necessity for France to readjust higher education and research activities in favour of the provinces (as opposed to the Paris region). The movement can be considered to be under way concerning higher education with 25 per cent of students in the Paris region now compared to 35 per cent in 1960 , but there is still a very long way to go as far as research is concerned, as over 50 per cent of research activities are still based in the Paris region. At the same time, this regional development policy has to be conducted with considerable caution due to very heavy pressure from local governments who would like to establish a university in almost every Department capital. It is obvious that it would not be possible for all of them to offer a sufficient choice of programmes to the students, let alone develop the level of research activity which is essential in the role of a university.

References

Pour une stratégie convergente du système éducatif et des entreprises
   Documentation française, 1985, 1988.
Education Economie. Quel système éducatif pour la société de l'an 2000?
   Documentation française, 1987.

Acknowledgements to Madame E. Janeau (Director of Student Counselling, Université Joseph Fourier, Grenoble) for her contribution to the completion of the statistical data contained in this article and to Madame S. Verdurand (Administrative Director of the International Affairs Department, Université Joseph Fourier, Grenoble) for the English version of this article.

Chapter 12

Inspiration of the Muse or Management of the Art?
Issues in Training for Academic Posts and Teaching in France

Guy Neave

Introduction

Anyone looking back on the past decade of reform in higher education, let alone the past quarter century cannot, I would suggest, help being reminded of the famous red-painted Russian dolls. One pulls off one Babushka only to find a smaller version of the same staring one in the face. In efforts to bring higher education into a closer fit first with social demand and more lately with the pressure from international competition, we have first reformed its structure – some have expanded the non-university sector, others have merged it with the universities. All of us have revised, often radically, the content of degree programmes. Some are engaged in foreshortening their length. Others are embarked on an even more radical fragmentation in the form of modular studies. The vocationalisation of higher education has become a leitmotif across most higher education systems. And right now, many, some in a state more advanced than others, are battling to put in place more accurate instruments for evaluating both individual and institutional performance.

Each of these successive reforms has revealed its limitations. As we dispose of the Babushka of structural differentiation, we are brought face to face with the need to go further into changing the content of the curriculum. And, as that proves to be but partially successful, we move on to the next layer.

There is a dynamic in reform that penetrates with increasing power into that area which one American policy analyst has termed 'the private life of academe'. Having set out 25 years ago with the belief that reform of the structures of higher education – and the differentiation between university and non-university sectors is not an atypical example – was the solution to massive and persistent

146

social demand for higher education, we have tended increasingly to turn our attention away from input to higher education and instead to concentrate on process and output. In all this, the issue of how one prepares individuals for an academic career has largely gone by default.

Incompatibilities

As our systems of higher education are faced with yet another era of expansion and growth in the student estate – an expansion every bit as spectacular as that which accompanied the transition of higher education in Europe from an élite to a mass model during the 1960s and 1970s – increasing disquiet is being voiced about the apparent incompatibility between teaching and research. This, of course, is a perverse way of describing this perception. In effect, it has to do with the natural response of academia when called upon to show itself productive and that is to seek to increase publication output or time spent on research. In the latter connexion, it is particularly interesting to note that in the survey carried out in 1988 by A.H. Halsey and his team at Oxford the numbers of British academics spending 50 per cent of their time on research had risen significantly over the 15 years since the appearance of his previous study, *The British Academics*, published in 1974. The so-called incompatibility thesis is particularly evident in the US where the current accusation is that academia is abandoning undergraduate teaching to a species of subacademic proletariat, variously composed of non-tenured instructors and graduate students.

If the American strain of this phenomenon may be seen as the most virulent, it is by no means an American exclusivity. Where the American version differs from some of its European counterparts lies in its being a phenomenon internal to academia; a species of professional responses to the rewards and pressures most evident in American research universities. In Europe, the incompatibility thesis takes a slightly different form, often in the formal division between institutions permitted to undertake fundamental research and those which may have to content themselves with 'scholarship' – that is, keeping abreast of their field by contemplating other people's work in place of doing their own. It is, in short, less a development internal to academia so much as a policy imposed from without the academic estate. Either way, whether a deplorable form of academic 'offloading' or a judicious measure to ensure the 'concentration of national research resources upon established excellence', the tensions that are gathering around the time-honoured, seamless web of teaching and research are present in most of Europe's systems of higher education. And if the issues it poses are shared, the measures taken to deal with it are not. On the contrary, they tend to be highly contextualised, governed by the patterns, practices and structures already in place.

Factors of Change and Perverse Effects

What are these issues? What are the factors which contribute to this tension? And what are their implications for current patterns of training for the academic estate and more particularly for teaching? The first of these factors is the massification of higher education itself and most particularly when the university *stricto sensu* was the prime recipient for demand for higher education. Of crucial importance were – and for that matter still remain – formal conditions of access to higher education, whether higher education could control student numbers or whether it possessed a form of capacity limitation or *numerus clausus*. Capacity limitation has an important indirect consequence for the training of academia and especially so in that dimension which has to do with the socialisation of the individual into disciplinary values, attitudes and culture which are no less important than the formal mastery of technique, methodology or investigative procedures.

Those systems which, like the British, could directly control the influx of student numbers could also ensure that the recruitment to the academic profession remained in keeping with the supply of trained young academics coming through what may be termed the 'traditional' system of training, which involved both preparation of a thesis and the process of anticipated professional socialisation that accompanied it [Clark 1993]. Part of this process included part-time, often non official employment of doctoral students in tutorials, practical or small group work. In other words, doctoral level studies in their traditional mode involved both socialisation and, as part of that overall process, gradual induction into the experience of teaching.

Consequences

The situation was very different in those systems where, formally, holders of the general secondary school leaving certificate had a constitutional right to a place in higher education and in which control over student numbers could only be exercised *en cours de route*. In France, Italy, and Spain, open access and subsequent high non-completion rates, brought about an immense shift in the overall burden of responsibilities towards the undergraduate level and most particularly in teaching. Even today, in French universities more than half the teaching contact hours are concentrated into the first two years (first cycle) (Comité National d'Evaluation 1993, p.36). Student demand, concentrated into the undergraduate or what has elsewhere been termed 'non-advanced' level, had two effects: one immediate, the other more long term. Both of them amount to nothing less than the break up of the traditional and incremental system of socialisation and induction into the academic life, though clearly it did not affect either the existence of national competitions or procedures for nomination to post.

In the immediate term, the need to fulfil teaching demands was met by bringing in a large number of graduate students as temporary instructors. *De facto*, though not *de jure*, the presence of large numbers of untenured assistants or precari, created a two strata academia. On the one hand, teachers/researchers with permanent appointments who had gone through the often long drawn out process of defending a thesis, or having been initiated in the traditional manner to teaching and to the discipline; on the other, an instructor class whose teaching obligations had not been prepared for and whose process of socialisation into the disciplinary culture was scarcely begun, let alone completed.

In short, the initial effect of massification, just as it broke up the reverse unity of research training as a means of acquiring the rudiments of teaching, also brought about a fundamental divorce between those for whom teaching was their sole *raison d'être* and those for whom teaching and research were their normal obligations. The evolution of a two-track academic body was not, however, uniform across the different subject areas. Those most drastically affected tended precisely to be the 'low paradigm' fields in the humanities and social sciences. By contrast, many of the 'high paradigm' fields – and often high cost disciplines: medicine, engineering, biology – were able to shelter themselves from the deluge by the presence of a *numerus clausus* admissions policy, by a high degree of internal selectivity and thus cleave, far more than was possible in the case of the humanities and social sciences to the established pattern of researcher productivity and to the established modes of disciplinary induction.

If this stratification with its attendant differences in task assigned to each, emerged most clearly in France, Italy and Germany in their transition from élite to mass higher education during the 1970s, it is not out of place to suggest that it is also present, though so far at a less developed extent, in contemporary Britain which is currently making the same transition.

Diversification in the Student Body

Massification of higher education places particular weight on teaching skills as an inevitable consequence of expanding student numbers. And in those systems with a high non-completion rate their apparent inefficiency in converting the unqualified adds to the clamour for improvements to be made in teaching. There are, however, other factors at play which rebalance this function and which are not uniquely dependent on sheer student enrolments. Amongst these, one of the more powerful long-term influences has been not merely the diversification in terms of curricular pathways, qualification patterns and age range of first time entrants. It also involves a significant diversity in the ability range, and motivation occupational intention of a student body which in certain countries – and remember that France with around 38 per cent of the age group enrolled in higher education represents a higher proportion of the age group than attended the academic grammar school or *lycée* twenty years ago.

Nor can one rely any longer on the basic assumption that those entering higher education will possess what David Reisman has termed the 'inner gyroscope' of self-direction, of being discipline-centred and possessing that necessary cultural baggage to make informed and judicious choices as to the areas of study most suited to whatever career plans they may have formulated. To put it another way, just as the process of disciplinary enculturation broke down for a part of the teaching body in higher education, so the relatively homogeneous process of preparation for higher education grounded on the assumption that the discipline was the constant and the student the variable, itself broke asunder. The move towards a 'student-centred higher education system' has not merely made the general task of teaching more complex. It has also added to the range of responsibilities that the university and its personnel must assume – guidance, counselling, orientation etc. – which in an age not too distant were seen as the responsibility of the individual student as well as the proof of his or her suitability for higher education and evidence of personal maturity (Teichler 1984).

Diversity in the social origins and future occupational ambition of students are the hallmarks of the mass university. But they also have fundamental implications for that most important of all functions – namely, the renewal of the academic profession itself, a matter of especial importance at present given the prospect that over the next ten years or so, upwards of one third or more of those currently in post in France will reach retirement age. Among the prime issues are how to recruit a sufficient number of students who will embark on the path towards higher learning, and how to retain them in higher education at a time when pressures from both industry and the private sector for the very highly qualified are as great, as the prospects they hold out are attractive. Second, and in this France is far from being alone, where to draw the boundary line between the research training system for future academics and those who will work outside the university?

Redrawing Boundaries

Unlike those countries which make a relatively clear-cut distinction between undergraduate and postgraduate studies, the structure of studies in the French university is more fluid, being based on a system of two-year cycles. In other words, the boundary layer or chop line between the research training system and advanced level taught degrees, which tends to be concurrent in those systems which follow an Anglo Saxon rationale, is in France consecutive and is marked off some five years after entry to university. To be sure, there are differences between the disciplines: some, like Economics, tend to accept students for research training only after completing the *Diplôme d'Etudes Approfondies* (at the end of the fifth year); others, like Physics, tend to select their future research students at the point of entry to the DEA (Neave and Edelstein 1993, p.204). Nevertheless, the tendency is increasingly towards drawing a line between the start of the research training system and what has sometimes been termed 'preadvanced training', thereby making the division within research training rather than between first degree and graduate studies. The creation of doctoral schools follows this rationale, though unlike the American graduate school, they are specifically geared towards research and more particularly to imparting a general research culture whilst attenuating much of the overspecialisation and fragmentation which is evident in DEA courses (Comité Nationale d'Evaluation 1993, p.44).

Restatement of Purpose

This deliberate emphasis on reasserting training *by* research as opposed to training *for* research comes, I would suggest, as a clear and unambiguous riposte to the situation which I touched upon earlier – namely, the *de facto* separation between research and teaching amongst certain strata of the teaching body which took place in the seventies under the pressure of massification. Simply to reassert the indivisibility of the two is certainly necessary. It is not, however, sufficient. For if those who teach must have research experience, it is no less important that those who research must also have teaching experience, unless that is, further expansion of the nation's higher education system is to fall victim, once again, to the *de facto* stratification within academia which accompanied the first student deluge in the 1960s and 1970s. History, as Karl Marx once remarked, repeats itself twice: the first time as tragedy and the second time as farce. It is wise to avoid both scenarios.

Key Measures

The key to strengthening these links as well as building up a reserve of young talent for the academic estate has been the policy progressively to expand the provision of research grants for doctoral students and, in certain cases, to attach a limited commitment to supervise tutorials – up to 64 hours per year – as part of the conditions attached to the award (Comité National d'Evaluation 1993, p.106) The latter, known as *monitorats d'initiation à l'enseignement supérieur* are of more than passing interest since they seem to involve, not simply the objective of ensuring that more doctoral students are drawn towards the academic profession. This particular scheme also seems to point to a reversion to the earlier model of teaching within research – a pattern of induction which formed part of what was alluded to earlier as the 'traditional mode' of apprenticeship to academia. In other words, it seems to reaffirm the unity of teaching and research as fundamental elements in the training of future academics and thus stands as a remedy to the separation between them which was the perverse effect of an earlier stage in the saga of massification in French higher education.

Finally, perhaps the most significant change in the training for the academic estate has been the restructuring of doctoral level studies in 1984. The abolition of four different types of doctorate – from the short cycle doctorate to the massively erudite *Doctoral d'Etat* – and their replacement by a single doctoral award gained at the end of between three to five years was certainly an act of determination and boldness. It was also a measure of rationalisation, not to mention harmonisation – which, seen within a broader context, stood as the first example in a trend which has subsequently gathered strength and not just in France (for Britain see Henkel and Kogan 1993, pp.71–114), as governments increasingly turned their attention towards reinforcing the place of the research training system within the mass university.

Implications

What do these changes to the research training systems and to the conditions under which today's candidates to the academic profession accomplish their training, tell us? The first message is, I would suggest, that the so-called incompatibility thesis between teaching and research does have some credence in France. But it is the mirror image of the situation in the United States. One of the main threats that the mass university posed in France – at least during its early years – was the risk that the sheer pressure to teach which came from spiralling student numbers, also brought in its train the risk of eating into both the individual's – and thus the university's – opportunity to research. Unlike the current situation facing the United States where the commitment to research seems to threaten the quality of undergraduate teaching, if we are to believe the conclusions of East Coast Foundations for the Advancment of Teaching, in France, the pressure to teach first and second cycle students threatens the university's ability to carry out research. The insistance on bringing back the unity of research and of teaching as part of revitalising the socialisation of research students is a clear attempt to restore this balance. Or, to put matters slightly differently, such developments as the doctoral school with its emphasis on instilling a general research-oriented culture, is an explicit commitment to the basic indivisibility of teaching and research – hence the equally explicit rejection of the incompatibility thesis.

Envoi

Whether the price that has to be paid for maintaining the quality of teaching and the principle of democracy of access as an increasingly rigourous line of demarcation or zone of protection around those schools and institutes where doctoral students and future members of the academic estate are trained, is something time will certainly tell. What it may also tell others is that democracy of access is far from being incompatible with Republican rigour. But then, it never has been.

References

Comité National d'Evaluation (1993) *Universités: la recherche des équilibres: rapport au Président de la République 1989–1993.* Paris: La Documentation Française.

Halsey, A.H. (1991) *The Decline of Donnish Dominion.* Oxford: Oxford University Press.

Halsey, A.H. and Trow, M. (1974) *The British Academics*. London: Faber and Faber.

Neave, G. and Edelstein, R. (1993) 'France.' In R.C. Burton (ed) *The Research Foundations of Graduate Education: Germany, Britain, France, United States, Japan*. Berkeley, Los Angeles and London: University of California Press.

Teichler, U. (1984) 'Germany.' In R.C. Burton (ed) *The School and the University: An International Perspective*. Berkeley, Los Angeles and London: University of California Press.

Chapter 13

University Autonomy and the Search for Quality

Juan M. Rojo

Introduction

Since their first appearance in Europe some time in the eleventh century, universities have shown a remarkable capacity for survival. In evolutionary terms, universities seem to have a formidable capacity for adaptation to the most different social and political environments. It is therefore hardly surprising that universities prize independence as one of their most valued possessions and often demand greater autonomy from governments.

Of course, autonomy of an institution does not necessarily lead to better performance. As more than 80 per cent of the budget commonly comes from the taxpayer, and European universities are not cheap, there is growing concern among citizens that autonomy must be somehow balanced by an adequate control of the quality of the services that the university provides. In this chapter, I briefly discuss the tension between autonomy and the search for quality using illustrations from recent developments in higher education in Spain.

Autonomy

Although at times it has been argued that university autonomy has deep ethical roots it is more commonly considered to be warranted on the basis of efficient management. This is due to the distinctive character of universities rooted in intellectual achievement. This gives rise to its own peculiarities, such as the key role of small units (departments) in initiative and decision, a tendency to collective management and to self-criticism. Higher education establishments other than universities are usually under much stricter governmental control.

I should stress that I am referring only to public universities. The borderline between public and private universities is not well defined; I shall define public universities as non-profit bodies open to any citizen, and in which student selection is solely based on academic merit. Whether fees are required is less relevant as long as an adequate scholarship system exists. In all European universities a major part of the cost is borne by the taxpayer.

Prior to 1982, all universities in Spain depended directly on the Ministry of Education, which approved the budget, managed them, selected the professors and so on. Even short leave of as little as a week at a foreign university required approval from the ministry. The Law of University Reform (1983) gave the universities considerable autonomy, for example, in the approval of the budget, in the definition of curriculum content, and in the appointment of most of their staff including Deans and Vice-chancellors (ICED 1988).

In the following decade many positive consequences have followed. Bureaucracy has been dramatically reduced (ex-post control has replaced ex-ante permission), an opening up to society has commenced and the universities are more aware that their research, their training, and even their image is saleable. Competition among universities has improved quality and stimulated the launching of new initiatives related to real user needs.

However, autonomy has also revealed some serious shortcomings; the most serious is the excessive tendency to appoint professors mainly from within the establishment. The bad effects are often not appreciated until long after the appointment has been made. This is not a problem restricted to Spain and has become more common everywhere under the pressure derived from shrinking staff size. Quality control in appointments is perhaps more important than in any other aspect of the university.

The Three University Assignments

Universities frequently complain that their pursuit of quality is in conflict with the expansion of student numbers. In recent years there has also been a growing concern of the disproportionate influence of industrial biased and government targeted research which might damage the structure of university research. To put these fears into perspective (EC Memorandum on Higher Education in the European Community 1991), I will recall the main tasks of higher education institutions in most of Europe.

In my view, there are three needs of modern society that need to be met by the higher education system:

1. To provide a high level cultural and scientific background to increasing levels of society, this includes adding a vocational element to those who are not at present progressing further up the educational ladder.
2. To provide efficient training for the top professionals which will provide the future backbone of society.
3. To carry out research not only contributing to the advance of the frontiers of knowledge, but also in support of industrial development.

These three assignments are not easily combined if quality is to be maintained and one must express a reasonable doubt whether universities are the optimum choice for all three.

Extension of General Education

In recent years, particularly in the past two decades, the numbers in higher education have been rising steadily, in some cases dramatically in every European country (Table 13.1). Most of this growth has been in the universities (in Spain virtually the whole (Pascal 1994). I am convinced that this extension of education is a great asset for the future of our countries. Nevertheless, the severe budgetary strain involved indicates the need for some reconsideration of the system. For instance, it is an illusion to think that the floods of students arriving for category (1) above can be taught by the same professors who are expected to handle (2) and (3).

A way out could be by proposing a separate institution for (1). Much effort has been devoted in a number of European countries to finding a satisfactory alternative to the university (OECD 1991), an example is the German *Fachhochschule* for vocational training. However, I believe that in our contemporary society there exists what is sometimes called 'university hunger'; people consider university education as a highly desirable course for their children. The fate of the Polytechnics in the United Kingdom is an example of the effects of this; after much discussion they have received university status without substantial change in the way they operate. We need to consider further how it is possible to retain the quality of the universities despite the pressure of numbers.

One can think of some 'first rank universities' to concentrate on (2) and (3) leaving the rank and file to deal with the 'flood'. These would not be very different from the colleges in the US, which have after all been very successful as can be judged from their increase in numbers from 679 in 1965 to 1296 in 1983 (OECD 1987). However, this might deprive some regions of both first rank universities and of

Table 13.1 Evolution in the number of higher education students during the eighties in eleven European Union countries

	A	A	'80–'81	'81–'82	'82–'83	'83–'84	'84–'85	'85–'86	'86–'87	'87–'88	'88–'89	'89–'90
B	271	1.97	26.3	26.8	27.4	28.2	30.7	31.2	32.2	33.2	34.2	37.2
DK	127	2.54	28.6	28.4	29.0	29.2	29.1	29.3	29.6	30.4	31.5	–
E	1169	6.41	24.3	24.0	24.4	26.5	26.9	28.6	29.7	31.5	32.4	33.5
F	1587	4.80	25.5	27.2	27.8	28.3	29.3	29.8	30.0	30.9	34.5	37.2
GR	188	2.81	17.4	17.7	19.4	20.9	23.3	26.2	26.9	28.0	28.9	–
NL	435	2.31	30.0	30.5	30.7	30.8	31.0	31.8	31.3	32.2	32.4	34.3
IRL	85	4.79	20.3	21.5	22.1	21.4	23.1	24.2	24.7	25.2	25.8	26.4
I	1358	2.82	27.7	25.7	25.4	25.4	26.2	25.7	24.6	26.0	27.3	28.6
P	157	6.79	11.2	11.2	11.5	11.5	13.1	12.1	14.0	–	14.5	18.4
UK	1178	3.19	20.1	20.4	22.7	22.6	21.7	21.8	22.3	22.7	23.5	25.2
D	1720	2.51	26.2	27.6	28.4	29.0	29.4	29.9	30.1	30.6	32.0	33.3

A   Total number of higher education students (in thousands) in 1989–90 (for Greece and Denmark one year earlier)

B   Mean percentual increase in the total number of students from 1984–85 until the last year in table

Rest   Colums '80–81 to '89–'90: Ratio between the number of higher education students and the population segment aged 20–24 years for the corresponding academic course nucleation centres for research and development. One must also not forget that these differentiated systems are liable to lead to discrimination with respect to social or economic background, which has been sometimes referred to as 'social apartheid' (OECD 1991).

An alternative is not to discriminate between universities but to rank high quality departments and give them special support and funding; from an administrative point of view it may be preferable to designate them as Institutes. This approach has its merits but can add a new stress to the academic community as has happened recently in the United Kingdom.

A third possibility relies on other bodies like the Centre Nationale de la recherche Scientifique (CNRS) in France or the CSIC in Spain to pair off their institutions with university departments. The mixed units that resulted could receive special consideration without interfering with university autonomy; the policy for appointment of staff could also be co-ordinated and might reduce the incidence of internal appointments. In summary, much ingenuity is required to shelter high quality groups within a university that otherwise must fulfil its mandate for mass teaching.

Professional Training

Professional training of the highest quality is a key requirement of society for doctors, lawyers, engineers etc., and this has always been the traditional task of the universities before the massive expansion. Some now argue that the university is no longer the best place for professional training and argue for special schools. This has certainly already happened in the many thriving business schools and I suppose that the French *Grandes Ecoles* are the archetype of this approach.

There are a number of drawbacks to the 'special school' approach. The schools tend to be too much closed in on themselves, and specialisation is achieved at the expense of the interdisciplinary learning which is so much needed in our rapidly evolving society. On the other hand, this objection no longer applies when the specialised knowledge is acquired in a graduate school as the previous degree course should have guaranteed a more multipolar approach.

It is often suggested that training in specialised schools have little esteem for research; they seem content with instruction of well-established knowledge and of case studies. The subtle intermingling of research with training so typical of the best traditional universities is often absent.

My final objection has a political bias. These schools promote 'old boy' networks which can evolve into a class bound system where admittance is strongly conditioned by social origin, which is much less apparent in the general university.

Research and Development

I will now consider the possibility that high quality research might be carried out more effectively outside universities.[1] I am thinking particularly of the multisectoral public institutes found mainly in the Latin countries (such as the CNRS in France, the CSIC in Spain and the CNR in Italy). I am sceptical that research quality *in toto* would be improved by a steady transfer of university research into an all-research environment. The hypothetical advantage of such a move in terms of the availability of equipment, central facilities and technical assistance is probably counterbalanced by the loss of contact with students and the narrowing of research interests consequent on the dropping of teaching. There is also a problem related to staff ageing. In universities it is well-recognised that staff may lose their research drive as they get older, but this does not mean at all that they equally lose their ability to teach; on the other hand, the researcher who loses his/her drive is a real problem in a research institute where there is probably no alternative role for him/her.

In some fields, research institutes might be advantageous; this is particularly true in technological areas such as microelectronics, or where non-publishable work, material confidential to industry is involved, or research with hazardous materials. There is also a question of size; very large research establishments would disturb the balance of a university. It is usually agreed that universities are best concerned with fundamental research but this can be profitably carried out in partnership with institutes.

Measuring Quality

Present economic difficulties, as well as concern about the age structure of the population, have raised questions about how far the welfare state can continue to grow and since the budgetary burden

---

1   It is worth recalling that a recent analysis of the situation in Britain led to a contrary conclusion. It recommended the merging of several research institutes with nearby universities. There were several comments in *Nature* in the summer of 1994.

of the universities is not a negligible proportion of the budget it is not surprising that there is public concern that universities should provide good value. This implies that regular evaluation needs to be carried out; the question is whether this evaluation can be carried out effectively.

Measuring quality means assessing the performance of a system with respect to previously determined specifications. It is obvious that the specifications need not be the same for the three functions of the university. Research is most accessible to evaluation and well-established patterns of evaluation exist. The broad foundations of assessing fundamental research are accepted even though there are some doubts about some aspects of peer review. Extending this from the individual to departments and whole universities is not very demanding, and in fact has been successfully used in various European countries.

Applied research is more difficult to evaluate; even such obvious measures as patents may be misleading, as a non-exploited patent is of little value; collaboration with industry entails confidentiality which is a further complication. The European Commission and others are trying to develop better procedures.

Teaching is much the hardest to evaluate; there is no agreement of when is the best time to carry out the evaluation: whether immediately after completing a course, at the end of university studies or after entering employment. How much weight should be given to the views of the students themselves and how much to employers? The European Conference of Rectors have proposed a model for quality assessment that can be regarded as a useful starting point (Conference of European Rectors 1993).

Even if procedures are much discussed and disputed there is no doubt that more work on evaluation is needed, nor that there is much doubt that figures of merit for universities will figure prominently in the coming century.

Supporting Quality

One of the claims intrinsic to arguments about university autonomy is that government financial support should come as a lump sum, with the university itself making the decisions how to distribute it among its various needs. My personal view is that universities can be funded in this way for all their infrastructure and extension budgets; this is not incompatible with a significant part of the lump sum being related to quality assessment.

This can be regarded as autonomy being made harmonious with accountability. While this is desirable, it is limited by the current deficiencies in the evaluation methodologies, which has tended to lead to premature interventions by funders. Unfortunately, the interventions have been more related to planning proposals than to real quality evaluation.

Professional training and research require a different approach. I favour separate funding of externally evaluated departments even if the funds are consolidated under one heading for managerial reasons. While some might prefer that all university support were lumped into one figure, there are difficulties due to conflicting claims in which, for example, extension funds were to absorb funds earmarked for professional training; the corrections to such imbalances are slow to correct and the detrimental effects can build up quite rapidly.

It is unlikely that the university evaluation methodology could be settled satisfactorily in a single step; rather it is likely to need progressive refinement. However, even a modest move towards evaluation as a basis for developing selective support can have a significant effect on the quality of a university. An example from Spain can be cited: all university professors are state employees with uniform salaries across the country. It was suggested that research would be stimulated if professors were to receive a part of their salary (up to 20%) in relation to an external periodical evaluation of the quality of their research, with an initial bonus based on past performance. That was started in 1989, since when 20,000 professors have been evaluated (Pascual 1991); about half were granted these allowances (Table 13.2). At the start there was much anxiety among the staff but this has subsided.

At the same time, an evaluation of teaching in the universities was undertaken. This was a responsibility of each university; the magnitude of the salary allowance was, however, uniform. It was not successful because the evaluations came out as almost 100 per cent positive. It became clear that academic authorities found great difficulty in making negative reports on people who had the power to dismiss them ! This illustrates one of the difficulties in matching autonomy with quality assessment. There are other matters with relevance to the development of quality one of which is mobility.

Table 13.2 Summary of action and some numerical results from the evaluation of individual research of Spanish Professors in the 1989–1992 period

The scheme: Each person with a tenured position at a Spanish University could ask for individual research evaluation. An *initial* evaluation was carried out in 1989, each person could apply for one *salary step* for every *six years* of past research. For every step with a positive evaluation the salary was increased by 4%. In the following years, the professors could apply for additional steps every time that a period of six years from the previous evaluation was completed.

The evaluators: First, the Spanish Ministry of Education and Science appointed a group of 17 scientists of the highest recognition (many of them foreign institutions). This group, apart from other tasks, were asked to appoint a few possible evaluators for each of the eleven thematic areas such as Chemistry, Earth Sciences, Art and History etc., from which the final five (for each area) were selected after discussion with University Vice-Chancellors and CSIC government bodies. Evaluators serve for a period of two years.

Numerical results:

	Number of Professors	Number of steps evaluated	Percentage of positive evaluations
Full Professors	5081	13,287	73.4%
Assistant Professors	16,428	20,603	53.4%
Demonstrators	7238	1448	15.4%

* Demonstrators: they are tentured staff dedicated mostly to teaching in short cycle (3 years) careers. Most of them do not have a PhD

Mobility

Parochialism is perhaps the single most adverse circumstance to the pursuit of quality, and as pointed out earlier, autonomy can favour parochialism. It is well-known that mobility is much greater in the United States. Often non-academic elements are involved. For example, in most European countries, university staff tend to buy rather than rent their homes and universities can counter this if they are able to offer rented property either on a short-term or longer-term basis. New supranational schemes within the European Union also appear to offer some help. However, it is up to universities to make a serious effort to promote mobility of staff.

Interaction with Industry and Services

Autonomous universities to an increasing degree look for partnership with industry and with services (EEC 1993). While involvement in R&D is so common that it does not require further comment, two other aspects of partnership do. Joint training programmes, particularly ones arising from developments in information technology, and taking into account the multidisciplinary approach that universities can provide seem especially interesting. Another matter is that many of the services being developed in modern societies, for example, environmental research needed for road or irrigation policies cannot be effectively introduced without serious research and this often is of a high order and interdisciplinary. This is also an interesting area of interuniversity competition.

Flexibility

The teaching responsibilities of universities will undergo considerable change in the near future. Training programmes will become a major activity, while the traditional face to face contact between teacher and student will be largely replaced by various forms of distance learning. An increasing number of students will spend their time at more than one university. This has been inhibited by curriculum rigidities, but the experience with European exchange programmes such as Erasmus and Comett should pave the way for easier exchange. Autonomy can be of substantial help in improving this kind of offer.

Publicity

The promotion of competition between universities requires the stimulus that can come from the publicising of the results of assessments and evaluations, with due care to prevent excessive self-laudation. In some European countries (e.g., in France, Spain and the UK), some evaluations have received press coverage and this is likely to increase and may be of value for the public. However, it can also easily become contentious.

Conclusions

1. Autonomy and independence are essential to public universities in stimulating good teaching, training, and research. These are best achieved if the universities have full

control of their own management. However, bearing in mind the high level of public funding, performance must be evaluated and the results freely disseminated. Evaluation is dynamic and should be made full use of to improve departments and institutions.

2. The number of university students in Europe is likely to continue to grow, even in the face of new alternative higher education schemes. Universities have to learn how to cope with growth without deterioration in teaching and particularly in professional training and research.

3. Professional training is carried out most successfully at universities (an exception may be postgraduate business studies). In order to protect professional training it is suggested that the funding received by the university for these purposes should be earmarked.

4. Research must be a major and permanent part of university activity, but it needs critical evaluation to ensure that only quality work is funded. Differential funding can result in some departments becoming essentially just teaching departments. It is important that the departments involved in professional training should be strongly linked to research. Involvement in research with industry should be encouraged.

5. More efficient methods of evaluating university performance are needed; different modalities are needed for extension activities and for professional training and for research.

6. Funding for infrastructure and extension is best through a lump sum transfer; that for professional training and research support through direct channels to departments.

References

EEC (1993) *Conference of European Rectors. View on the Memorandum on HE in the EEC.* Brussels.

EEC (1993) *IRDAC Opinion on Education and Training for European Competitiveness.* Brussels: EEC.

EEC *Memorandum on Higher Education in the European Community*, Brussels, 1991

IECD (International Council for Educational Development) (ed) (1988) *The Spanish University Reform.* Madrid: MEC-Consejo de Universidades.

OECD (1991) *Alternatives to Universities.* Paris: OECD.

OECD (1987) *Universities under Scrutiny*. Paris: OECD.

Pascual, P. (1991) 'Evaluation and the improvement of quality.' *CRE-Action 96*, 95–102.

Pascual, P. (1994) *Universities and Research in Spain*.

Chapter 14

Higher Education in Central and Eastern Europe
An Approach to Comparative Analysis

Wolfgang Mitter

Introductory Remarks: Central and Eastern Europe in Transformation

The fundamental changes that have seized the whole region of Central and Eastern Europe have already left their first impact on the education systems, in general and higher education in particular. It is true that up to now these changes have not yet led to stabilising measures, let alone comprehensive reforms. Even the legal provisions, in the form of laws, decrees and directives, which have been recently made, give evidence rather of immediate reactions to the collapse of the 'socialist' regimes than of expressly determined goals or perspectives. This appraisal can be exemplified by the contents of the Higher Education Acts which were passed in (former) Czechoslovakia on May 3rd 1990, in Poland on September 12th 1990 and in Hungary on July 13th 1993. As far as Russia is concerned, the comprehensive 'Law on Education' of July 10th 1992 includes fundamental references to higher education.

The present-day stage of the transformation process is still hardly discernible; all the more so as all initiatives and efforts aimed at revising goals, structures and contents of higher education are involved in the overall economic and socio-political scene. In this connection, the foreign observer takes notice of priorities which are given to the overcoming of elementary hardships, concerning subsistence and medical treatment as well as civil unrest, let alone martial actions in former Yugoslavia and in some regions of the former Soviet Union. Different though all the recent initiatives and actions have been in the individual countries, they signal the departure from the socialist past and the search for alternatives which are oriented to 'democratic' and 'pluralistic' concepts (cf. Anweiler *et al.* 1990; Mitter 1992).

Looking for insight into current trends and problems, foreign observers must not restrict their inquiries to the analysis of legal documents and expert comments, whose publication in journals for the interpretation of topical events are frequently overtaken by the reality of actual change. A wider range of sources is provided by programmes and pamphlets which are issued by political parties, professional associations and other social groups; a good number of which are accessible in the form of brochures or articles in the daily press.

Such publications, ephemeral as they often are, are informative in a particular way, as they record successions in leading management and administrative positions, from ministries 'down' to faculties and chairs, and they give insight into developments at the 'grass roots' of individual universities and, furthermore, into local working conditions characterised by lack of up-to-date textbooks, technical instruments and other learning aids and appliances. Finally, excursions to the countries concerned and talks to visitors from Central and Eastern Europe – scholars, politicians, administrators, lecturers, but also students and, generally speaking, representatives of the 'educationally engaged public' – enrich the access to the oscillating scene which is characteristic of higher education in Central and Eastern Europe today. This paper is based upon the pluridimensional evaluation of available sources as just outlined. The author is aware of the transitory character of his approach which comes nearer to a 'snapshot' than a systematised analysis. This restriction appraisal applies even more to the predictive considerations and postulates.

These introductory remarks should be completed by the author's comment concerning his understanding of 'Central' and 'Eastern Europe' with regard to its geographic dimension. Contrary to the German custom, the English medium academic terminology makes a distinction between 'Eastern Europe' and the 'Soviet Union'. This is ambivalent, because while it points to clarity it also risks confusion.

Excluding the former Soviet Union from 'Eastern Europe' minimises the effort to draw 'appropriate' demarcation lines inside that multinational agglomeration which was, even under Stalinist totalitarianism, rather a region than a State, though based upon a common and imperial history of a few centuries. Yet, this approach neglects the question of how to identify the 'European' components of that multinational Union both in sociocultural and political terms and to define the criteria against what came into the debate under the category of its 'Asian' components.

The term 'Eastern Europe', as applied in West Germany between 1945 and 1989, suggested the idea of a homogeneous region which, in fact, had never existed. It is true that the history of the 'socialist period' permitted its application as long as it was limited to the factors of ideological doctrinairism and political uniformity as common features of identification and demarcation against the 'West'. Even under the socialist umbrella, however, it obscured, first of all, the deep boundary line demarcating the 'Catholic' (East) Central from the 'Orthodox' (and 'Muslim') Eastern and South East Europe which passed through the contemporary State of Romania and the collapsing Federation of Yugoslavia. In this historical respect, the restitution of the Baltic Republics as entirely independent States has formally restored their (East) Central European relation to 'Eastern' Russia.

The collapse of the Socialist Bloc in general and of the Soviet Union in particular has, on the one hand, effected the restitution of the term 'Central Europe'. In the interim period between World Wars I and II that connotation included Germany and Austria, while the recent shift has restricted it to the belt of countries between Germany, Austria and the Commonwealth of Independent States. The recent debate about a revival of the historic connotation of Central Europe (including Germany, Austria and sometimes even North East Italy) is not to be discussed in the context of this paper. It is true that, according to the German tradition, this term *per se* has been widely adopted to the region 'East of Poland'. However, this shift leaves the allocation of the aforementioned 'Asian' components of the Commonwealth of Independent States, in particular the Siberian region of the Russian Federation, unclarified.

These tentative reflections on terminological aspects should not be taken too far. Since higher education, and education *in toto*, is involved in this book, these introductory remarks are necessary all the more so as they set the framework of the following comparative approach. At the same time, they should be taken as permission for using the term Central and Eastern Europe as a working concept, covering both the member countries of Commonwealth of Independent States, Central Europe (within its recent demarcation) and also South East Europe. This working concept comes near the philosophy and practice of UNESCO (United Nations Educational, Scientific, and Cultural Organisation) which has included the whole of the former Soviet Union in its East European subregion.

Eastern Germany will be only slightly tackled in this paper; none the less, a few remarks seem to be needed. The former German Democratic Republic (GDR) must be identified as a unique and exceptional case, insofar as the overthrow of her 'socialist' regime has been followed by reunification with the established and democratic structures of her Western counterpart. Since this process has been constitutionally legalised by the accession of the former GDR to the

Federal Republic of Germany, the impact of this decision on present-day higher education and its prospects differ from those in the other previous socialist States. On the other hand, references to the former GDR will be useful in illustrating the socialist higher education policies.

The Historical Departure

Since the end of the 1940s, higher education in most Central and East European countries was oriented to the Soviet model. In principle, this determined its continuity inside the Socialist Bloc. At the same time, Yugoslavia developed its own socialist conception, built on the principle of self-management. Albania maintained a separate course, chosen in the Chrushchev era, until the collapse of her socialist regime. In the 1960s and 1970s, Albania's peculiar way was underlined by adjustment to certain policies of the People's Republic of China, with special regard to an extreme tie of training schemes and courses to the needs of socialist production.

However, higher education inside the Socialist Bloc shared a number of common features which were based upon the following fundamental principles and guidelines (cf. Mitter 1978, pp.29–38; cf. Hegedüs, von Kopp and Schmidt 1982; Novikov 1981).

1. The place of higher education in the socialist society was entirely defined by its societal function. Therefore, goals, structures and contents of higher education were dominated by the political monopoly and ideological monism of the State. The dovetailing of the authorities for ideological indoctrination and for the political exercise of power in the central organs of Party and State leadership bound practice and theory to the directives of a State policy, which for its part was to be understood as an element of a comprehensive societal policy. In the socialist variant of higher education, the degree of commitment in policy decisions which, for example, were contained in the official pronouncements of the highest organs of Party and State (Party Congress decisions, etc.) was intrinsically higher than is the case with corresponding manifestations in Western countries, even when the educational policy was directed centrally. This form of political monopoly given, the existence of Federal State structures, such as in the Soviet Union and Czechoslovakia (since 1968), entailed only slight, if any, limits to centralised governance and control which was in

principle operated by hierarchically organised bureaucracies and supported by dense and impervious security and intelligence networks.

2. Higher education was considered as the uppermost stage of vocational training. Consequently, the capacities of the sector as a whole and of its individual institutions were adjusted to the economic parameters centred on the five-year plans and their subordinate arrangements. These overall directives had immediate impacts on the admission policies. The GDR and Czechoslovakia excepted, the applicant had to acquire secondary school graduation (of academic quality) in the form of a 'maturity' certificate and to pass an entrance examination consisting of written and oral tests according to the requirements set by the faculty he/she wanted to be enrolled in.

The exceptional cases of Czechoslovakia and also of the GDR were due to the monopoly of the *Abitur* (maturity certificate) as the sole criterion to a higher education course – which, however, did not include the claim to enrol in the chosen course of studies. In the GDR, this unique position of the Abitur was, furthermore, underlined by the rigid selection mechanisms concerning the admission to the *Erweiterte Oberschule* (Extended Secondary School), representing the university-bound track of upper secondary education. The education reform in Yugoslavia of 1974, on the other hand, was aimed at the integration of upper secondary and higher education as a concomitant of the 'professionalising' policy to be dealt with later.

In all the other East European countries the discrepancies between comparatively open admission policies in the university-bound upper secondary education stage and the restrictive selection for higher education were never solved, thus having remained part of the socialist heritage which, in this particular respect, shares many similarities to policies in the West. Anyway, the strict admission practised everywhere was related to the expected needs of the individual branches of the national economies. This explains why the drop-out rates were rather low both during the training courses and in the terminal examinations. On the other hand, this system was characterised by comparatively low proportions of university students (1989) within the corresponding age-groups (18 to 23), e.g., 21.4 p.c. in the Soviet Union and 16.2 p.c. in Czechoslovakia, to be compared with 27.9 p.c. in Western Europe (Straka 1991, p. 94).

3. The subordination of higher education to the political monopoly of Party and State was reinforced by direct control exercised by the corresponding ministries, as a rule organised as separate units (Ministry of Higher Education, Ministry of Science and Higher Education, etc.) and having overstaffed bureaucracies at their disposal. Overstaffing in this sector included the management inside the higher education institutions. Academic autonomy which had been a privilege of universities before, was abolished or, in some cases reduced to purely nominal competencies. For instance, in Bulgaria the universities had the right to elect their rectors and deans restored in 1958, yet, since no election could take place before the supreme Party authorities had given their 'recommendations', the *de facto* range of responsibilities remained as it had been installed at the end of the Second World War (Bachmaier 1991).

The Hungarian scholar Istvan Bessenyei has proposed the term 'Prussian-Soviet Model' to define the hierarchical and bureaucratic character of higher education management in the Socialist Bloc (Bessenyei 1991, p.152; cf. Pribersky 1991). The applicability of this term, however, is doubtful insofar as the Prussian-German university was not directly steered by the State authorities. Instead it was marked by a considerable degree of inner autonomy, though, as in most European countries, distinctly restricted by State supervision and decision-making with regard to the appointment of professors (but out of lists submitted by the faculties) as well as in the provision and control of the budgets. The supremacy of the State authorities in socialist European Europe was particularly evident in their right to introduce, revise and withdraw syllabi and training schemes, at least for all obligatory courses which were uniform throughout the individual countries. This was also the case in the federal Soviet Union.

The most striking manifestation of the State (and Party) supremacy was seen in the ideological penetration of the syllabi, in particular in the humanities and social sciences. Furthermore, the obligatory programme included extra disciplinary courses for students of all faculties, such as Marxism-Leninism, History of the Communist Party, etc., let alone military training for men.

4. Higher education in Central and Eastern Europe in the 'pre-socialist' periods had been structured on a binary line with universities and polytechnics as main pillars. The universities were, apart from their legal status as 'autonomous bodies', privileged by the acknowledged philosophy and practice of linking teaching and research with a distinct dominance of the latter. Under the socialist concept, the binary structures were abandoned as a corollary of the subordination of all higher education establishments both to the political and ideological dominance and to economic planning. This change entailed the transformation of the universities to mere teaching institutions, research being reduced to a minor position. This was especially the case in most of the newly founded universities at the periphery (above all in the Soviet Union), which were not given any research opportunity; in any case the staffs were loaded (and often overloaded) with teaching obligations.

5. Where research was included in universities, it was usually incorporated in 'national research plans', normally under the chairmanship and management of State agencies or extra-university research institutions. In each country, the top of the pyramid in this sector was represented by the National Academy of Sciences under the direct responsibility of the Council of Ministers. While the Academies were focused on fundamental research with (natural) sciences dominating, applied research fell into the domain of so-called 'branch institutes', each under the direct supervision and control of one of the numerous specialised ministries or authorities (industrial branches, agriculture, navigation, forestry, mining, trade and commerce, social services, medical care, education, etc.). Within the branch groups, the Soviet Union and the GDR held an exceptional position with Academies of Pedagogic Sciences as centres for educational research, curriculum development and ideological instruction in the area of general education. Yet, it was their subordination to the Ministries of Education – and not to the Councils of Ministers – which determined their lower rank in comparison to the 'big' Academies of Sciences.

In the last years of the socialist period, the branch institutes increasingly had to compete with special research institutes which were emerging inside the production sector itself, particularly within the big State firms. The tying of training schemes to the specialised needs of the national economy were considered as a constitutive component of the syllabi and examinations. Nevertheless, this orientation did not lead to the total abandonment of 'academic' conceptions, all the more so as the Academies of Sciences insisted on the availability of qualified researchers (in the pure sense). In this context, one should mention the university of Novosibirsk which was established as a research university alongside the Branch of the Soviet Academy of Sciences in the late 1950s (with only about 4,000 students at the end of the 1960s).

In the regular universities and, even more, the polytechnics, the production-oriented training was reinforced by contracts between higher education establishments and firms comprising, special research programmes, extended learning-by-doing periods and practicals for students in the production sector. In this respect, Romania developed the most ambitious models, followed by Bulgaria and Yugoslavia (Bachmaier 1991; Soljan 1991). This one-sided policy neglecting the training of theoretically qualified scientists, met with harsh criticism – in Yugoslavia already during the late 1980s, in the two other countries after the overthrow of their socialist regimes.

6. Resulting from the loss of academic autonomy, universities were deprived of the right to confer academic degrees. The GDR continued with her German two-tier system with doctorates and habilitation doctorates. In Czechoslovakia and Hungary the universities retained the right of conferring so-called 'little' doctorates, while the scientific degrees of Candidate and Doctor became the responsibility of the Central Examination Committees under the direct supervision of the Ministries of Higher Education. Since the awarding of degrees was no longer a prerogative of autonomous academic bodies, the doors were opened to manipulation in form of political degrees as a means of rewarding praiseworthy Party or State functionaries (and sometimes, also, ministerial officers who had incurred their superior's displeasure). On the other hand, one should not forget that the big Academies of Sciences were often able to

keep out interventions from their research programmes and achieve outstanding scientific achievements, although frequently needed to show obedience to ideological and political 'campaigns', such as peace appeals, struggle against inner or outer enemies, etc. This, admittedly restricted, privilege could be maintained particularly by those which could base their case on a long established reputation, such as the Soviet Academy of Sciences (founded in 1725 as Imperial Russian Academy of Sciences).

7. Finally, the inclusion of higher education in ideological indoctrination and economic planning led to the loss of universities as centres of multidisciplinary thinking and communication. The remaining universities were frequently reduced to the faculties of humanities and sciences, while the extra-university higher education sector was broadened by the transformation of the former faculties of laws, medicine and economics into separate units alongside the existing and emerging polytechnics for engineering. Since this sector, in its turn, underwent further subdivision, the whole higher education system was characterised, compared to its counterparts in Western countries, by an extreme degree of specialisation.

Quantitative growth can be registered as the chief asset in the development of higher education during the socialist period. This statement holds true even when one considers the lag in numbers of establishments and students compared to developments in Western countries, particularly in the United States with her totally different higher education system. The increase in numbers of institutions and students reached its comparatively highest extent in the Soviet Union and the developing countries of South-East Europe, while the developments in Czechoslovakia and, especially in East Germany, indicated much slower growth. In this respect one has to add that in the whole Socialist Bloc the development of higher education was paralleled by the extension of upper secondary and post-secondary technical and vocational schools which, especially in Czechoslovakia and East Germany, exercised compensatory effects with regard to the professional training of the younger generation.

In all the countries the quantitative growth was accompanied by the foundation of many new establishments, especially at the periphery of the individual countries which resulted in what the Croatian educationist, Nikola Nikola Soljan, has identified as 'demetropolisation' (Soljan 1991; cf. Weilguni 1991). Compared to Western parameters, universities and polytechnics in Eastern Europe were rather small in enrolments with only a few thousand students as a rule. This trend of distributing higher education all over the territories doubtlessly had positive effects on the development of intranational infrastructures. On the other hand, it led to discrepancies in quality between metropolitan and peripheral establishments concerning the qualification of teaching staffs, the admission of applicants and equipment. In order to fill such gaps in the main centres of higher education, such as Moscow and Leningrad in the Soviet Union, special in-service courses were held for professors and lecturers from peripheral places.

In the years following the collapse of the socialist systems, higher education has been subjected to wide internal criticism. Critical comments concentrate on the backwardness and overspecialisation of training programmes for students, low qualification of teachers, unreliable admission policies, and insufficient remuneration of staff. Most comments end up in complaints about the bureaucratic rigidity of the management and, again, the low level of material equipment.

The reasons for all these deficiencies trace back to fundamental misarrangement in the planning, which had caused permanent gaps between aims and objectives on the one hand, and realities on the other. As regards the Socialist Bloc as a whole, this failure was aggravated by the surprising lack of effective co-operation among the comparatively isolated individual national systems. This policy was favoured by the Soviet Union which preferred bilateral agreements with the individual satellite States each to close multilateral ties. The assumption may not be wrong that there was resistance in the satellite States against coercive pressure, Bulgaria excepted.

Fundamental common features did not prevent the existence of variations which were characterised by specific types of structures and curricula. Divergences became manifest and indicated to what extent and how Western experiences were adopted. Moreover, one has to pay attention to the historical reasons for the continuity or survival of specific national or regional traditions. Points of orientation for an explanation of differences in this domain are reached through consideration of the following peculiarities:

1. In the comparison of higher education between the Soviet Union and the other countries we must take into account the duration of the socialist development up to the end of the eighties, which resulted in the Soviet Union's function as a model, to which we have already referred. One must also bear in mind the fact that the transformation of higher education in Russia that became sovietised after the October Revolution was comparatively radical. In the other countries

after the Second World War, however, there followed a step by step adaptation of the 'bourgeois' universities which already existed in the capitals and big cities, to the new social and political conditions of the socialist order of society to be erected – speeded of course to a greater or lesser extent by the authorities responsible. Higher education presents a good example of differences resting upon debates, whether and to what extent elements of the inherited academic autonomy could be tolerated beside the dominant guidelines of adjusting teaching and research to the changing requirements of economic planning. In this respect, Poland and Hungary were most distant from the Soviet model.

2. The establishment of priorities in higher education policy was conditioned essentially by the level of industrial development and the state of education of the population at a particular time. This factor was significant especially from the point of view of the initial conditions which prevailed when the socialist period in educational history began in the individual countries. It distinguished the comparatively highly developed and established structures of universities and polytechnics in Czechoslovakia and the GDR from those of the other countries which were industrialised to a lesser degree or hardly at all.

But here we must also point to the inflexibility, characteristic of the policy of pursuit of uniformity in the early 1950s, in which the basic features and details of the Soviet higher education system were imitated even when this included a retrograde development. This statement can be strikingly related to the Central European systems in Poland, Czechoslovakia, Hungary and the GDR. In this context the exceptional position of Yugoslavia is worthy of special attention. In spite of the steering role of the Union of Communists which ensured party rule there as well, the federalisation of the State and the practice of self-management laid the ground for bureaucratic decentralisation. The concept of self-management was implemented by the arrangement of associated work between universities and firms which, in their turn, were organised according to this main principle. It is true that the comparatively decentralised structure saved Yugoslavian universities from overcentralised bureaucracies. On the other hand, the lack of ability of the elected delegates also resulted in the establishment and growth of bureaucracies, although within the framework of smaller administrative units. Finally, the local decentralisation was to a good extent invalidated by far-reaching standardisation of the higher education system of the whole federation, by which the previously diversified universities and polytechnics were reduced to two types of four-year faculties and two-year higher schools (at post-secondary level) (Soljan 1991).

3. The question of the level of the economy and the state of higher education directly indicates the specific historical antecedents of the individual national systems which refer not only to the pre-revolutionary bourgeois period but also extend back into previous centuries. Their after-effects are distinguishable even today in the shape of national and supranational traditions. This factor, which will be refered to again later, directly affects the present-day battles, patterns of national identity and their implications for reform of higher education. Therefore, it may suffice here to outline a few exemplifying cases. Thus the Hapsburg-Austrian policy, which can be traced back to Maria Theresa and Joseph II and which produced the establishment of a highly developed and efficient university system in the nineteenth century, has left its traces not only in the higher education of Czechoslovakia, Hungary, Slovenia and Croatia, but also – in competition with French influences had also left some imprint on developments, in Poland and Romania, whereby the previously mentioned internal border between Transylvania and old Romania should be recalled. The heritage of the Tsarist past has not been entirely extinguished by the Soviet system. It is still most alive in the Academy of Sciences. Finally, one has to take into account the impact of the Prussian-German university idea which was conceived by Wilhelm von Humboldt and had a tremendous impact on university development all over Eastern Europe. The survival of certain traits of academic autonomy must be seen in this light, waiting for in-depth inquiries after the opening of the archives.

Summing up, the comparative educational research which has been conducted in Western countries in the past decades has, on the one hand, in principle criticised the political and ideological monism of the socialist systems in form of a system-transcending judgement. On the other hand, however, the system-immanent appraisals have laid the ground for positive conclusions concerning certain attainments of higher education policies and drives in Central and Eastern

Europe. Such positive conclusions can be found in studies of the quantitative growth, and also in sectoral innovations. However, one cannot put forward this statement without emphasising that all these investigations were, to a large extent, conducted from an outside point of view which was aggravated by the lack of access to primary sources and field work. Thus after the radical changes in Central and Eastern Europe, comparative educational research is challenged to tackle new tasks consisting of reanalysis and scrutiny of the past socialist period from an insiders view which has been offered, by the availability of hitherto inaccessible sources and data (cf. Anweiler 1990; Mitter 1992).

Sectoral Initiatives Towards Reform in the 1980s

This presentation would be incomplete, if we neglected the fact that certain tendencies signalled the beginning of a departure from rigid and doctrinaire positions. They can be already noted in the 1970s. Such examples indicate attempts at reform of teaching methods, for instance by replacing the traditional frontal lecturing and memorisation by group and laboratory work and by activating students to independent learning. Another area of reform concerned the admission policies where, particularly in Hungary, attempts were made at integrating secondary school leaving and entrance examinations, thus overcoming the stress of organising two examinations within a few weeks (in May and June). The farthest-reaching march into the future could be observed in Hungary (Lukàcs). There the Education Act of May 2nd 1985, included features of reform in higher education, although the supremacy of the party organs was not restricted. In particular, this Act confirmed the first steps towards decentralising the network of responsibilities in management; it also stressed the need for inner autonomy to be granted to the organs (rectors, senates, faculties, etc.) of the individual universities. The Act as a whole became obsolete as a corollary of the overall socio-political changes, but the innovatory drive inherent in it has been appreciated in Hungary up to today.

In Poland, where communication to Western universities and research institutions had also been relatively open, though characterised by continual swings between progress and regression, reforms were mostly stimulated by various inquiries of the Institute for Science Policy and Higher Education (*Instytut Polityky Naukowej i Szkolnictwa Wyzszego*) (which was closed in 1991). Its comparatively open orientation became particularly evident by its co-operation with Western and international institutes and organisations. Furthermore, the 'Report on State and Trends of Education in the People's Republic of Poland' which was completed by the second Expert Committee immediately after the Round Table had reached its first success in overthrowing the socialist regime (1989), contained a chapter devoted to the need of reforms in higher education (Kupisiewicz 1991).

Finally, one should not neglect the attempts at modernising organisational and curricular components of higher education in the Soviet Union since the middle of the 1980s. In this connection, special mention has to be made of the research done by the Institute on Problems of Higher Education (*Institut problem vyssego obrazovanija*, today the Institute of Higher Education) in Moscow. Its efforts have not reached, however, visible outcomes, involved as they became in the controversies and oscillations of Perestroika. Certain steps towards more flexibility and openness to cautious co-operation with Western higher education institutions could be even made out among the hard-liners, Bulgaria, Czechoslovakia and GDR – although mainly in theoretical debates and hardly in practice. Summing up, however, all these pre-revolutionary initiatives towards sectoral reforms were finally rolled over by the fundamental changes of the late 1980s and early 1990s.

Present-Day Issues

To come back to our introductory remarks, observation of the present situation gives evidence of multifarious approaches to innovations and reforms in the higher education systems of the Central and East European countries (Reuhl 1992). The diversity of the transformation processes, taken as a whole, can be traced back, on the one hand, to the different national and regional traditions coming out in the deliberations of policy-makers and educators. On the other hand, they mirror the comprehensive scope of the fundamental changes which have seized the political, social and economic frameworks related to higher education. In general one can state a situation which is characterised by rolling developments. In an attempt at proposing a tentative typology, one can make a distinction between three fundamental frames of reference.

The first is represented by the Commonwealth of Independent States. As long as the Soviet Union existed, the changes which were on the way were related to 'Perestroika', i.e., to reforms inside the socialist system. Nonetheless, the cases of system-transcending departure need special attention. This approach was involved in the turbulences of the 'Putsch' of August 1991 and the following four months of wavering actions and intentions characterising the agony of the Soviet Union. Nevertheless, it is worthwhile to refer to Gorbachev's decree of May 15th 1990, because it opened new perspectives, including radical departure from rigid admission policies and highly restricted access to information. The main goals, as proclaimed in that decree, should be, 'to guarantee that the citizens of the USSR exercise their rights and liberties in the field of higher education...to create the prerequisites for raising the quality of higher education and to ensure the effective use of the scientific potential available in institutions of higher education' (Savel'ev 1992, p.41). In principle, the post-Soviet higher education policy in Russia has been oriented to these goals (Directory 1994).

Within the second frame of reference we find the Czech and Slovak Republics, Hungary and Poland (Bessenyei 1991; Cerych 1990; Kouchy and Hendrychova 1993; Krankus 1991; Lajos 1993; Mühle 1994; Pribersky 1991; Scharf 1991; Straka 1991). In these four Central European countries the evolutionary developments typified by the 'velvet revolutions' to use Vaclav Havel's slogan have already reached genuinely democratic standards, particularly with regard to the universities' academic autonomy. In principle, the three Baltic republics could be included in this frame of reference, but for the time being, there remains the open question of how to tackle the integration of the Russian-speaking minorities (in Estonia and Latvia) which suggests caution.

The third frame of reference is represented by countries where the contours are hardly clear yet, system changes having more or less been limited to eliminating all explicit references to the previous regimes and to proclaiming the democratic nature of the post-socialist order. In this category, one has to allocate Romania, Bulgaria (Bachmaier 1991; Bizkov 1991) and Albania, while the successor states of former Yugoslavia (Soljan 1991; Weilguni 1991) seem to look for individual strategies, orienting themselves to their specific pre-socialist traditions.

In a wider framework, East Germany could be considered as a fourth category, specified by her integration into the socio-political system of the Federal Republic of Germany. The continuing existence of structural, curricular and, above all, attitudinal features of the socialist inheritance indicate, however, that East Germany will remain a unit with both German-German and German-Central East European dimensions.

Since uncertainty is present, we must refrain from offering any definitive analysis. Constantly observing the scene, however, we feel encouraged to draft some contours which may help in identifying some trends. The following list of items should be understood as only tentative.

1. All the innovative approaches are focused on the removal of all indoctrinating pressures to which the socialist systems were subjected by political power and ideological doctrinairism. It goes without saying that the opening towards democratic and pluralistic self-awareness of higher education is greatly dependent on the degree of political revolutionism. The state of the revolutionary process becomes, for example, manifest in the closing down of universities, institutes and chairs which were devoted to one-sided investigation and transmission of the Marxist-Leninist ideology (or, when this is thought to be possible, in their transformation to institutes of sociological research, etc.), in the elimination of the obligatory area of courses in ideological education and in the purification of curricula and syllabi in general and in subjects such as history and literature. Thus, university teachers and examination boards have to tackle emergency situations in the everyday practice, which are not only caused by the cancellation of certain syllabi and the withdrawal (or at least selected application) of hitherto valid textbooks, but also by the suspension of certain parts of the examinations before new alternatives are conceived.

2. The attainment of spiritual freedom and plurality is closely connected with a new way of handling the steering mechanisms of the higher education system and therefore with the role of the State in higher education policies. It should not raise any astonishment that the removal of bureaucratic and ideological suppression, has led to calls for democratisation and to efforts in restoring traditional academic autonomy. Yet, the current debates on how this conception should be put to practice in laws, decrees and statutes, are often distinguished from similar approaches in Western Europe by the radicality of the models and propositions. The establishment of self-governing bodies immediately following the political changes gave evidence of such swings to all-round participation, e.g., the 50 per cent proportion of students at Czechoslovakian universities on university committees. There the pendulum has swung towards the middle again and has resulted in the students' proportion of one third. In general, the debates about the quorum refer to the representation of professors, lecturers, students and management personnel in the governing bodies.

3. The Hungarian sociologist, Tamas Kózma, identified the
    socialist society as an 'educational affluent society' (Kózma
    1989). His thesis is worth quoting in this connection still
    because it points to one of the essential reasons explaining
    the inflexibility and rigidity of the education systems in the
    countries of the former socialist bloc. As a concomitant of the
    intended and initiated departure from comprehensive
    planning by the State authorities to the re-establishment of
    the market and to the restitution of private property, one has
    to study all models and arguments which dominate the
    discussion under the heading of decoupling education and
    the employment system. Above all, this issue is particularly
    relevant because of the necessity to remove the ties between
    school-leaving certification and job guarantee. This
    desideratum needs to be fulfilled; all the more so as job
    guarantees were even allocated to some of the employment
    hierarchy.

The conclusions to be drawn from this change relate to their
remarkable impact on the admission policies at the levels of
upper secondary and higher education, and they confront
policy-makers in the areas of economy and education with
tasks they are not accustomed to (Kuebart 1990). Moreover,
one has to consider that young people with higher education
certificates have to care about finding jobs themselves and to
take into account that in the current situation the available
job need not congrue with one's formal qualification. The
issue of de-coupling has been intensively discussed in
Western countries too. However, such linkage was only in
some sectors of the employment system, and even there it
has been abandoned long ago. On the other hand, at least in
their fundamental extent, unexpected changes at the end of
the 1980s explain why in some former socialist countries,
above all in Hungary, the pendulum swung the other way
(Halasz and Lukacs 1990; Lajos 1993).

The high esteem of free market philosophies has encouraged
another socio-political trend which directly influences
higher education policies. Having got rid of the tight
budgetary and organisational fetters of socialist planning,
pleas for including higher education in the rules of supply
and demand meet with interest and acceptance.
Overestimation of the possible speed of such a radical
change in systems with strict state-supervised management
and financing, inevitably leads to disappointment and

failure. The development in Hungary, at the end of the 1980s of radical decentralisation of higher education management and free financing, exemplifies the return to a different State responsibility.

4. Structural and curricular reforms are, above all, aimed at the concept of modernisation. Efforts have been made to overcome the rigid grading systems by which students are promoted from one year to the next. Instead, open arrangements are proposed, and recommendations have been given to adjust the existing standards of degrees of higher education (with their terminal certifications) in order to make them conform with Anglo-Saxon education standards demarcating undergraduate from graduate study courses. Aleksandr Ja. Savel'ev has summarised the need for structural reform of higher education in Russia with reference to:

   • the education levels and number of terms
   • the types of education (universities, academies, specialised institutions)
   • the educational forms (full-time, part-time and correspondence courses)
   • the subordination of institutions of higher education and different levels of the administration system (union, republic, local) (Savel'ev 1992, p.42).

Savel'ev's considerations can be called exemplary, apart from his reference to the 'union' (e.g., federal) level which, however, has not become obsolete with regard to the Russian Federation.

5. The universities emphasise the need for the restoration of research to their work as an essential component to be linked with teaching. Yet, this demand raises complex problems. The extra-university research institutions, in particular the Academies of Sciences, are not willing to see their capacity restricted and to share it with the universities (cf. Josephson 1994). Therefore, they have started campaigns in order to prove the benefits of their contributions to the national science outcome. Secondly, the universities, being involved in tremendous internal troubles with regard to their teaching obligations in a period of apparently increasing enrolments, are little prepared to cope with the new challenge. Thirdly, they often lack scientists with that experience which lays the ground for the development of

research capacities, let alone the non-availability of material equipment. Finally, the reorganisation of the national research system must be seen in connection with the reform of interrelations between research and the economy under free market conditions.

6. The free market orientation of higher education policies have an immediate impact on structures and curricula of the individual institutions and their units, as well as on the system as a whole. On the one hand, competition has become an important item, related to the assessment of individual achievement (concerning students and teachers) and to the evaluation of single institutions. Approaches to developing ranking orders have come into the picture. They include the rivalry between universities and polytechnics and, moreover, tend to the formal organisation of élitist corporations, as practised by the rectors of traditional and central Russian universities.

7. Higher education has to (re)identify its place in society. This search is determined, on the one hand, by the aforementioned principles of 'academic autonomy' and 'free market' policy. On the other hand, in order to meet the challenges of modernisation, universities have to become again integrated, which means the reincorporation of the separated institutions (institutes of law, economics, medicine, etc.) as faculties and university departments. Legal provisions of recent years indicate that this path has been taken. Furthermore, modernisation means an openness to new tasks with special regard to the development of pluridisciplinary projects, for instance in the area of economic studies and research in connection with ecological problems.

8. There is a more or less articulated trend to privatisation which can be regarded as the top of free market activities (cf. Schmid 1994). In the beginning of the 1990s, many private institutions were established, frequently supported by foreign sponsors or direct foreign, mainly American, involvement; the latter in particular in Bulgaria. In a great number of cases, however, such initiatives have already turned out to be ephemeral, since they lack both material solidity and curricular coherence. The recruitment of qualified staff raises further problems, whose solution widely depends on how far professors and lecturers at state institutions can acquire second jobs by comparatively better

working conditions and attractive salaries. According to the poor situation at most state institutions, it should not raise any surprise that such appeals are successful. Furthermore, state institutions, in their turn, tend to include private sectors in their own activities; they rent out rooms and equipment to private educational institutions (or even to firms) and organise special training courses on a fee-paying base for students who have not passed the competitive (concours) entrance examinations. On the whole, the private sector is far from being consolidated, some universities such as the highly respected Catholic University at Lublin (Poland) excepted (which is a *de facto* public institution, all the more so as it is entirely financed by the State). The somewhat chaotic picture is complicated by the lack of legal provisions, particularly with respect to the formal acknowledgement of changes in status and in examinations and certifications.

It goes without saying that all the initiatives which have been taken in order to overcome former stagnation and backwardness, are linked with efforts to find partners for co-operation in the Western world (cf. Kallen 1993; Last and Schaefer 1994; Mühle 1994). One mainstream goes to North America, where many universities and research institutes have established extended scholarship programmes for lecturers and students from Central and Eastern Europe. Western Europe is the goal of the other mainstream. Here the European Union has taken initiatives in creating exchange programmes between West and East European universities within the project TEMPUS. Bilateral forms of co-operation have also been initiated (e.g., Stand und Perspektiven 1994).

Concluding Remarks

The crisis into which higher education has been driven in the whole region of Central and Eastern Europe has been recognised by prominent representatives of these countries, both in the academic and in the political and economic sector. Savel'ev's appraisal may be typical of the situation in all countries of the former Socialist block:

The analysis of the higher education system of the USSR shows that it is not dynamic and flexible. The alteration of the nomenclature of professions resulted only in the elimination of apparent duplication and the normalisation of their distribution with respect to professional groups. Stipulating uniform standards of instruction in practically all fields of specialisation causes unnecessary expense because different specialists with different levels of training are required in practice, and often education received at institutes of higher education appears to exceed that essential for a given type of work and so remains unused (Savel'ev 1992, p.47).

Recalling the enormous problems on the economic scene, one can conclude that the march into the future is more than complex. The internal political and social problems, reinforced by widespread moral uncertainty in all East European countries aggravate the crisis probably even more than the economic austerity as such. One has to take into special consideration the dissolution of the Soviet Union and the collapse of Yugoslavia. Each of these countries has to cope with multinationality issues resulting from their 'pre-revolutionary' inheritance and from the Soviet migration policies.

In the Commonwealth of Independent States, higher education is particularly concerned because in all the Republics the number of Russian lecturers and students is very high which results in the Russian language as the dominant instruction medium. Even at many non-Russian universities, lectures are given in Russian; to some extent this is due to the stage of the academic and scientific standard of Russian against that of many idioms and languages, particularly in the North and South East of the Commonwealth. On the other hand, it does not mirror the current amalgamation of multiethnic populations. This is why higher education is closely involved in the multinational and multiethnic issues seeking a solution on the basis of peaceful coexistence.

Universities and polytechnics must cope with structural stagnation and innovate content which have become obsolete. Democratisation and autonomy can be identified as basic concerns. Illusory expectations must give way to realistic appraisals showing that many problems can only be solved by continuous effort. Warnings against hasty and ill-considered borrowing of Western models are highly relevant, including an overestimate of the structural and curricular achievements of Western universities; frequently the Eastern counterparts do not take regard of the conditions under which these examples exist. This ignores the long and hard experiences before such achievements were attained and the fact that they are often far from being consolidated in the West.

Regarding the relation between higher education and the world of work, the socialist experiences, though based upon the principle of merging training, research and production, are unlikely to be helpful in the future. These must follow the idea of a free partnership between universities and firms, in which transitional solutions are inevitable.

Higher education is likely to play an essential role in democratising Central and Eastern Europe. Memory of pre-socialist achievements which often resulted in high level scholars and solid specialists may turn out to be a promoting factor, as long as it is not over nostalgic. Whether higher education is able to take its expected and necessary role in the socio-political progress of the Central and East European States, will depend on how and to what extent a balance between initiatives and realistic expectations can be achieved and maintained. Western expertise and advice is needed on all levels. Exchange of lecturers, students and, last but not least, managers and administrators can support innovative efforts to a remarkable degree and is probably more important than material help. This does not mean neglect of the need to provide modern equipment and means of information, teaching and learning. Finally, Western support can be fruitful only on the base of mutual tolerance and respect. Western partners have to take into account the historical fact, that despite all the current troubles, Central and Eastern Europe are regions where higher education, in particular universities, can look back on a rich tradition of scholarly achievement and excellence. One should not forget, that the Charles University in Prague (founded in 1348) and the Jagiellonian University in Cracow (founded in 1364), together with the Vienna University (founded in 1365), mark the beginning of higher education in Central Europe and that the Lomonosov University in Moscow is approaching its 250th anniversary. This list could be easily extended.

The collapse of the socialist regimes in Central and Eastern Europe has broadened and intensified the foundations for a universal development of higher education to be built upon international communication, understanding and co-operation. This challenge can only be met, if all the internal and international obstacles are identified and removed.

References

Anweiler, O., Mitter, W., Peisert, H., Schäfer, H.-P. and Stratenwerth, W. (eds) (1990) *Vergleich von Bildung und Erziehung in der Bundesrepublik Deutschland und in der Deutschen Demokratischen Republik* (Comparison of education in the Federal Republic of Germany and the German Democratic Republic). Küln: Verlag Wissenschaft und Politik.

Bachmaier, P. (1991) 'Hauptetappen in der Entwicklung des bulgarischen Bildungswesens 1944–1989' (Main stages in the development of the Bulgarian education system 1944–1989). In P. Bachmaier (ed) *Bildungspolitik in Osteuropa. Systemwandel und Perspektiven* (Educational policy in Eastern Europe. System change and perspectives). Wien: Jugend und Volk.

Bessenyei, I. (1991) Modernisierung, Hochschul- und Wissen-schaftspolitik in Ungarn (Modernisation, higher education and science policy in Hungary). In P. Bachmaier (ed) op.cit., pp.150–160.

Bizkov, G. (1991) *Bildungsreformen in Bulgarien. Hoffnungen und Realitëten* (Educational reforms in Bulgaria. Hopes and realities). In P Bachmaier (ed) op.cit. pp.195–200.

Cerych, L. (1990) 'Renewal of central European higher education: issues and challenges.' *European Journal of Education 25*, 351–359.

Directory of higher education institutions in Russian Federation (1994) Moscow: ICIEP.

Halász, G. and Lukács, P. (1990) *Educational Policy for the Nineties. Theses for a New Concept of State Educational Policy.* Budapest: Hungarian Institute for Educational Research.

Hegedüs, L., von Kopp, B. and Schmidt, G. (1982) *Hochschulstudium und Berufseingliederung in sozialistischen Staaten* (Higher education and job adjustment in socialist countries). KÜln/Wien: Böhlau-Verlag.

Hochschulkooperation (1994) *State and Perspectives of Cooperation with Higher Education and Scientific Institutions of the Ukraine.* Bonn: Hochschulrektorenkonferenz.

Josephson, P.R. (1994) 'Russian scientific institutions: Internationalisation, democracy and dispersion.' *Minerva 1*, 1–23.

Kallen, D. (1993) 'Western Europe and the reconstruction of higher education in Central and Eastern Europe.' *Higher Education Policy 6*, 3, 22–27.

Koucky, S. and Hendrichova, S. (1993) *Higher Education and Research in the Czech Republic: Major Changes Since 1993.* Wien: Institut für die Wissenschaften vom Menschen.

Kozma, T. (1989) 'An educationally affluent society: Key issues in the Hungarian educational policy.' *Perspectives in Education 5*, 4, 223–232.

Krankus, M. (1991) 'Die Reform des slowakischen Schulwesens. Probleme und Perspektiven' (The reform of the Slovak education system. Problems and perspectives). In P. Bachmaier (ed) op. cit., 101–114.

Kuebart, F. (1989) 'Soviet education and comparative research – a German View.' *Comparative Education 25*, 3, 283–292.

Kuebart, F. (1990) 'Kader für die Perestrojka. Zu Konzeption und Verlauf der sowjetischen Hochschulreform' (Cadres for Perestrojka. Comments concerning conception and course of Soviet higher education reform). *Osteuropa 40*, 10, 947–962.

Kupisiewicz, C. (1991) 'Die Expertenberichte von 1973 und 1989 zum Stand des Bildungswesens in Polen – Entstehung, Inhalt und Funktion' (The Expert Reports of 1973 and 1989 concerning the state of education in Poland – Emergence, contents and function). *Bildung und Erziehung 44*, 39–52.

Lajos, T. (1993) 'Perspectives, hopes and disappointments: higher education reforms in Hungary.' *European Journal of Education 28*, 403–413.

Last, B. and Schaefer, H.-D. (1994) Die Wissenschaftsbeziehungen der Hochschulen in den neuen Bundeslèndern mit Mittel-/Osteuropa im Zeitraum 1989 bis 1993 (The scientific relations between the new Federal Laender and Central-/Eastern Europe 1989–1993. Berlin: Projektgruppe Hochschulforschung Berlin-Karlshorst 1994 (=Projektberichte 2).

Mitter, W. (1978) *Secondary School Graduation: University Entrance Qualification in Socialist Countries. A Comparative Study.* Oxford: Pergamon Press.

Mitter, W. (1992) 'Education in Eastern Europe and the Soviet Union in a period of revolutionary change.' In W. Mitter, M. Weiss and U. Schèfer (eds) *Recent trends in Eastern European education.* Proceedings of the UNESCO workshop held at the German Institute for International Educational Research, Frankfurt am Main, 5–7 June 1991. Frankfurt am Main: German Institute for International Educational Research, 121–136.

Mühle, E. (ed) (1994) *Perspectives on the Reform of higher education in Central and Eastern Europe.* Bonn: Hochschulkonferenz 1994 (= Dokumente zur Hochschulreform 90/1994).

Mühle, E. (1994) 'Rückkehr nach Europa'. Zur Reform der ostmitteleuropëischen Hochschulsysteme seit 1989 (On the reform of the higher education systems in East Central Europe). *Osteuropa 44*, 10, 907–925.

Mühle, E. (1994) Hochschulreform in Ungarn. Das ungarische Hochschulgesetz vom 13. Juli 1993 (Higher education reform in Hungary. The Hungarian Law on Higher Education of July 13th, 1993). Bonn: Hochschulrektorenkonferenz 1994 (= Dokumente zur Hochschulreform 93/1994).

Novikov, L. (1981) *Hochschulen in der Sowjetunion* (Higher education in the Soviet Union). Küln/Wien: Böhlau-Verlag.

Pribersky, A. (1991) Hochschulpolitik und politische Kultur – Thesen zur Rolle von Hochschulpolitik und Intelligenz in der politischen Entwicklung Ungarns seit 1945 (Higher education policy and political culture – Theses concerning the role of higher education policy and the intelligentsia in Hungary since 1945). In P. Bachmaier (ed) op. cit., pp.161–173.

Reuhl, G. (1992) *Wissenschaftskonkurrenz. Hochschulorganisation in den US, Europa und der Sowjetunion* (Competition in the area of sciences. Organisaion of higher education in the US, Europe and the Soviet Union). Frankfurt am Main/New York.

Savel'ev, A. Ja. (1992) 'Problems in the development of higher education in the USSR.' In W. Mitter, M. Weiss and U. Schëfer (eds) op. cit., pp.41–56.

Scharf, R. (1991) Zum Verhëltnis von Hochschulforschung und Wirtschaft in osteuropäischen Staaten. Aspekte der Reformdiskussion vor dem Hintergrund westlicher Erfahrungen (Concerning the relation between research on higher education and economy in East European countries. Aspects of the reform debate against the background of Western experiences). In P. Bachmaier (ed) op. cit., pp. 126–137.

Schmid, U. (1994) Das russische Hochschulwesen in der Krise. Am Beispiel der Lomonossow-Universitët in Moskau (The Russian higher education system in crisis. Exemplified by the Lomonosov University in Moscow). *Neue Zürcher Zeitung*, July 19th, 8.

Soljan, N.N. (1991) 'The saga of higher education in Yugoslavia.' *Comparative Education Review 35*, 1, 131–153.

Stand und Perspektiven der Zusammenarbeit mit Hochschulen und Wissenschaftseinrichtungen in der Ukraine (State and perspectives of co-operation with higher education and scientific institutions in the Ukraine). Bonn: Hochschulrektorenkonferenz 1994 (Materialien zur Hochschulkooperation 2/1994).

Straka, J. (1991) Die Hochschul- und Wissenschaftspolitik in der Slowakei (Higher education and science policy in Slovakia). In Bachmaier, Peter (ed.), op. cit., pp. 93–100.

Weilguni, W. (1991) Zwei Systemmodelle des Bildungswesens in Jugoslawien als Grundlage für Reformen im Hochschulbereich (Two system models of the education system in Yugoslavia as base for reform in the higher education sector). In Bachmaier, Peter (ed.), op. cit., pp. 215–219.

Chapter 15

Higher Education in Japan

Ulrich Teichler

Introduction

About three decades ago, Japan was hardly addressed, if international conferences or books aimed to provide an overview on recent
developments of any societal issues in major industrial societies. In
the mean time, knowledge on Japan has become so widely spread
that it is difficult to add anything new to it. As regards higher
education in Japan, for example, four characteristics tend to be
stressed in academic publication, reports by journalists, as well as
accounts by other observers.

- First, Japan is generally viewed as one of the most strongly
  expanded systems of higher education, as far the quota of
  beginner students of the respective age group is concerned.
- Second, the range of quality and reputation among Japanese
  universities seems to be wider than that among universities
  in European countries.
- Third, competition for admission to the most prestigious
  universities seem to overshadow all the activities in schools
  and institutions of higher education.
- Fourth, many experts point out that achievement standards
  for university students, in contrast to university-bound
  youth in secondary schools, do not seem to be very high.

One should be aware of the fact, however, that higher education in
Japan was similarly characterised already one or two decades ago.
One might ask whether these characteristics have remained more or
less stable over time or whether there is a tendency to overlook major
dynamics and recent issues.

In this presentation, first, a short descriptive overview on Japanese
higher education will be provided in a few sections (see Teichler 1975;
Cummings, Amano and Kitamura 1979; Amano 1989; Muta 1993).

Second, some issues will be addressed in more detail which have been a focus of debate over the last few decades and might be salient as well, when we address the future of higher education.

Institutions and Enrolment

When the structure and organisation of the Japanese education system was reformed after World War II closely in tune with the US education system, initially universities (*daigaku*) were established as the only type of higher education institutions. In 1993, the total number of universities was 534; among them 98 national, 46 local and 390 private institutions. They enrolled altogether 2,390,000 students; 73 per cent at private institutions (see Ministry of Education, Science and Culture 1994).

Universities provide as a rule four-year course programmes to students who have completed 12 years of primary and secondary education. The programmes lead to a *gakushi* which is considered internationally equivalent to a bachelors;in medical fields, the course programme requires six years.

Three hundred and fifty-nine universities, about two thirds, established graduate schools (*daigakuin*). Among them, 242 award doctoral degrees (*hakushi*) whereas 117 confer master's degrees (*shushi*) only – many not in all fields of study provided in undergraduate education. Master courses take two years as a rule and doctorate courses three years. It is possible, though, to be awarded a doctoral degree upon submission of thesis without prior enrolment at the daigakuin. In 1993, altogether 122,000 students were enrolled at daigakuin.

Junior colleges (*tanki daigaku*) were initially established on a provisional basis in 1950 because not all institutions could comply to the standards of a university. In 1965 they became a permanent feature of the higher education system. They provide mostly two-year and in some fields three-year courses to students who have completed 12 years of primary and secondary education. In 1993, altogether 530,000 students were enrolled at 595 junior colleges, in which the private sector comprised 84 per cent (502 as compared to 37 national and 56 local) of the institutions and 92 per cent of the students.

Colleges of technology (*koto senmon gakko*) were established in 1962 as a third type of higher education institution. Upon completion of the middle school and altogether nine years of school education, students are provided with a five-year programme in which the final two years are considered to be part of higher education. The 62 colleges (54 national, 5 local and 3 private) have altogether 55,000 students, among them only 5 per cent at private institutions.

Since 1976, the better equipped among the so-called 'miscellaneous schools' (*kakushu gakko*) were upgraded to special training colleges (*senshu gakko*). The 3431 special training colleges (161 national, 198 local and 3072 private) are considered to be part of the post-secondary education system in Japan. They provide one-year to three-year predominantly full-time courses for specific vocational areas, mostly requiring 12 years of prior education. Of the total of 859,000 students, 94 per cent were enrolled at private institutions.

In recent overviews, miscellaneous schools have also been named post-secondary institutions. A further 3055 institutions (among them 3 national and 75 local) report 367,000 students (among them 98 per cent at private institutions) comprising such different institutions as driving schools, cram schools for entrance examinations, vocational schools, foreign educational institutions residing in Japan etc.

There are some colleges for special professions which are not under supervision of the Ministry of Education, Science and Culture, but under other ministries, for example the Ministry of Labour and the Self-Defence Agency. A few years ago, the Ministry of Education, Science and Culture established an office in charge of examining the qualifications acquired at these institutions and the possibility of awarding a higher education degree.

Governance and Financing

All institutions of higher education are supervised by the Ministry of Education, Science and Culture. Whereas national higher education institutions are directly established by the government, local and private institutions have to be approved by the Ministry upon recommendation by the Council for University Chartering and the School Juridical Person. The Council also recommends standards.

The highest decision-making body at national universities is named the 'Senate' and is composed of academics, and that of private universities the 'Board of Trustees', comprising mostly of external representatives and possibly owners of the institution. Presidents and deans of faculties in Japan are both in formal function and power less influential than at U.S. institutions of higher education, though more influential than in many European countries. Traditionally, presidents of national universities have to respect decisions regarding academic personnel, research and teaching on the part of faculties, and the Ministry has to respect the final decisions by the senate regarding academic matters. Experts point out, however, that the government has a strong say in detailed bureaucratic regulations, through the provision of the head of administration from among its staff, as well as through informal deliberations prior to the formal decisions by the universities.

According to the White Book on Education 1990, about 1.8 per cent of the gross national product was spent on higher education in Japan in the late 1980s. The government provided altogether 41 per cent of the income of universities (60 per cent of that of national institutions and 13 per cent of that of private institutions); tuition and other fees comprised 34 per cent (about 15% at national and about 65% at private institutions). Though tuition and other fees at private institutions are almost three times as high as at national institutions, national universities eventually spend about two and a half times as much per student as private universities (Ministry of Education, Science and Culture 1990).

University students spent in 1992, on average, more than 1.8 million yen for a study year, of which about 42 per cent was for tuition and fees. Only about 6 per cent of their costs were covered by governmental grants and loans.

Access, Admission and Institutional Hierarchy

Upon completion of nine years of compulsory education – six years at primary school (*shogakko*) and three years at middle school (*chugakko*) – 96 per cent of the respective age group transferred to upper secondary education or to colleges of technology in 1993. The number of those completing upper secondary education in 1993 corresponded to 89 per cent of those completing compulsory education three years earlier.

Whereas most compulsory schooling is taken at the respective school closest to one's home, upper secondary education is highly stratified, and almost one third of high school students attend private institutions. Pupils of the ninth year are permitted to take an entrance examination at a public high school (*koto gakko*), the results of mock tests help choosing the respective school. More than 70 per cent of upper secondary school students take general courses, more than half of which are viewed as college-preparatory, and the remaining less than 30 per cent courses with a vocational emphasis, notably in technical, commercial, agricultural and home economics areas. All successful applicants for upper secondary education are entitled to apply for admission at institutions of higher education. High schools vary substantially in the success of their students in enrolment at prestigious universities.

Students have to apply at individual faculties (*gakubu*). Opportunities for multiple applications to universities are wider than at the time of application for upper secondary education. However, they are limited in the public sector, because national universities cluster their examinations around two dates. Those wishing to enrol at public universities have to take standardised tests administered by the National Centre for University Entrance Examination. The individual universities decide upon the subjects to be taken in this framework, and they administer their own examination as a second stage of selection. About 20 per cent of the private universities make use of this standardised test as well. Some universities take into account teachers recommendations and undertake interviews themselves, but the more prestigious a university the more it relies solely on examinations, mostly in the five subject areas – Japanese language, foreign language, social studies, mathematics and science.

Japanese youth spend many years preparing themselves for the fierce competition which tends to be characterised as 'examination hell'. The majority take lessons in private tutoring institutions (*juku*). More than one third of university students initially decide not to enrol at a university, but to spend one or more years as a ronin (literally, a samurai without a master) in order to try again to be admitted at a university of their choice, possibly after attending a cramming school (*yobiko*).

Learning, Teaching and Research

After World War II, Japan introduced a credit system as in the US. One hundred and twenty-four credits had to be collected to be awarded a degree; a credit corresponds to 45 hours of lectures and individual study. Initially, all course programmes had to comprise more than one third of the required credits in general education, foreign languages and physical education. These regulations were abolished in the early 1990s.

More than 90 per cent of students actually complete their studies successfully, and more than 90 per cent of them do so in the required period. Average prolongation beyond the required period amounts only to 0.2 years. Many experts, however, claim that this regular completion is due to lenient standards in higher education.

It has been argued frequently that Japanese universities do not expect students to work extraordinarily hard. In a comparative study undertaken in the mid-1980s on education in the US and Japan, US experts praised the quality of Japanese primary and secondary education (see also Husén 1991), but strongly criticised the quality of Japanese higher education (Dorfman 1987). In fact, surveys suggest that Japanese university students spend only about 25 hours per week on study and almost 15 hours on *'arubaito'*, i.e., work at earning money. One should bear in mind, though, that the number of hours spent on study varies in Japan more strongly by field of study than it does, for example in the US or in Germany. Many Japanese students enrolled in humanities or social sciences obviously believe that neither the field of study nor the level of achievement will matter substantially as far as career opportunities are concerned.

At almost all national universities departments are divided into chairs (*koza*). A chair usually comprises of one full professor (*kyoju*), one associate professor (*jokyuju*) and one or two assistants (*joshu*). Lecturers (*koshi*) are more frequent at private universities. Most of the positions at national universities are not allocated to individual chairs. Whereas almost all professors at national universities are permanent full-time employed civil servants, the majority of teaching staff at private universities are part-timers, notably academics doing a side job. Many professors at private institutions took up their position after retirement from a public institution.

According to an international survey undertaken in 1992, Japanese professors consider themselves to be more strongly research oriented and actually report that they spend a higher proportion of their time on research than their colleagues in the US and in the European countries included in the survey. However, the survey shows as well that the proportion of those not involved in research projects, as well as those not receiving an external research grant is higher than in the other countries referred to above (see Enders and Teichler 1995).

As in most other countries, the tradition of a close link between teaching and research is only upheld in a small part of the research sector. At major national universities, a substantial proportion of professors have only a research function and are allocated to research institutions outside the departmental structure.

Issues of Expansion and Stratification

The number of Japanese youths continuing education beyond nine years of compulsory schooling was about 50 per cent in the 1950s and grew to more than 90 per cent within two decades. Upper secondary education became not a legally, but a socially mandatory period of schooling. More than 90 per cent of those starting upper secondary education complete this three-year phase and are eventually entitled to transfer to higher education. The proportion of those qualifying for higher education, upper secondary education school leavers completing the third year of colleges of technology, among those completing compulsory schooling three years earlier reached 89 per cent in 1993.

The enrolment ratio in higher education, i.e., the proportion of beginner students among the respective age group, in Japan was around 10 per cent during the 1950s. It increased to 38 per cent in 1975. After it had more than doubled within one decade it remained more or less constant until about 1990 (see Ernst, Demes and Post-Kobayashi 1993). Thereafter, it began to increase moderately to 41 per cent in 1993 (about 28% at universities, almost 13% at junior colleges and about half a per cent fourth-year students at colleges of technology) (Ministry of Education, Science and Culture 1994).

The number of first-year students in courses requiring 12 years of prior schooling at special training schools corresponds to about 18 per cent of the respective age group.

From the mid-1950s to the early 1960s, various governmental agencies co-operated in the establishment of human resource requirement forecasts and in the recommendation of related policies. The forecasts came to the conclusion that both the total number of upper secondary educational school leavers and university graduates were surpassing the demand of the employment system by far, whereas shortages were to be expected of school leavers in technical fields and university graduates in science and engineering. The government expanded those fields in public institutions, but did not undertake any measures to stop expansion in other areas (see Teichler 1976).

The period of expansion was accompanied by economic progress as well as by an increased belief of large groups in society that they had become part of the middle class and that their children could successfully compete for educational success. Enrolment at private universities increased overproportionally, and private institutions could raise tuition and fees beyond average wage increases for a long period. The trend of expansion was not even challenged by the fact that wage differentials according to educational attainment levels decreased substantially during this period. Rather, small differences in reputation of the educational institution seemed to be worth all the effort.

There are not any comprehensive explanations of the causes of the long period of non-expansion of higher education in Japan after 1975. The most frequently stated explanation is the least convincing one. It is often claimed that special training schools were the growth sector of post-secondary education. A closer look, however, reveals that the growth of senshu gakko was a mere upgrading phenomenon, for enrolment in miscellaneous schools decreased in tune with the growth of senshu gakko.

The end of higher education expansion in Japan in the mid-1970s certainly was linked to the government's decision to subsidise private higher education on the condition that the intake of students far beyond official capacity standards was discontinued. National subsidies covered only 7 per cent of the expenses borne by private institutions of higher education in 1970; this increased to 30 per cent in 1980, but declined again to less than 15 per cent in the early 1990s (see Ministry of Education, Science and Culture 1990). One might ask whether the decreased subsidies will continue to put a ceiling on expansion.

The current debate in Japan, however, points in a different direction. Due to demographic reasons, the number of secondary school leavers started to decline in 1992. It is generally expected that higher education institutions will be more or less successful in recruiting the same total number of students, thus the quota of new entrants among the corresponding age group will increase to more than 50 per cent during the first decade of the 2000s.

There is one area of expansion in higher education which deserves attention, though small in total numbers. In 1975, less than 10 per cent of Japanese science and engineering graduates advanced to graduate schools, but this proportion has now passed 20 per cent. Major Japanese production companies recently changed their recruitment policies in favour of an increasing intake of science and engineering graduates from masters courses.

Since the late 1980s, the proportion of women entering higher education has overtaken that of men. However, they tend to enrol at less prestigious institutions. Of the respective age group, 37 per cent of men began to study at universities in 1993, 2 per cent at junior colleges and 1 per cent at the fourth-year courses of colleges of technology, while 19 per cent of women went to universities and 24 per cent to junior colleges. There is a difference, though, as regards enrolment at special training colleges.

There are various speculations in Japan as regards further development of the stratification of the system. Most experts conclude that the institutional hierarchy might even become steeper. On the one hand, the least prestigious institutions might, as a response to the decreasing age cohort, lower standards in order to enrol the same absolute numbers of students as they did in the past. There are recent indicators that the government is loosening its pressure on private institutions of higher education, as far as minimum quality is concerned. On the other hand, the Japanese government has made various decisions in favour of promoting the research capacities of the most renowned universities.

The Degreeocracy Debate

The fierce competition for educational success, notably for being admitted to a prestigious university, is possibly the characteristic of Japanese education most frequently referred to in the academic, as well as in the popular literature. In many cases, one does not talk about this phenomenon solely, but rather about a set of conditions which is usually called *'gakureki shakai'* or in the last two decades also as *'kogekureki shakai'*. This might be translated as society of (long) educational paths or might be explained as credential society or degreeocracy (see Dore 1976; Teichler 1976; Amano 1990).

There is a strong belief in Japan that occupational opportunities largely depend on the educational institution one was admitted to and eventually graduated from. Large Japanese companies which are most likely to ensure the ideal of lifelong employment and which promise other benefits tend to prefer graduates from the most prestigious universities and to take the reputation of the institution into account beyond the competence the students actually reach. Also, the rank of the university seems to affect the opportunity of passing the most demanding entrance examinations for top careers in the public sector. Researchers are divided over the issue whether educational investments in Japan pay off in terms of human capital (cf. Kaneko 1992), but most Japanese seem to be willing to put enormous efforts into education even for marginal career gains.

Competition for educational success is reinforced by the strong belief that the Japanese educational system provides more or less equal opportunity for ambitious youth. This belief is not based so much on 'equality of results', i.e., on knowledge of actual educational success according to socio-economic background. Available research suggests that about half of the students at the most prestigious universities belong to the highest quintile in terms of parental occupational status. This does not seem to be exceptionally open in international comparisons. Faith in the openness of the educational system, rather, seems to be reinforced by the modes of selection. The decision about one's opportunities rests on success in entrance examinations, i.e., provisionally the entrance examinations to the high school and definitely the entrance examinations to the university.

This selection is generally considered to be extraordinarily fair and notably provides opportunities for those who put most effort into preparation.

The hierarchy of universities is the obvious link between educational opportunity and the determination of careers by educational success. Tokyo University, Kyoto University and Tokyo Institute of Technology are most frequently named as ensuring top careers in the private sector; according to some surveys, more than a quarter of top managers are graduates of one of these three institutions. Almost half of those passing the examinations for the top administrative careers are graduates of Tokyo University or Kyoto University. Keio University and Waseda University are the most prestigious among the private institutions. What might be more significant, though, is that competition for admission to higher education, in contrast to the US, is not only directed toward the top institutions, but differences in reputation also play a substantial role in the choice among the least prestigious institutions.

Political efforts made to reform the admission system to higher education have not been successful in the past. About every ten years – most recently in 1979 and 1990 – the Ministry of Education, Science and Culture dissolves the existing test institute and establishes a new one, each somewhat different in the thrust of the tests and the mode of operation. Dates might have changed and also phases of examination. What has remained constant, though, is at least a final stage of examination to be administered by the individual university as well as the selection decision resting with the individual university or its departments. For some period, alternative modes of assessment got some momentum, notably among the less prestigious institutions: some introduced essay examinations instead of and in addition to multiple-choice examinations; others introduced oral examinations, reduced the number of subjects to be examined and took into account teachers' examinations. Recently, those practices have been frequently criticised as undermining the fairness of the system.

Even if possible major changes in the relationships between socio-biographical background, education and career are envisaged, they do not promise a substantial impact as regards the 'examination hell'. Three changes might be worth consideration.

First, changes in women's education and career became a major focus of the debate. The women's advancement rate to upper secondary education surpassed that of men already around 1970 and that to higher education around 1990. However, still the majority of women opt for junior colleges whereas more than 90 per cent of men proceeding to higher education opt for universities. Almost one quarter of women studying bachelor's programmes are enrolled in women's universities, and women comprise less than 20 per cent of students at the most prestigious and most research-oriented universities.

Since 1985, legislation aims to guarantee equal opportunity for women in employment. This, in practice, has led to an even clearer division between top careers in major private enterprises, the so-called comprehensive track (*shogo shoku*), filled 90 per cent or more by men, or the career general track (*ippan shoku*), filled 100 per cent by women. Enterprises underscore equal opportunity for those on the same track, but most women graduating from universities are informally advised to accept employment in the ippan shoku sector, traditionally provided for junior college graduates. Women are not yet formally compelled anymore to leave the firm after a few years, yet the practice of employment for a few years remains widespread.

Second, major industries became increasingly interested in recruiting scientists and engineers who have been awarded a master's. In contrast to the US, access to graduate education is not viewed to have any significant redistribution effect in the selection taking place at entry to undergraduate programmes. This is due, in part, to the still relatively small advancement rate to graduate education. In addition, most students heading for graduate education do so in the university where they took their first degree.

Third, most experts agree that substantial changes in the 'examination hell' could only come about, if hiring and promotion of staff in employment de-emphasised educational credentials. In the mid-1970s, recruitment practices as regards university graduates changed significantly. Whereas individual universities previously were told to recommend a limited number of students which the companies would take seriously into account in their recruitment process, now any student may apply to any enterprise, and recommendations are believed to play an important role nowadays only in science and engineering fields. This change of recruitment mode, however, does not seem to have resulted in a much weaker link between the university one has graduated from and the subsequent career.

The economic problems since the early 1990s fuelled again a debate about a possible end of the ideal-type modes of lifetime employment and seniority promotion. It is premature to conclude whether careers will be less predetermined by prior education. Currently, the increased employment problems for graduates even underscore the importance of the individual university.

Changing Profiles of Study and Competences

Japanese institutions of higher education are relatively free to change their curricula. Legislation provided, after World War II, that a course programme had to comprise of 36 credits of general education (12 each in humanities, social sciences and natural sciences) as well as 12 credits in foreign languages and physical education. During the early 1970s, regulations regarding the proportions of fields in general education were scrapped, and early in 1991, all framework regulations for curricula were dropped.

Institutions of higher education were also relatively free to shape their curricula, because neither employers nor most professional organisations expected universities to establish common cores for individual disciplines. The Ministry of Education, Science and Culture has to approve the establishment of new course programmes both in public and private institutions, and it certainly has a strong informal influence on the denomination of individual chairs at national universities, but universities can opt for specific solutions if they want to do so. On the other hand, they hardly felt pressed, because preparation for a career was expected to be general rather than strongly disciplinary or specialised and because preparation for future academic careers was rather viewed as being based on individual chairs and respective sub-specialisations than on disciplines and departments. Also, pressure in this direction might be low, if it is true that students in many subjects and at many higher education institutions might get awarded credits on the basis of relatively low effort and quality of achievement.

Any generalisation about trends in the development of curricula and of the substance taught can be made only with caution, because those changes are less publicly visible than those structural and quantitative developments and the system of governance. Most experts agree that the student unrest in the late 1960s has triggered off the establishment of numerous committees and the writing of the broad range of curricula reform proposals, but the impact of these activities fell short compared to the initial ambitions. The discontinuation of any general education and foreign language requirements in the early 1990s has revived debates on the curriculum. More than half of the universities reported to a subsequent survey that major curricular reforms are being debated at their institution. It is also worth noting that the government shifted its support to private universities in part from general subsidies toward reward of innovative programmes in teaching and research. It is premature to assess the outcome of this new wave of curricular debates. There are indicators, however, suggesting a favourable climate for curricular change.

In 1984, a National Council on Educational Reform (*Rinkyoshin*) was created by Prime Minister Nakasone in order to emphasise the importance of educational policy. Various recommendations of the Council met with mixed reactions, but three proposals were widely approved as urgent and timely:

- Education should strongly emphasise the development of the individual.

- Education should prepare students to act successfully in international environment.

- Education should provide lifelong education for a gradually ageing society (National Council on Educational Reform 1986).

As regards internationalisation, measures to ease the employment of foreign teaching staff in the early 1980s, as well as efforts to encourage increased enrolment of foreign students, are more visible changes than curricular efforts for internationalisation. Already in 1983, the Japanese established a plan, according to which the total number of foreign students should increase from less than 20,000 to about 100,000 in the year 2000. In 1993, the number of foreign students at Japanese institutions of higher education surpassed 50,000 of whom more than 80 per cent came from China, Korea and Taiwan (see Abe 1995). On the other hand, more than 120,000 students left for study abroad, most of them individually and a substantial proportion to branch campuses of Japanese universities. In contrast to Europe and the US, organised student exchange between Japanese and foreign universities plays a marginal role.

Additionally, there are some indications that a certain degree of specialisation has gained momentum. As a rule, enterprises tend to consider graduates to be 'raw material' for in-company training rather than being trained for specific professions. Many large enterprises, however, recently established careers for specialists, though up to the present mostly on a small scale. As already mentioned, a growing number of enterprises began to encourage science and engineering graduates to take a master's course prior to application for employment. The recent boom in computer science also indicates a growing reward for specialised courses.

Growing Importance of Graduate Education and Research

Graduate education in Japan was undertaken in the past on a very small scale. In recent years, however, it has expanded significantly. The ratio of first-year students in master courses to that of bachelor's increased from less than 5 per cent in 1980 to about 10 per cent in 1993. The ratio varies from less than 3 per cent in social sciences to almost a quarter in engineering and more than one third in natural sciences. Graduate courses in humanities and social sciences almost exclusively serve the reproduction of the academic profession, and many study places in graduate education remain vacant. On the other hand, private industry currently employs the majority of science and engineering graduates from master programmes, and it aims to increase recruitment of masters substantially.

Enrolment in doctoral courses has increased at about the same pace in recent years. In 1993, it corresponded to almost 3 per cent of those awarded a bachelor's three years earlier. One has to bear in mind, though, that more than half of the doctorates are awarded after submission of thesis without prior enrolment in a doctoral programme.

If there is no change of function of graduate programmes in the humanities and social sciences, one might expect a growing discrepancy in enrolment between the major disciplinary groups. For on the one hand, the demand for new academics in humanities and social sciences is expected to stagnate or to decline due to the demographic changes referred to above. On the other hand, demand for doctors in science and engineering is expected to rise further.

In recent publications on the state of research in Japan, it is generally pointed out that expenditures for research in Japan match those of other major industrial societies. Altogether, R&D in private companies seems to take a bigger share than in other comparable countries, whereas research in higher education seems to be relatively poorly funded. According to the Japanese government's Science and Technology White Paper 1992, research funds per researcher in the university sector are only about one third of that in other national research institutes and in private institutes. One has to take into account that these ratios would look even more unfavourable, if the considerable number of institutes at universities was excluded the staff of which serve only research functions.

According to this international comparative study of the academic profession, Japanese professors express about the same degree of satisfaction regarding their profession in general as their colleagues in the US, the United Kingdom, Sweden, the Netherlands and Germany, but in three respects they express clearly more negative views.

First, Japanese professors are least satisfied with their salary – a fact which might be viewed as surprising, if the salaries were compared to those in other countries looking at the exchange rates only, but certainly reflects the purchasing power of the salary, notably in metropolitan areas.

Second, Japanese professors consider their profession most frequently as a personal strain.

Third, Japanese professors rate the resources for teaching and research available at their university – rooms for teaching, laboratory, computer equipment, library, secretarial service, etc. – clearly more negatively than their US and European colleagues. This holds true for Japanese professors in science and engineering fields, as well as for those in social science and humanities fields. It also holds true for Japanese professors at prestigious, research-oriented universities (Enders and Teichler 1995).

In the wake of recent government initiatives of increasing public spending as a countermeasure to an economic recession, universities obviously were viewed with a favourable eye, notably in respect to the infrastructure of most prestigious universities. Some experts claim that the lack of funds for research is the most salient current issue of higher education in the 1990s, and the government must eventually take measures to redress this situation. It is premature to state whether this is more than wishful thinking.

Steering and Governance – A Low-Priority Issue

If one had to choose the single issue in higher education in Europe, which was in the forefront of discussion and reform efforts in many countries during the last ten years or so, one would certainly point at the triangle of procedural deregulation by government, the growing importance of management of higher education institutions and the establishment of evaluation systems. These issues were not overlooked in Japan, but they do not play a similarly prominent role in public debate.

The history of governance of Japanese national universities is shaped by strong emphasis on typical modes of an 'academic guild' on the part of the academics. Decisions jointly approved at the level of the faculty have to take into account the strong position of the chairs, which are supposed to be respected by the senate and the president, and this strong decentralised emphasis is viewed as the most efficient counterbalance to the traditionally strong governmental power which tends to exercise informal pressures in academic matters and to control the administration through an abundance of bureaucratic regulation combined with a control of the administration personnel at national universities.

Private universities in Japan have, as in other countries, a higher degree of autonomy as far as the government is concerned; although the government can intervene at the time when a new university is established. The introduction of subsidies for private institutions of higher education opened up further opportunities for governmental steering. Private universities in Japan, however, make less impressive use of their freedom than those in the US, because their financial means are as a rule smaller and their reputation as a rule lower than that of major national universities.

Repeated efforts were made to introduce managerial models of higher education, i.e., to strengthen the executive power of the president and to introduce boards. Recommendations by the US occupation forces were eventually shelved after heated debates, and after protests on the part of most academics. Again, after the student protests in the late 1960s, the Central Council of Education (*Chuo Kyoku Shingikai*) suggested the strengthening of the powers of the president and to establish an advisory body of external representatives. The government, however, suppressed all reform steps in favour of substantial participation rights of students and junior staff. It established the University of Tsukuba as a model of reform of governance. Departments were supposed to have stronger say *vis-à-vis* the individual professor, and the presidents and vice-presidents were entrusted with increased powers. Views differ about the success of this experiment, but certainly this model did not spread. In the mid-1980s, the National Council on Educational Reform recommended a system of university governance similar to that proposed previously by the Central Council for Education.

The fact that the relaxation of curricular regulations in the University Standards established in 1991 was combined with the insertion of a paragraph on assessment and self-evaluation of institutions of higher education, is viewed by some experts as a first step towards a steering and governance model, which was influenced by US managerial approaches, but has taken a spate similar to those underway in various European countries. At present, however, we note reservations prevailing similar to those in Germany rather than changes of governance similar to those in the United Kingdom, Netherlands or Nordic countries.

Views might vary with respect to the strengths and weaknesses of managerial approaches. However, debates on the goals and functions of higher education are more vital if they are not overshadowed by debates on the modes of operation of university governance.

Moderate Concerns

The current debates on higher education neither express complacency nor serious worries. We observe a state of moderate concern. It is not the time of protests nor a time of absolute silence.

The current climate of Japanese higher education is in various respects similar to that in Germany. We observe many issues calling for reform, but efforts in favour of reform lack the sense of urgency that could be observed around the 1970s. Substantial improvement is viewed as desirable, but we at most observe incremental changes here and there. The public tends to criticise universities for being resistant to change. This might be correct as far as dramatic revisions are concerned, but is certainly an exaggeration as far as change in the substance of teaching and research is concerned and also in respect to smaller modifications of structures of higher education. The Japanese higher education expert, Kitamura, summarised this state of affairs in a conversation as follows:

> 'Japanese universities are not innovative in running their institutions, but they are not resistant to change in this respect, they just tend to be afraid of missing the bus.'

References

Abe, Y. (1995) 'Japan and international academic mobility in Asia and the Pacific.' In P. Blumenthal, C. Goodwin, S. Smith and U. Teichler *Academic Mobility in a Changing World: Regional and Global Trends.* London: Jessica Kingsley Publishers.

Amano, I. (1989) *Kindai koto kyoiku kenkyu.* Tokyo: Todai shuppansha.

Amano, I (1990) *Examinations.* Tokyo: Tokyo University Press.

Cummings, W.K., Amano, I. and Kitamura, K. (eds) (1979) *Changes in the Japanese University.* New York: Praeger.

Dore, R. (1976) *The Diploma Disease.* London: Allen and Unwin.

Dorfman, C.H. (ed) (1987) *Japanese Education Today.* Washington, DC: U.S. Department of Education.

Enders, J. and Teichler, U. (1995) *De Hochschullehrerberuf im internationalen Vergleich.* Bonn: Bundesminister für Bildung, Wissenschaft, Forschung and Technology.

Ernst, A., Demes, H. and Post-Kobayashi, B. (1993) *Beziehungen zwischen Bildungs- und Beschäftigungsystem in Japan 1970 bis 1991: Eine Datensammlung.* München: ifo Institut für Wirtschaftsforschung and Deutsches Institut für Japanstudien.

Kaneko, M. (1992) *Higher Education and Employment in Japan*. Hiroshima: Hiroshima University, Research Institute for Higher Education.

Ministry of Education, Science and Culture (1990) *Japanese Government Policies in Education, Science and Culture 1990*. Tokyo.

Ministry of Education, Science and Culture (1994) *Education in Japan 1994: A Graphic Presentation*. Tokyo.

National Council on Educational Reform (1986) *Summary of Second Report on Educational Reform*. Tokyo: Government of Japan.

Teichler, U. (1976) *Das Dilemma der modernen Bildungsgesellschaft*. Stuttgart: Klett.

Further Reading

Arimoto, A. and de Weert, E. (1993) 'Higher education policy in Japan.' In L. Goedegebuure, *et al.* (eds) *Higher Education Policy: An International Comparative Perspective*. Oxford: Pergamon.

Demes, H. and Georg, W. (eds) (1994) *Gelernte Karriere: Bildung und Berufsverlauf in Japan*. München: Judicium.

Ehara, T. (1984) *Gendai koto kyoiku no kozo*. Tokyo: Todai shuppansha.

Georg, W. and Sattel, U. (ed) (1992) *Von Japan lernen?* Weinheim: Deutscher Studien Verlag.

Kobayashi, T. (1992) 'Japan.' In B.R. Clark and G.R. Neave (eds) *The Encyclopedia of Higher Education*. Oxford: Pergamon Press.

Muta, H. (1993) *Koto kyoiku ron*. Tokyo: Hoso daigaku kyoiku shinkokai.

OECD (1990) *Historical Statistics: 1960–1988*. Paris.

OECD (1993) *Education in OECD Countries: A Compendium of Statistical Information*. Paris.

Teichler, K. and Teichler, U. (1994) 'Der Übergang vom Bildungs- in das Beschäftigungssystem: Erfahrungen in Deutschland – Vergleiche zu Japan.' In H. Demes and W. Georg (eds) *Gelernte Karriere: Bildung und Berufsverlauf in Japan*. München: Judicium.

Teichler, U. (1991) 'Towards a highly educated society.' *Higher Education Policy 4*, 4, pp.11–20.

Teichler, U. (1992) 'Equality of opportunity in education and career: Japan seen in an international perspective.' *Oxford Review of Education 18*, 3, 283–296.

Chapter 16

Conclusions

An expansion of higher education is in full swing everywhere in Western Europe. It is not clear whether it will end in practically all young people continuing beyond high school with some form of higher education, or whether it will stabilise somewhere near the American level of about 70 per cent. This extension of education is perceived as a virtue without any clear definition of either its aims or the means by which it is to be accomplished. The phrase an 'educated population' is used, which implies that some 12 years of education to the age of 18 has been ineffective and contains the further implication that young people of this age are unprepared to face the outside world and need to be cocooned for a further period. These are striking changes in attitude to those of the quite recent past and indeed to the whole previous history of humankind. Certainly, there is not the necessity to scrape a living out of a marginal economy that was the usual situation in the past; further, the balance of the population has shifted dramatically from the rural location of the past to a predominantly urban existence today. Noting this change helps to clarify our ideas. Formerly in a rural environment, young people had to play their part in the heavy work involved in running the farm early and often intensively and this usually became their life work. Rather, few exceptional individuals escaped into higher education and were mostly destined for the professions. This situation changed with the growth of industry; much of the rural population moved into the towns where the population expanded greatly and became engaged in industrial production. They needed better education and this was satisfied by the development of the schools, universal education and the eventual lengthening of the school period. However, we are now in a period when industrial employment is rapidly decreasing due to progressive automation. There has been a compensatory increase in desk and administrative jobs but even these have changed as a result of the spread of personal work stations. Also, the balance between those in employment and those supported (young and old) is changing, so that a decreasing minority of the population is in employment. Clearly this situation 'makes room' for further education, although the burden on those in work supporting a growing part of the population will become increasingly heavy.

The highest population involvement in higher education over the past 50 years has been in America, and it is also a fact that over this period productivity in America has continued to run at about twice that of Western Europe. Is there a causal relationship between these? It would be hard to establish, but the suspicion that there is a causal relationship is certainly one of the reasons for political interest in the extension of higher education.

What kind of higher education should be offered and in what kind of institution? Views differ sharply from those who, regarding higher education as simply an extension of universal schooling, believe that the same largely undifferentiated pattern should be applied through a greatly enlarged university system, expanded both in numbers and the size of the universities. Others argue for a diversified system, retaining the old universities as centres of learning and research and at the same time creating new institutions, new universities and colleges with less elevated academic aims and usually with little involvement in research, as well as vocational colleges specialising in various aspects of the employment sector. While both approaches have both their own dynamism and problems, it is worth noting that it is largely the second of these patterns that has emerged in America. The Harvards, Princetons, and Stanfords have remained small and élitist and the enormous expansion has occurred elsewhere. Many would argue that mass education and high quality are not compatible and that we have to accept a trade-off. There is also the argument that as the higher education expands and in consequence the state's financial commitment grows, the autonomy of the higher education system is bound to be curtailed, and this has been seen almost everywhere.

We must assume that the new graduates will find appropriate posts and that somehow their improved education will be matched by appropriate occupations – this is something that is not yet ready for a detailed examination because after all, those we teach today will not have found their niche in the marketplace for several years, but it needs to be reviewed and analysed on a continuing basis. There is today a very proper concern that we are changing educational practices in the space of a fraction of a working lifetime. We can all see that the changes in society are proceeding at a very rapid rate and that somehow the students of today are going to have to adapt to those changes which will involve their work. We ought to be teaching in such a way that encourages flexibility and ready adaptation to change. Therefore, we need to decide what training and which institutional arrangements will encourage such attitudes. This is not a simple matter; we can emphasise the teaching of principles as opposed to excessive attention to detail, but even this assumes that principles do not change too much; the past gives us little confidence in this. A serious alternative is learning spread over a longer period while the individual is in employment. Distance learning (note 'learning' not 'teaching' which implies a necessary active approach) has an advantage here in its inherent flexibility to adapt to the individuals evolving requirements, although it can be argued that the loss of the community aspect of university and college life mitigates against its effectiveness. However, the considerable success of the Open universities suggests that this may have been overemphasised. It is certainly likely that programmes to support adaptation to changing technology and to provide for mid-life changes in job will be increasingly important. This workshop has taken place in the midst of very fluid and confusing changes: 'we are here as on a darkling plain swept with confused alarms of struggle and flight where ignorant armies clash by night'.

The contributors

Professor Daniel Bloch is President of the Université Joseph Fourier in Grenoble. He was previously Director of Higher Education in France, Rector of the Orléans-Tours education area, President of the National High Committee for Education-Economy and President of the Institut National Polytechnique in Grenoble.

Arnold Burgen is Editor of the European Review and was the first President of *Academia Europæa*. He was formerly Professor of Pharmacology at the University of Cambridge and Director of the National Institute for Medical Research, London

Professor Erik de Corte is Professor of Education, University of Louvain

Professor Staffan Helmfrid Department of Human Geography, University of Stockholm

Professor Karl Ulrich Mayer is co-director of the Max Planck Institute for Human Development and Education in Berlin and Head of its Centre on Sociology. He is an Adjunct Professor of Sociology at the Free University, Berlin and principal investigator of the German Life History Study.

Professor Wolfgang Mitter is Director of the German Institute for International Educational research, Frankfurt. He has been involved in many international bodies in education and is President of the World Council of Comparative Education Societies. He has had a special interest in the educational systems of the European communist states.

Professor Henk J. van der Molen is an endocrinologist, was Professor of Chemical Endocrinology (1966–1990), Dean of the Faculty of Medicine (1980–1) and since 1990 President of the Erasmus University in Rotterdam. From 1982–1990 he was Director-General of the Netherlands Organisation for Scientific Research (NWO).

Dr Guy Neave is Director of Research at the International Association of Universities, Paris and was previously Professor of Comparative Education at the University of London. He is Editor of *Higher Education Policy* and was Joint Editor in Chief (with Burton R Clark) of the *Encyclopaedia of Higher Education* 1992.

Walter Perry (Lord Perry of Walton) was the first Vice-Chancellor of the Open University 1969–1980. He is a Fellow of the Royal Societies of Edinburgh and London and was previously a member of the staff of the Medical Research Council and Professor of Pharmacology, University of Edinburgh 1958–1968. He is a Social Democrat in the House of Lords.

Professor J. Rojo is Professor of Physics, Universidad Complutense, Madrid. He has been Scientific Director, Spanish Agency for Research and Development Funding 1983–5 and Secretary of State for Universities and Research in Spain 1983–92.

Professor Peter Scott is Professor of Education in the University of Leeds and Director of the Centre for Policy Studies in Education and of the Research School in Education. He is a member of the Lord Chancellor's Advisory Committee on Legal Education and Conduct and a member of the Management Board of the Further Education Development Agency. He was editor of the *Times Higher Education Supplement* 1976–92.

Professor Stig Strömholm is Vice-Chancellor, Uppsala University, former President, Swedish Academy of Letters, History and Antiquities. Professor Jurisprudence, Private and Private International Law, Uppsala. Order pour le Merite, Germany. He has written numerous books on law, and works of fiction.

Professor Ulrich Teichler is Professor of Education and Director of the Centre for Research on Higher Education and Work, University of Kassel. He is also a Professor at the College of Europe, Burges and Chairmen of the Consortium of Higher Education Researchers.

Professor Martin Trow is a Professor in the Graduate School of Public Policy at the University of California, Berkeley, having trained in Mechanical Engineering and then Sociology. He was the Founding Director of the Center for Studies in Higher Education at Berkeley. He is a Trustee of Carleton College and a Foreign Member of the Royal Swedish Academy of Science and is a Past Vice-President of the National Academy of Education.

Subject Index

References to figures and tables are italic

bourgeois 177
charter 24
eligibility 11
France 141–2
in Higher Education
14–6
idea of 15
institutional models
15
international 104
legislation (1991–4) 11
students evolution
according to field
of study *142*
values 16
see also individual
names
University of the Air
63
University of the
Third Age 87
Uppsala University 39

values
and culture, changes
87
structures 37
video-conferencing 33
Vienna University
(1365) 188
vocational training 171
Volkshochschule (adult
education centre) 85

welfare 71
societies 79
welfare state 48, 51, 59,
85, 160
Wenner-Gren
Foundation 2
White Book on
Education (Japan
1990) 195
woman's movement 74
women 27, 74

and higher education
199, 201, 202
work experience 109
World Bank report
(1994) 21

youth education 81

Names Index

Austen, J. 33

Beaty, E., (Marton, F. *et al*) 122
Becker, R. 82
Bessenyei, I. 172
Bevan, A. 64
Bielinski, H. and Strumpel, B. 74
Bismarck, O.E.L. 69
Boekaerts, M. 119
Buchberger, F. *et al* 112

Chi, M.T.H.
et al 115
and Glaser, R. 114

Dalbey, J. and Linn, M.C. 118
Dall'Alba, G. (Marton, F. *et al*) 122
De Corte, E. (Buchberger, F. *et al*) 112
De Jong, T. and Ferguson-Hessler, M.G.M. 115

Edding, F. 81
Entwistle, N.J. (Marton, F. *et al*) 122

Faber, G. 86

Feltovich, H. (Chi, M.T.H. *et al*) 115
Ferguson-Hessler, M.G.M. and De Jong, T. 115

Gellert, C. 37, 47
Glaser, R.
and Chi, M.T.H. 114
(Chi, M.T.H. *et al*) 115
Globerson, T. and Salomon, G. 120
Gorbachev, M. 181
Groombridge, B. (Buchberger, F. *et al*) 112

Halsey, A.H. 147
Havel, V. 181
Hegel, G.W.F. 77, 78
Hounsel, D.J. (Marton, F. *et al*) 122

Janssen, P.J. and Minnaert, A.M. 115
Jay, E. (Perkins, D.N. *et al*) 118

Kennedy, M. (Buchberger, F. *et al*) 112
Kerr, C. 24
Køzma, T. 183
Kruse, A. 76

Lee, J. 64

Marton, F., *et al* 122
Marx, K. 78, 152
Miegel, M. 74
Millar, R. and Prosser, M. 123

Minnaert, A.M. and Janssen, P.J. 115
Mittelstrass, J. 76

Negt, O. 77–8

Perkins, D.N., *et al* 118
Perkins, J. 22
Peters, O. 82
Prosser, M. and Millar, R. 123

Reisman, D. 150

Salomon, G. and Globerson, T. 120
Savel'ev, A.J. 184, 186
Schoenfeld, A.H. 117, 118, 125
Smith, A. 28
Soljan, N.N. 175
Strumpel, B. and Bielinski, H. 74

Tishman, S. (Perkins, D.N. *et al*) 118
Trilling, L. 33

Unckel, P. 56

Vermunt, J.D.H.M. 124
Vèhèsaari, J. (Buchberger, F. *et al*) 112
Veysey, L. 26
von Humboldt, W. 76, 178

Weber, M. 31, 35
Wilhelm, F. Ist 69
Wilson, H. 63